An
Excursion
into
Creative
Sociology

An Excursion into Creative Sociology

Monica B. Morris

New York   Columbia University Press   1977

Library of Congress Cataloging in Publication Data

Morris, Monica B   1928–
An excursion into creative sociology.

Bibliography: p. 191
Includes index.
1. Knowledge, Sociology of.   2. Phenomenology.
3. Social interaction.   I. Title.
BD175.M67   301.1   76-19023
ISBN 0-231-03987-5

Published in the United States 1977
by Columbia University Press, New York

Published in the United Kingdom 1977
by Basil Blackwell, Oxford

Printed in the United States of America

Acknowledgments

GRATEFUL ACKNOWLEDGMENT is made to the following publishers and individuals:

To Grove Press, Inc., for permission to reprint from *Endgame,* by Samuel Beckett (© 1958 by Grove Press, Inc.); *Waiting for Godot,* by Samuel Beckett (© 1954 by Grove Press, Inc.); *The Bald Soprano,* by Eugène Ionesco (© 1956 by Grove Press, Inc.); and *The Dumb Waiter,* by Harold Pinter (© 1960 by Harold Pinter; published 1961 by Grove Press, Inc.).

To Faber and Faber Ltd. for permission to use material from *Endgame* and *Waiting for Godot,* by Samuel Beckett, and from "Burnt Norton," in *Four Quartets,* by T. S. Eliot.

To Eyre Methuen Ltd. for permission to use material from *The Dumb Waiter,* by Harold Pinter.

To Calder and Boyars Ltd. for permission to use material from *The Bald Prima Donna,* by Eugène Ionesco, in *Ionesco Plays,* Vol. I.

To the heirs of Luigi Pirandello and to E. P. Dutton & Co., Inc., for permission to quote from *Six Characters in Search of an Author,* from the book *Naked Masks: Five Plays,* by Luigi Pirandello, edited by Eric Bentley (© 1922, 1952 by E. P. Dutton & Co., Inc.; renewed 1950 in the names of Stafano, Fausto, and Lietta Pirandello). Reprinted by permission of the publishers, E. P. Dutton & Co., Inc.

To Harcourt Brace Jovanovich, Inc., for permission to quote from "Burnt Norton," in *Four Quartets* by T. S. Eliot (© 1943 by T. S. Eliot; © 1971 by Esme Valerie Eliot). Reprinted by permission of Harcourt Brace Jovanovich, Inc.

To Viking Press, Inc., for permission to reprint from *Mr. Sammler's Planet,* by Saul Bellow.

To Alfred A. Knopf, Inc., for permission to reprint from *Something Happened,* by Joseph Heller.

To John Cushman Associates, Inc., and Jonathan Cape Ltd. for permission to use material from *The Summer Before the Dark,* by Doris Lessing (© 1973 by Doris Lessing. Published by Alfred A. Knopf, Inc.).

To 20 Century Music Corp. for permission to reprint lyrics from "It's a Sin to Tell a Lie," by Billy Mayhew (© 1933, 1936 by Bregman, Vocco & Conn, Inc.; renewed 1960, 1963). All rights reserved.

To Warner Bros. Music for permission to reprint lyrics from "Old Man," by Randy Newman (© 1972 by WB Music Corp. and Randy Newman). All rights reserved.

To Dick James Music for permission to use lyrics from "Talking Old Soldiers" and "Sixty Years On," both by Elton John and Bernie Taupin (© 1969 by Dick James Music Limited). All rights reserved.

To Blackwood Music for permission to reprint lyrics from "Old Forgotten Soldier," by Harry Nilsson (© 1974 by Blackwood Music, Inc.).

To Paul Simon for permission to reprint lyrics from his "Old Friends" (© 1968 by Paul Simon).

To ATV Music Group for permission to reprint lyrics from "When I'm Sixty-Four," by John Lennon and Paul McCartney (© 1967 by Northern Songs, Ltd.). All rights for the United States, Canada, Mexico, and the Philippines controlled by Maclen Music, Inc., c/o ATV Music Group. Used by permission. All rights reserved.

To Profit Music, Inc., for permission to use material from "Morning Side," by Neil Diamond.

. . . even the most solid and powerful social institutions,
though they may imprison us, impoverish us, or kill us,
are fundamentally mythical constructions
    designed to hold chaos
    and formlessness
      at bay . . .

                         —MICHAEL NOVAKS

Preface

"CREATIVE SOCIOLOGY" includes ethnomethodology, symbolic interaction, neo-symbolic interaction, phenomenology, and existentialism—terms that trip impressively off the tongue but are understood clearly by only a relatively few initiates. The most recent among these approaches is ethnomethodology, which has its foundations in Schutzian phenomenology. Its proponents present their programmatic statements in language so obscure that many readers become quickly confused, frustrated, and discouraged. Terminology is introduced that is far from self-explanatory, sentences are tortuous, much chaff surrounds the wheat of wisdom that awaits those patient enough to sift through the terrible wordiness.

This book has developed from my efforts over the past years to "demystify" these approaches to the study of society for my students. I cannot claim that this is the definitive work in phenomenology, symbolic interaction, ethnomethodology, or any of the other approaches that belong in the category "creative sociology"; neither do I pretend to present a comprehensive and complete explanation of any one of them. My aim is to simplify profoundly complex concepts without rendering them simplistic and to encourage readers to venture into the deeper waters of the original writings.

As its title suggests, this book is intended as an appetizer, a fancy-tickler—a trip, if you will—an introduction to some intriguing ways of looking into what is so familiar that we do not consider it in any way problematic. Creative sociology takes the familiar, the ordinary, the commonplace, taken-for-granted world and examines it as though it were strange. For creative sociologists, the "solidness" of social structures is illusory, mythical, fleeting. Social organization, as well as the human self, is seen as a process, analogous to a river: flowing, changing, ever moving, altering direction over a period of time. In the village of Bramber in Sussex, one can see several old houses with jetties projecting into open, green fields. Centuries ago, when the houses were built, they backed onto the river Adur, but over the years the river has changed its course and now flows hundreds of feet away. In the same way human beings are constantly moving, changing, becoming. We are different persons from those we were ten years ago, last year, yesterday, this morning. Each is a different person to his mother, his wife, his child, his employer, the shopkeeper, the doctor. It has been said that we have as many selves as we have acquaintances. Just as the self is perceived as a multiplicity of selves, so is society seen differently by different persons, depending upon time, place, company, and countless other factors. The spoken word may be understood differently by each who hears it; the written word may have a different meaning for the reader from that intended by the writer.

If there are so many "realities," how do we make sense of our world? How do we get through each day? It is to this amazingly ordinary phenomenon of daily life that creative sociology addresses itself. For most of the time, for most of us, the world seems to make sense. Or do we make sense of it?

Although many kinds of approaches are included under the rubric "creative sociology," they are not the same. Part One of the book is concerned with pointing out first the similarities and then the differences among the various creative sociologies, as well as showing the manner in which they differ from other kinds of sociological perspectives. Part Two branches off into some tributaries, rivulets, and by-ways; it touches such areas of interest to creative sociologists as the theater as sociology, the meaning of age to the creative approaches to social phenomena, and the special ways in which language and language acquisition are studied from these approaches. The final part of the book takes up some of the criticisms of creative sociology. Is it inherently conservative, as some commentators claim, or is it inherently revolutionary, as others maintain? Is it science—or philosophy? Perhaps it is both, perhaps it is neither.

A book of this kind is never solely the work of one author. One's thinking is influenced and shaped by a lifetime of experiences and by the words and ideas of countless people, some of whom wrote centuries ago. Among the many to whom I am indebted I would like to thank, above all, Stanford Lyman and Marvin Scott, who, as teachers in my undergraduate years, first helped me to see the world from a sociological perspective. Among other teachers, colleagues, and friends, special appreciation and affection are given to Vern Bengtson, Ralph Bolton, Sarane Boocock, Cathy Cameron, Arlene Daniels, Jon Driessen, Bob Gilbert, Bob Herman, George Hesslink, Michael Lustig, Fred Lynch, Bob Nicholson, Helmut Wagner, Steve Warner, and more students than I can possibly name. All of these people, and others, have helped and encouraged me in more ways than they realize. Everything useful to be found in the following pages stems from them; the flaws are entirely my own.

My appreciation goes, too, to the Haynes Foundation for a Summer Research Fellowship in 1974 that gave me the luxury of time to prepare this book. I would also like to express profound thanks to Corinne Bybee, whose patience and advice during several typings of the manuscript encouraged and sustained me, and to my editors at Columbia University Press, Judith Bean and John D. Moore, who were kind, witty, and patient guides along every step of the way from manuscript to bound books.

Finally, to Manning Morris, to whom this book is dedicated, thank you, luv.

Contents

PART ONE
Moorings

Life is like music,
It must be composed by ear, feeling, and instinct,
not by rules.
Nevertheless one had better know the rules.

—SAMUEL BUTLER

CHAPTER ONE

Why "Creative" Sociology?

The Distinction between "Creative" and "Natural Science" Approaches to Social Behavior

WHEN WE LOOK at social behavior and social interaction, we are looking at the very subject matter of sociology: man among men, human beings among other human beings, the individual within the group. How are we to study such phenomena? Are we going to use the tools of the physicist, the biologist, the geologist? Or are human beings different from rocks and rats? The issue touched upon here is one that has concerned social scientists throughout the history of each of the social and behavioral sciences.

Most people are aware of the sharp divisions in, for instance, psychology. Some psychologists—those who run rats through mazes—maintain that we can learn a very great deal about human behavior from investigating animal behavior. Others, the humanists, argue that human beings, while they have some things in common with all animals, are different from other animals. Human beings have speech, the ability to reason, they have culture—and what we can learn about human beings by studying other animals cannot be applied to that which is essentially human in the human animal.

The same polarity is found within sociology. We have the positivistic-naturalistic approach on the one hand and the humanistic-culturalistic approach on the other. There are those, for example, who believe that one can observe, count, put the data in a computer, have them analyzed statistically, and in that way gain valuable knowledge about human beings. Such scientists feel, in fact, that *only* those items which can be observed and then verified by other professionals can be considered proper data for the social scientist, arguing that if we cannot use the same methods to study human behavior as those used by natural scientists, the only reason is that ours is still a young science and we have not yet perfected our instruments. They point out that chemists, physicists, and geologists have been working in their fields for hundreds of years, while sociology dates since only the early 1800s. As practitioners of a new science, we cannot be expected to have developed refined tools. Scientists on this side view social action as not different from the subject matter of the natural and physical sciences in terms of its analysis and explanation.

Extremists in this "objectivist," "positivist," or "naturalist" camp are well represented by George A. Lundberg, who maintained that a man flying before a pursuing crowd and a leaf flying before the wind can be explained by the same general laws; that sufficiently general principles can be found within the framework of the physical sciences to cover both cases. They can each be interpreted as "the behavior of an object of *specified characteristics* reacting to a stimulus of *specified characteristics* within a specified field of force." [1] Those who adopt the natural science approach to the study of society take as their task the discovery of relationships between causes and effects. They assume that there are uniformities which are discoverable and from which some order can be seen to exist in the flux or chaos of social activity. Among these uniformities are rules and guidelines that human beings have developed over time, such as "norms," "statuses," "customs," and the like, which become "internalized" so that people come to *want* to do what they *must* do if order is to be gained and maintained.

The other view is that social behavior cannot be studied by the methods of the natural sciences, for human beings are not comparable to plants or planets, rocks or rats. For those who take this stance, social action is defined in Weberian terms. For Max Weber, social action includes all human behavior, either overt or inward, active involvement or passive nonintervention, *insofar as the actor attaches a subjective meaning to it;* that is to say, such action takes account of the behavior of other actors and is thereby oriented in its course. [2] Human beings, unlike other creatures, do not simply respond mechanically to stimuli. The actions of human beings can be understood only if cultural definitions and the meanings implicit in personal emotions and feelings are taken into account, together with consideration of the situations in which the behavior occurs. The aspect of human beings and human behavior requiring examination is that which *is* human—that which no other animal or inanimate object demonstrates—the ability to interpret stimuli and to respond according to the interpretation.

For instance, the doorbell rings and you go to see who is waiting outside. As you open the door, someone rushes at you and punches you on the nose. What do you do in return? Punch blindly back? Slam the door in the person's face? While you might, indeed, act firmly, you are not likely to respond without first interpreting the action. Let us reconsider the situation. What if the "someone" who rushes at you is a four-year-old child, your nephew, to whom you have been giving boxing lessons?

The very different ways in which social scientists approach the study of social phenomena depend to a great extent upon their particular philosophical view of the social world, a view resting in part upon their assumptions concerning the very nature of human beings and their relationships with their fellows. Thomas Hobbes, for instance, saw life for human beings as likely to be "nasty, brutish, and short," unless their competitive instincts were firmly restrained, while Karl Marx saw humans as infinitely perfectible, able to change and improve their circumstances if only they were allowed to develop freely. There are those who see humans as basically evil, needing rigorous constraints if they are not to dismember their fellows, and others who see man as neutral, as self-actualizing, born a tabula rasa and *becoming* by interacting with other human beings.

Another, and slightly different, issue dividing social scientists is that of freedom versus determinism. Are human beings able to decide their own destinies, to make their own choices among alternatives, or is everything they do predetermined by something outside themselves and beyond their control? Do we study people as beings totally manipulated by circumstances, as did Émile Durkheim, or do we consider them totally free, as does the existential philosopher Jean-Paul Sartre?

Social facts, not *social action,* is the subject matter of sociology for Durkheim. The kinds of social facts he sees as general in a society depend upon the state of evolution in that society, and he sees them as exercising exterior constraints over the individuals in that setting. The density of the population would be seen as a social fact, as would the prevailing religion or the level of industrialization, and it is to these social facts that we must look for determinants of the behavior of the people in a society. Thus rates of suicide are explained not as manifestations of personal desperation, but instead by such social facts as the level of social integration.[3] Sartre, on the other hand, would claim that each person is master of his own fate. "Man is condemned to be free. Condemned, because he did not create himself, yet, in other respects is free; because, once thrown into the world, he is responsible for everything he does."[4] In the same way, the Enlightenment thinkers presented an image of human beings as reasonable, thinking creatures, able to perceive their circumstances, plan, and bring about change in rational and orderly manner, in contrast to earlier thinkers who saw the fate of the human race as predetermined by God and beyond redirection by mere human beings.

Whether human beings are acting creatures or are acted upon by circumstances beyond their control has been the subject of discussion through the ages.[5] According to Paul Tillich, the existentialist movement, which has as one of its basic premises that human beings are autonomous creatures able to direct and shape their lives, was started in the seventeenth century by Pascal, carried on by a few prophetic minds in the nineteenth century, and has come to full victory in the twentieth century. Tillich writes:

> Existentialism, in the largest sense, is the protest against the spirit of industrial society within the framework of industrial society. The protest is directed against the position of man in the system of production and consumption of our society. Man is supposed to be the master of his world and of himself. But actually he has become a part of the reality he has created, an object among objects, a thing among things, a cog within a universal machine to which he must adapt himself in order not to be smashed by it. . . .[6]

The contrary views of free will and determinism can be seen, then, as a continuing argument. A few thinkers have attempted to reconcile this dichotomy: both Marx and Weber tried to demonstrate the ties between "subjective" man and "objective" reality. Until recently it was popular to discuss the "early Marx," whose concern was with "alienation" and individual consciousness, and the "later Marx," who was seen as totally objective and positivistic in his view of society.[7] With the recent English translation of Marx's *Grundrisse*, however, some scholars are beginning to see continuity rather than division in Marx's lifework.[8]

Although the respective positions in the debate have been presented as mutually exclusive, it must be acknowledged that few contemporary social scientists would place themselves at either extreme. As a graduate student studying statistics I was told that it is "a sin to dichotomize," for "nothing in the world can be divided into either positive and negative, present or absent." Contingency tables should never be "two-by-two," but at least "three-by-three," because the presentation of only polar extremes must lead to the treatment of data with injustice. Well, you might ask, surely gender can be dichotomized into male and female? Surely one is either dead or alive? Matters of life and death, however, are becoming harder to decide day by day, as are matters of masculinity and femininity. Clearly, there are all kinds of shadings between any extremes. For the sake of this discussion, the basic assumptions underlying the "creative" approaches in sociology are: that human beings are not merely acted *upon* by social facts or social forces; that they are constantly shaping and "creating" their own social worlds in interaction with others; and that special methods are required for the study and understanding of these uniquely human processes. The term "creative sociology" has been newly coined to refer to the study of these socially creative enterprises.

The group of social scientists with whom we shall be concerned in this book has been elsewhere termed "interpretive," the methods they use to study social interaction being largely and loosely known as "subjective," for these scientists insist that in order to understand what is happening in any social setting or social situation, it is necessary to attempt to see the situation from the point of view of those who are being studied rather than imposing the observer's view of what is going on upon the situation. Another term for "subjective under-standing" is *Verstehen,* a German word which, simply translated into English, means "to understand," but which in sociology has a much more profound meaning. The concept of *Verstehen* is usually associated with Max Weber (1864–1920) but actually predates him slightly. It is to Wilhelm Dilthey (1833–1911) that we must turn for the classic statement in reaction to the posi-tivism of Auguste Comte and John Stuart Mill, both of whom felt that the methods of the natural sciences, which had proved so fruitful, should be gener-alized to the social sciences.[9] Both Dilthey and Weber were far from clear about the method of *Verstehen;* later, Alfred Schutz (1899–1959) clarified Weber's thinking considerably and, more recently still, Harold Garfinkel, the founder of ethnomethodology, has attempted to further erase ambiguities in Schutz's writ-ings about Weber.

As the debate between the naturalists and the humanists proceeds, one sees the term *Verstehen* replaced more and more in some fields by reference to "the phenomenological perspectives of the actor." Alfred Schutz is known as a phe-nomenologist. The concern of phenomenologists is (as is the concern of all *verstehende,* interpretive, or creative sociologists) the understanding of the cog-nitive perspective of the social actor upon his subsequent behavior. Included among this group, besides phenomenologists and ethnomethodologists, are symbolic interactionists, neo-symbolic interactionists, and "sociologists of the absurd." In the pages that follow, these different approaches will be defined and their similarities and differences will be discussed.

Background to the Phenomenological Approach: Husserl, Weber, and Schutz

We will begin with phenomenology because it is both the oldest of the approaches with which we shall grapple and it is at the heart of the newest creative sociology: ethnomethodology.[10] Further, phenomenology is probably the most difficult of the approaches to understand, and familiarity with its terminology should simplify the task of clarifying the others.[11]

Edmund Husserl (1859–1938)

What is phenomenology? In spite of countless books and articles that purport to answer this question, a clear-cut answer appears to be elusive. In order for an approach to be legitimately called phenomenological it should have some recognizable relation to the central thesis of Edmund Husserl.[12] Husserl was born in 1859 in Czechoslovakian Moravia, then part of the Austrian Empire. During his education at the universities of Leipzig, Berlin, and Vienna his major area of study was mathematics, but his greater interest was in philosophy and as a postgraduate scholar he studied philosophy under Franz Brentano at the University of Vienna. In 1866 he went to the University of Halle as an assistant to Carl Stumpf and the following year became a privatdocent on the philosophy faculty. He remained in Halle until 1900, when he transferred to the University of Göttingen. During the following sixteen years he produced some of his most important works; his new philosophy, which he termed "phenomenology," was taking shape between 1904 and 1907 and attained its final form by 1913. In 1916 Husserl went as full professor to the University of Freiburg, where he remained until his retirement in 1928. The years at Freiburg were fruitful ones, as were the years between 1929 and 1938, the year of his death.

Husserl's life work can be divided into four periods: the pre-phenomenological period from 1887 to 1900, which culminated in the ideas formulated in the first volume of *Logical Investigations;* the period of phenomenology as a limited epistemological enterprise (1901–1906); the period of pure phenomenology, during which he formulated a new kind of transcendentalism and a new kind of idealism (1906–1928); and the last period, in which the

Lebenswelt ("life-world") idea gradually emerged and began to occupy a more central place in his phenomenology (1928–1938).[13]

The central thesis of Husserl's mature work was that of the life-world, a term that refers to the concrete reality of an individual's lived experience, in contrast to the interpretation of that reality made by the scientist. That this was a concept never fully clarified by Husserl may be the reason that phenomenology, as it continues to develop, is a moving philosophy, comprising several currents that have a common point of departure but move out at different speeds and in different directions.[14]

What do such diverse thinkers as Brentano, Heidegger, Husserl, James, Merleau-Ponty, Sartre, Scheler, Schutz, and Weber have in common, even though some do not consider themselves phenomenologists? The difficulty of pinpointing the concept of phenomenology is illustrated by the fact that Husserl himself shifted his thinking several times during his lifetime. What remained constant throughout was his search for a rigorous philosophical science divorced from the prevailing positivistic science of the time. Originally, his stress was on "going back to the things themselves"—searching for the essences of phenomena in order to understand them—but this interest gradually shifted to include an emphasis on the wonder of the fact that beings exist in the world who are aware of their own being and of other beings. Husserl ultimately came to emphasize the subjective aspect of phenomenology.[15]

Herbert Spiegelberg claims that it is their method of study which forms the common core uniting all phenomenologists. If human beings live in a reality built out of their interpretations, the task for the phenomenologist is to reconstruct the ways in which human beings go about this interpreting in their daily lives, a task which involves *direct intuition* as the source and final test of all knowledge, and *insight* into essential structures derived from such intuition.

To be able to intuit directly what other persons are doing and why they are doing it is surely a difficult (some might say impossible) task. Phenomenologists have not yet given a clear working description of what such a method involves, although some scholars have attempted to set out the method in a series of steps: Spiegelberg presents seven steps, the first three of which he maintains are used by all phenomenologists, the rest being used by only a small group.[16] Each of these seven steps presupposes those prior to it and each involves a progressively deeper investigation. Phenomenological study begins with a profound disbelief in the theories and taken-for-granted assumptions handed down from other traditions. It attempts to see with "innocence," to observe as though for the first time and then to analyze and describe what is seen. John Wild, while admitting that there are no recipes, no fixed procedures, says that three steps may be clearly distinguished, these three incorporating most of Spiegelberg's seven steps.[17] Each of these steps requires the performing of an *epoché*, or a "bracketing" or "reduction," these terms being used interchangeably.[18] As the phenomenological enterprise is to reveal and clarify phenomena, all disguises must be penetrated, all taken-for-granted, unquestioned usages must be put aside, in the attempt to perceive what phenomena really mean; this putting aside of common usage is what is meant by "bracketing," "phenomenological reduction," "transcendental reduction," "performing the epoché."

We live in an everyday world of things and activities, a social reality comprising cultural objects and social institutions, a world that we, as ordinary human beings, accept without question because we were born into it as it exists. As social creatures, we suspend doubt in the paramount reality of our society. We take the *natural attitude* toward the world of everyday life; we accept it naively. We do not pause and marvel as the days run by. To a Martian, much that we take for granted would appear strange; it might even seem illogical, stupid, or insane. One need not, in fact, travel as far as outer space to find a stranger; those who emigrate to new lands do not share the basic presuppositions of their adoptive society. The necessary adjustments are frequently halting and painful; culture shock must be overcome.[19]

For phenomenologists the very commonplace, common sense, unclarified, taken-for-granted features of the world in which we pass our everyday lives are the subject matter of a science of society. This is the *Lebenswelt*. Because we live in this world as ordinary people, as well as scientists, it is difficult for us to remove objects from their usual settings for examination. We must bracket our own present attitudes and presuppositions—put them to one side, hold them in abeyance—and, as the first step, try to grasp the meaning of a phenomenon as it is lived through by the people involved. It may be, for instance, that I, as an ordinary human being, am an atheist, but as an investigator I wish to examine religion to discover, if I can, its meaning and influence upon society. For these purposes, I must put aside my own prejudices, biases, opinions, beliefs—or lack of them—and try to grasp what religion means for the persons I study. This requires the ability to play the role of the other, to use my imagination, my feeling, all the artistic capacity I possess, to put myself in the other person's place, to feel as he feels, to follow his actions and attitudes as he concretely lives them.

An understanding of the phenomena from within, as they are lived through by others, is the first step in a disciplined investigation of human experience. Subsequent steps aspire to higher levels of abstraction. The second step requires another epochē.[20] I must now ask, in the hypothetical investigation, not what the religious experience means for the people living through it as individuals, but what it means for human beings in general and for humanity as a whole. Questions regarding the nature of religion must be asked. Is it a protest against human beings' inability to control certain aspects of life? Is it a defense against the capriciousness of nature and the elements? Is it a response to the inevitability of death? What is its significance?

The third step or task requires a final epochē, or transcendental reduction. The attempt now is to separate the universal, lasting essence of the phenomenon—the *eidos,* as Husserl terms it—from the fleeting and the incidental. Each human being has a view of the world that usually includes a religious element. What is it about religion that is common to all worlds?

While some contemporary thinkers do not agree that all three steps of the epochē should be, or can be, attempted, the effort to study things not as entities or essences in themselves but as they are perceived by human beings in a social world demonstrates the importance of *meaning* for phenomenologists, as for many creative sociologists. The phenomena of phenomenology are not the *facts* of experience but the *meaning.* When we "bracket the existence" of the content of any given experience, we put aside all questions of fact—of truth or falsity— to concentrate exclusively on the meaning of the experience to the one or ones experiencing it.[21] When I, as investigator, study religion, the question of whether or not God exists becomes irrelevant (even if proof were possible), just as does the question of whether or not witches are real. Questions of meaning can be answered whether such things are real or imagined. The phenomena to be described are meanings. According to Husserl, when we bracket existence we become "disinterested" spectators. This does not mean that the phenomenologist does not care about what is observed, or that he ceases to remain a natural human being, but that he must adopt an objective or detached attitude.[22] When existence is bracketed, or when the epochē is performed, what was previously taken for granted without scrutiny is discovered in the fullness of its meaning for *someone.* Objects do not simply have meaning in themselves, they have meaning *for someone*. The intelligibility of an object or an experience depends upon what someone makes of it; this is what Husserl meant by the discovery of *intentionality*. Consciousness is *intentional*. Human beings do not merely possess consciousness but consciousness *of* some thing or some event. To discover intentionality is to discover the meaning of something for someone as that something is simply and concretely experienced.

Max Weber (1864–1920)

For Max Weber, too, the understanding of the meaning of an act *for the actor* was of foremost importance. He wrote: "Action is social insofar as, by virtue of the subjective meaning attached to it by the acting individual (or individuals) it takes account of the behavior of others and is thereby oriented in its course." [23]

Max Weber is acknowledged as one of the major founders of contemporary sociology, as are Marx and Durkheim. There is, however, no "Weberian school" to parallel the "Marxists" or the "Durkheimians." This is due, in part, to the ambiguities in his work; he presents no systematic view of society, no hint of Utopia, but it is his insight, his "interpretive sociology," that provides the theoretical bridge between Husserlian philosophy and Schutzian phenomenological sociology.

Weber was born in Erfurt, Thuringia (now East Germany), of a well-placed family. His father was a lawyer and politician, a right-wing liberal; his mother was cultured and pious. Although he demonstrated great capacity for learning in his youth, his time at the university was stormy. After being withdrawn and bookish until his late teens, he went to the University of Heidelberg at eighteen and soon followed the German fraternity pattern of dueling, drinking, and carousing. His mother is alleged to have been deeply offended by the new coarseness she observed in her son. His scholarly work continued despite his boisterous youthful activities and he chose an academic career, but ill health dogged him throughout his life, causing him to abandon the pressures of full-time teaching.

Although a prodigious scholar whose encyclopedic knowledge included subjects as varied as history, economic law, religion, art, politics, and science, his illness was such that deep depression and anxiety thrust him into prolonged periods of inactivity, one such breakdown incapacitating him for nearly four years. In 1889 he spent several weeks in a mental institution. The barren stretches of his life were interspersed with periods of intense scholarship and travel.

For Weber, the search for knowledge is never complete; it is, rather, always a striving towards understanding, each new discovery destined to be discarded or changed by subsequent knowledge. The imposition of any framework by the scientist provides only a limited way of seeing, as it inevitably hides from view countless aspects of the phenomenon. Weber considered it impossible to understand reality in its total richness—questions may be asked but answers can never be other than partial. His statements are rarely declarative or definitive but are qualified by numerous clauses and footnotes. Given these reservations, it is not surprising that his view of society appears to his readers as a somewhat untidy parcel, held together loosely by social relations or social interactions.

This does not mean that he was anything other than meticulous in his scientific and scholarly endeavors. His careful conceptual formulations have provided inspiration and impetus for analysis of a number of aspects of society for countless sociologists and political scientists. The Weberian concepts of most importance to the discussion of the bridge between Husserlian philosophical phenomenology and Schutzian phenomenological sociology are *social action, Verstehen,* and *ideal types.*

Social action, or social behavior, as already defined, is action that has subjective meaning for the actor. To be termed "social" such action must involve cognizance of others or another. Understanding of social action can be of more than one kind: It may be purely intellectual—at the rational-logical level—or it may be interpretive—empathic.

A methodological device for rational understanding is the *ideal type,* or *pure type.* To develop an ideal type one regards all irrational, seemingly purposeless, emotional elements of conduct as deviations from purely goal-oriented behavior and determines how a rational course of action would proceed given what is known about the participants and their goals. Weber's model of bureaucracy is one example of an ideal type. It includes all the elements a bureaucracy would comprise if it were to operate at the highest level of efficiency. As we all know from experience, though, inefficiency and irrationality appear to be as usual in modern society as do their opposites. How are we to explain behavior that seems to be irrational, that does not appear goal-oriented, that may even be harmful or destructive to the actor? How are we to explain contradictions in people's actions? Unless the actor is insane, surely his actions have meaning for him? Weber saw the task of sociology as attempting an interpretive understanding of social action using the method of *Verstehen* in combination with ideal types. *Verstehen* searches for the actor's intention and in so doing can help to explain, for instance, the conflicting goals of management and workers in bureaucratic organizations which may slow down production or interfere with management's aims. *Verstehen* may help explain why certain religious ethics go hand in hand with particular kinds of economic arrangements.[24] Just as the performance of the phenomenological epochē requires "indifference," or objectivity, on the part of the observer, so does the use of *Verstehen* as a research device call for a bracketing. The researcher's own belief in the morality or immorality, truth or falsity of what is observed must be put aside. What is to be sought is the meaning to the actor.

Alfred Schutz (1899–1959)

Alfred Schutz was born in Vienna, where he spent his childhood and youth. He studied law and the social sciences at the University of Vienna under Ludwig von Mises, Friedrich von Wiese, Hans Kelsen, and others, and he remained in Vienna for his early professional life in law and banking.[25]

His first major book, the only one published during his lifetime, was *Der Sinnhafte Aufbau der sozialen Welt.*[26] The book was read by Husserl with considerable appreciation. When the two men later met, Husserl offered Schutz the opportunity to become his assistant at the University of Freiburg, but Schutz could not accept the offer. He and his wife left Austria in advance of the Nazi occupation and, after spending a year in Paris, in 1939 emigrated to the United States of America, where Schutz reestablished his career in law and business. He soon began lecturing at the New School for Social Research in New York, where he accepted a full professorship in 1952, curtailing his business activities. His students and colleagues speak of him with great affection and admiration as a warm, delightful person.

Schutz's work can be seen as a clarification, a synthesis, a transformation, and an advancement of the work of both Husserl and Weber, with further inspiration drawn from the ideas of Henri Bergson, William James, George Herbert Mead, Georg Simmel, W. I. Thomas, and several others. For Schutz, the subject matter of sociology is the manner in which human beings constitute, or create, the world of everyday life; the task of sociology is to develop both a theory of this creative social activity and a rigorous method for its study and description. He begins with the Husserlian notion of the *Lebenswelt,* the world of everyday life, the taken-for-granted world into which we are born and which we accept, taking the natural attitude toward it. Other people inhabit this world with us; somehow we live our daily lives among them, taking them into account as we proceed with our mundane business. How do we manage this with such seeming ease? Weber had made a start in solving this problem but, Schutz felt, had broken off his analyses of social action, *Verstehen,* and ideal types too soon, without fully explaining how humans *do* orient themselves to others, or how we, as social scientists, can use the methods of *Verstehen* and ideal types to understand this social action.

"IN-ORDER-TO" AND "BECAUSE" MOTIVES

Schutz agrees with Weber that to understand action one must discover meaning; the first step, therefore, is to define "meaning." How do we interpret, or find meaning, in our everyday activities—in what we see and hear and touch and smell and taste? In and of themselves, Schutz says, our lived experiences mean nothing to us unless we possess a vast stock of previous experiences upon which we draw and reflect to explain each new experience, this latest experience then becoming part of our mental stock. To most experiences, meaning is ascribed in retrospect, although we also think projectively in terms of future experiences. These two kinds of ascriptions of meaning Schutz terms, respectively, *because motives* and *in-order-to motives.*

An *in-order-to motive* involves a measure of planning, a reasonable notion of how a goal is to be achieved. This kind of motive is a context of meaning that is built on the stock of experience available at the time of projecting. Schutz writes, "Every in-order-to motivation presupposes such a stock of experience which has been elevated to an 'I-can-do-it-again' status." [27] He gives as an example the dialing of a telephone number. The caller anticipates that a number of events will occur, leading him to be able to speak to the person being called. The entire procedure is taken for granted, the caller not necessarily understanding or thinking about the electronic processes he will trigger. The caller projects an idea of the call in the future perfect tense as "something I will have done soon," and then simply dials. He dials a number *in order to* speak to a friend.

With a *because motive,* meaning is generated by an already experienced event. For instance, I put up my umbrella because I have perceived that it is raining. To be sure, I could say, "I put up my umbrella in order to stay dry," but the timing of experiences is important in discriminating between genuine because motives and in-order-to motives. In-order-to motives refer to some experience in the future; because motives refer to past experience, even though that experience may have occurred a mere fraction of a second ago.

RECIPROCITY OF PERSPECTIVES, MODES OF RELATEDNESS,
SOCIAL DISTRIBUTION OF KNOWLEDGE

We live in the world not as isolated atoms but as social beings. How do we take into account the meaning, or intention, or motives, that experiences have for the others to whom we relate? How do we move from an understanding of subjective meaning, meaning to the individual, to intersubjective meaning, meaning between and among people?

One of the ways we understand another is by assuming the other's standpoint. This is simple when dealing with experiences that are common to most people. If I see you put up your umbrella, I can readily determine that you are attempting either to keep dry or less likely, to keep cool, depending upon the weather. You can understand that if I am running it is probably so that I can get where I am going as quickly as possible. Schutz's term for this ability for each of the parties to an encounter to be able to put himself in the place of the other is *reciprocity of perspectives.* We can watch others in action and, drawing from our stock of experience, or knowledge, perceive what they are doing and why they are doing it.

It is also relatively easy to interchange standpoints with those with whom we are familiar. We are then reasonably safe in assuming that our interactants do perceive objects in much the same way as do we. Schutz points out, however, that the ways in which we relate to others differ greatly depending upon whether we know people intimately, in face-to-face relationships as consociates, or whether we know them impersonally. Our relationships also vary temporally. We know people here and now as consociates, but others whom we do not perceive directly fall into one of three classes: the world of contemporaries (*Mitwelt*), who live and experience at the same time as do we and who might conceivably become consociates; the world of predecessors (*Vorwelt*); or the world of successors (*Folgewelt*).

The ways in which we relate to others also depend upon an infinite number of characteristics that affect the stock of experiences, or stock of knowledge, which we bring to a situation. Women know things that men do not know, just as men know things of which women are not aware. Social standing and education, one's position in the work world, whether one is single or married, has four children or none, one's understanding of music, sports, or technology—all of these and much more contribute to a person's stock of knowledge. Knowledge, says Schutz, is socially distributed.

TYPIFICATIONS

Given the difficulties of interacting with others who possess varied stocks of knowledge, how do we "get by" in ordinary day-to-day encounters? How can we assume another's standpoint? Schutz says that the stocks of knowledge actors possess, much of which has been handed down to them by their parents and teachers, are in the form of *types,* or *typicalities,* or *typifications.* The knowledge that the ordinary person possesses is not homogeneous, it is incoherent, unclear, and contradictory, but for members of a particular group it takes on an appearance of sufficient coherence, clarity, and consistency to give anybody a reasonable chance of being understood. This is so because any person born or reared within a particular group or culture accepts a ready-made, standardized scheme of behavior in the culture as an unquestioned and unquestionable guide in all the situations that normally occur within that social world. This scheme comprises a series of recipes for interpreting and handling situations with a minimum of effort. These recipes include *of course* assumptions, which we accept even though we may not know their origins or their real meanings.

Although one can rarely know another's motives, meanings, goals, and plans, one can experience them in their *typicality* by constructing typical patterns of motives and ends of which the other's actions appear to be an instance. This is similar to the ideal type of Max Weber but at the common-sense level, for one's own purposes, rather than at the level of the scientist, whose propositions are subjected to rigorous examination by other scientists. It is fairly safe to assume, in the world of everyday life, that the life-world of one's fellows is similar to one's own life-world. Schutz suggests that these types are "vacillating approximations," generated in terms of the purposes at hand. They are arbitrary and may bear little relation to the "facts." Again, though, matters of "truth" or "falsity" are not being questioned. By and large, members of groups feel that they experience and interpret the world in similar ways. If they did not, social life would rapidly crumble.

Whenever we pass from situations in which we have an intimate knowledge of the other interactants, we employ types to understand others' actions. These are the common-sense constructs of ordinary people making sense or meaning of their world. These typicalities have a measure of anonymity in that they belong to no one person but are believed by the members of the group to be shared by all.[28]

FROM COMMON-SENSE CONSTRUCTS TO SOCIAL SCIENCE CONSTRUCTS

So far, we have examined Schutz's theory of the manner in which actors in the world of everyday life interpret the actions of their fellows. What methods does Schutz propose for the scientific observation and description of these phenomena? [29]

In the discussion of the natural attitude of the life-world, it has been noted that human beings suspend doubt in the paramount reality of that life-world. We take for granted that our world is orderly, that other human beings exist and are conscious, just as we are conscious, that others live in similar ways to ourselves so that, for all practical purposes, we can understand each other. As we live in this paramount reality, we modify and add to the stock of knowledge we each have to hand, that knowledge being passed to us by parents and teachers largely in the form of types or typicalities.

The life-world is our major province of meaning, or province of reality, but it contains other provinces of meaning that we can enter either by drifting into them, as into the province of dreams or fantasy, or we can enter purposefully, as into the province of science, or religion, or theater. When we enter one of these provinces, or subworlds, we impart to it "the accent of meaning," suspending doubt in *its* reality and, for the time being, bracketing the other provinces of meaning. As we become fully absorbed in the actions of the characters in a film or a play, the world in which they live becomes our world. Our return to the life-world when the lights go up is sometimes shocking in its abruptness. To move from province to province requires a leap of consciousness. [30]

The world of science is one such province of meaning. To enter it requires the bracketing of the life-world, the performance of an epochē. The scientist must leave aside all presuppositions about what is *of course* real and "true" to examine the subject matter indifferently and objectively. All that the scientist as a human being in the life-world takes for granted becomes the object of study for the human being as scientist.

The research methods scientists use are governed by their subject matter. The world of nature explored by the natural sciences does not "mean" anything to molecules, atoms, and electrons; on the other hand, the life-world, which is the observational field of the social scientist, has specific meanings for those who inhabit it. Schutz uses *first-level constructs* to refer to the common-sense types used by human beings in understanding the everyday world and *second-level constructs* to refer to ideal types, or constructed types, used by the social scientists to explain social reality. Second-level constructs, like first-level constructs, must include reference to the *Verstehen* of the actor's action from the actor's point of view, the meaning an action has for the actor.

The second-level, scientific constructs must be objective in the sense that their propositions are subjected to controlled verification and must not refer to private, unreachable experience—but *Verstehen* has been accused by its critics of being a totally introspective activity, unsuited to scientific method because unverifiable. Schutz, in response to these accusations, insists that *Verstehen* is neither introspective nor private, even when used at the common-sense level. *Verstehen* is the knowledge of the meaning of human actions which we have gained in our experience of life. It is a result of processes of learning or acculturation and is controllable at least to the same extent that any other method is controllable. It can be used as a scientific method and is, in fact, used continuously in such arenas as courts of law. In court, decisions must be made regarding whether, for instance, the defendant has shown "premeditated malice" or "intent" to kill, and whether he was capable of knowing the consequences of his act. Schutz points out that we even have certain rules of procedure furnished by rules of evidence in the legal sense, and a kind of verification of the findings resulting from processes of *Verstehen* by, for instance, courts of appeals. Predictions based on *Verstehen* are always being made with a high measure of success. For instance, Schutz says, there is an excellent chance that a properly stamped and addressed letter put in a New York mailbox will reach the addressee in Chicago. We know this, not through deep introspective study of the motives of post office workers, but through our general stock of knowledge about our society.

The second-level constructs of the social scientist are constructs of the constructs made by the actors in the social scene. The in-order-to motives and the because motives—the "course-of-action" types of the life-world—must be replicated as course-of-action types for the social scientist. A second-level construct is a model of a sector of the social world consisting of typical human action, but it is formed from an entirely different standpoint from common-sense constructs. The scientist brings to the task a body of scientific knowledge, which includes rules of procedure; he himself is not "of" the setting being studied but has replaced the personal biographical situation with a scientific situation. He cannot organize the observed world in layers around himself at the center, nor can he interact as a consociate with one of the actors without temporarily abandoning his scientific attitude.

Models, or typifications, are abstracted from the totality of social action to include only those elements pertinent to the performance of course-of-action patterns. Social science typifications, then, are not of actors as human beings living in the richness of their everyday lives but are of "puppets" to be manipulated by the scientist for his scientific purposes. A type is limited by the scientist's purpose just as a puppet is limited by the puppeteer. In such a simplified model of the social world and the actors within it, rational choices from rational motives are possible, just as in the Weberian ideal typical model of bureaucracy.

To be considered scientific, constructs must fulfill certain requirements. They must be formed in accordance with the postulates of *logical consistency, subjective interpretation,* and *adequacy.* Logical consistency implies the highest degree of clarity of the conceptual framework and compatibility with the principles of formal logic. It is their strictly logical character that distinguishes second-level constructs from the constructs of common-sense thinking in daily life. Subjective interpretation insures the possibility of referring back to the meaning an act had for the typified actor, since the construct must relate types of persons and types of actions in a plausible way. Finally, compliance with the postulate of adequacy means that the action implied by the construct would be understandable to the actor and his fellow actors in terms of their common-sense interpretations of everyday life.

Once the models are constructed it becomes possible to manipulate and change situations in endless ways in order to predict how particular puppets with specific underlying goals and motives might behave under varied sets of circumstances, and to discover and explain observable regularities.

Existential Phenomenology and Other Phenomenologies

Existential Phenomenology

The existentialist movement is not new. As was mentioned earlier, Pascal, who wrote three hundred years ago, has been described as an existentialist thinker. Existentialism is a phenomenological mode of thought in that it attempts to approach the problem of being by a careful study of personal existence as it is concretely lived, as it is perceived by the individual consciousness. Existentialism is phenomenological in that it describes what is experienced without imposing preconceived notions and prior categories upon that which is examined.

The foundations of modern existentialism may be said to be rooted in the work of Søren Kierkegaard (1813–1855). Kierkegaard, a Danish philosopher, was almost unknown outside his homeland during his lifetime, but his work later exerted a great influence upon Protestant theology and the philosophy of existentialism. In his work on religion, Kierkegaard maintained that if we are to understand religion as a peculiarly human manifestation of man, we must understand it in relation to the thinker of the thought, as the guiding light of his existence. By grasping the nature of existence—life as it is lived—we can understand consciousness, or thought, but by consciousness alone we can never understand existence. Kierkegaard discussed religion not in abstract or rational terms but as a personal, deeply felt, emotional experience of flesh-and-blood human beings.[31]

Among modern existentialists are Martin Heidegger (1889–   ), whose best known disciple is Jean-Paul Sartre (1905–   ), and Maurice Merleau-Ponty (1908–1961). Heidegger worked closely with Husserl, as his assistant, at Freiburg from 1920 to 1923. He was also friendly with Max Scheler (1874–1920) and Karl Jaspers (1883–1969), both phenomenological philosophers. Merleau-Ponty was influenced by the work of Husserl and of Schutz. For many years he and Sartre were colleagues in the founding and production of a journal, *Les Temps modernes,* in which they expressed their ideas and versions of existential phenomenology.

Interest in existentialism was renewed and grew to popular dimensions during and after the holocaust of Nazism. The literature of the modern existentialists, in the form of the novels and plays of the absurd as well as in philosophical writings, is saturated with a sense of the uncertainty, fragility, and finitude of human existence. All of life is lived in situations. We struggle to understand one situation, only to move on to another, to begin again our search for understanding. We are always moving, our struggle to attain some kind of assurance of permanence leading only to the next situation. If there are any rules and guidelines by which one may live, they are shifting, ambiguous, elusive; they vary from situation to situation. Camus' Sisyphus personifies the human condition, ever pushing his huge burden toward the top of the hill, only to have it roll to the bottom when, once more, he must push it upward.

The Sociology of the Absurd of Lyman and Scott

Deriving its name from the theater and literature of the absurd, Lyman and Scott's sociology of the absurd is clearly founded upon existential-phenomenological foundations. The sociology of the absurd asks how social order is possible. By "social order" is envisaged "the meaning social actors attach to events, persons, self, and others" to make sense of their world, for "absurd" implies that "real" or "essential" meaning is nowhere to be found; each must strive to carve out meaning for himself. All systems of belief are arbitrary.[32]

Although the sociology of the absurd rejects the notion of "essential" meaning, it does recognize that there is a common ground upon which we stand—a set of rules, norms, guidelines by which we live. These guidelines, though, are blurred. They must be negotiated, especially in unfamiliar situations. In familiar situations the rules are much less problematic. The meaning an actor gives is situational, "situation" including the social characteristics of the actor. Actors, however, are not necessarily forced to act in given ways because of these characteristics; this is not a deterministic philosophy. Human beings are seen as both constructing, and being constructed *by,* social reality in every situation.

The view of human beings held by the sociologists of the absurd is of creatures who are capable of making choices among alternatives, who have a large measure of autonomy. Yet, drawing from Georg Simmel, this sociology sees *conflict* as underlying all social action. Even two lovers in an embrace may be regarded as being in conflict since each may be seeking to outdo the other in demonstrating affection or providing the other with pleasure.[33] An element is added here that does not appear as a stated presupposition in Husserlian or Schutzian phenomenology, although Weber certainly considered matters of power in his sociology. Weber saw society as composed of a loosely knit collection of interest groups, each vying to maintain or to enhance its advantage over other groups. In the absurd, human beings are seen as goal-oriented, as seeking the best way to realize their goals while at the same time presenting themselves to others in the best light. All human relations have the quality of a game. There are winners and losers, depending upon one's skill at interpreting and manipulating the rules. The sociology of the absurd addresses the question of power, of subordination and superordination, and the ways in which this is perceived by actors in their continuing attempts to realize their goals.

If, say Lyman and Scott, the theater of the absurd illustrates the essential meaninglessness of the world, the sociology of the absurd describes man's constant striving for meaning. "It is the meaningless-world-made-meaningful which is the strategic research site for the Sociology of the Absurd." [34]

The Sociology of Knowledge of Berger and Luckmann

Like the sociology of the absurd, Peter L. Berger and Thomas Luckmann's work has been profoundly influenced by the teaching and writing of Alfred Schutz. Luckmann is joint author with Schutz of *The Structures of the Life World*, published after Schutz's death; Berger was associated with the New School for Social Research for a number of years. Their widely read treatise on the sociology of knowledge, *The Social Construction of Reality*, takes as its central concern the ways in which human beings construct reality—produce society—so that it becomes an objective reality for them. Society, say Berger and Luckmann, is a human product, an ongoing production, created and sustained by the processes of *externalization, objectification,* and *internalization,* these processes not necessarily being temporally separated or in this sequence.

Our subjective interpretations and meanings are externalized in speech and other symbols. We talk about ourselves, and in the talking we crystallize who we are and what we are as objects, both for ourselves and for others. As we talk, we externalize and objectify our reality, this reality being limited by our stock of knowledge which, following Schutz, is socially distributed. As does the sociology of the absurd, the sociology of knowledge of Berger and Luckmann acknowledges the importance of power in the ability of some to impose their definitions of reality upon others.

Human existence is an ongoing externalization. As humans externalize *themselves,* they construct and objectify the world around them.[35] The internalization of humanly constructed reality indicates that the objectified world becomes subjective reality; it means that humans come to understand, accept, and share definitions of reality. Only when we are able to participate in each other's being do we become social beings, members of society.

We become members of society through processes of socialization, "the comprehensive and consistent induction of an individual into the objective world of a society or a sector of it." [36] Through socialization we internalize social reality.

The varying kinds of contents objectified and internalized from culture to culture are a clear indication that the "realities" of societies are socially constructed rather than physically or biologically determined.[37] Notions of "proper" sexual behavior, for instance, have varied through the ages and from culture to culture, as have images of maleness and femaleness. Homosexuality was considered noble and moral among many Greeks of Plato's time, including soldiers, whereas at present homosexuality will provoke immediate discharge from most nations' military services.

Marxist Phenomenology

A marriage between Marxist thinking and phenomenology may appear to be an unpromising union; many sharp distinctions can be found between the two theoretical approaches. Phenomenology, as we have seen, takes the actor's meaning or interpretation as its central datum, while Marxism is concerned with the nature of the economic substructure of a society and its effect upon other social structures. Such simplifications do justice to neither school of thought. Phenomenology is by no means a clear-cut philosophy; similarly, the work of Marx is multidimensional. Marx's writings are rich in humanism, the emphasis on the importance of the linkage between existence and consciousness showing concern with issues that are also central to existential phenomenology, while a phenomenological analysis of subjective and intersubjective experience need not exclude discussion of the social implications of such study.

The blending of Marxism and phenomenology requires the abstraction from each philosophy those elements that are compatible. From a Marxist dialectical perspective, for instance, the seemingly static structures of society undergo continuous change, continuous reconstruction. Both the Marxist dialectic and existentialism stress the temporary character of reality. What exists at any given moment is destined to be transformed by its inner contradictions. What appears an orderly arrangement is neither permanent nor necessary. Dialectic, though, is not inexorable. Human beings affect the process by their choices among the actions they perceive as possible. The person is at the center of both philosophies.

The writings of Marx stress the creative, self-determining relation of human beings to their circumstances. Human beings can change the conditions of their existence, hence Marx's emphasis on *praxis*—action. In changing circumstances, in creating their social world, human beings make possible new ways of knowing that world, new ways of being conscious of their existence, of being human.

For Marx, human beings become real and as objects to themselves only in and through their relationships with other human beings. The nature of these relationships can change their views of themselves. They can be separated from their humanness—they can live as animals, meeting their animal needs but failing to realize their human potential—or they can be "species beings"—aware of themselves as active, creative beings, and conscious of other human beings as similarly productive and creative.[38]

This aspect of Marxist thought is clearly compatible with those elements of phenomenological sociology which hold that human beings are fully human only in their relationships with others. The social world is an intersubjective world, the social beings within that world interpreting actions in the light of the stock of knowledge they bring with them to each situation. Knowledge is socially distributed; it depends upon family background, education, and employment, among many other factors. Changes in circumstances bring with them changes in ways of seeing the world. Thought and experience, consciousness and existence, are closely related in both Marxist thought and in phenomenology.

Among those who have attempted a synthesis of the two schools of thought are Sartre, Enzo Paci, George Gurvitch, and the young Herbert Marcuse, but the task is not complete and, because change is continuous in the existentialist and the dialectical viewpoint, the task can never be completed.[39]

The phenomenological approach, in all its varieties, is concerned with the meaning, or intention, that social action has for actors, the ways in which individuals interpret their worlds. To discover the actor's intention, research methods are used which themselves require interpretive skills, and a special form of detachment and disinterest, as these terms are uniquely defined within the phenomenological framework.

Symbolic Interaction: From Mead to Goffman

Although symbolic interaction developed separately from phenomenology, in the United States rather than in Europe, the two approaches are similar in a number of ways. Indeed, according to some of its interpreters, symbolic interaction is concerned "with the 'inner' or phenomenological aspects of human behavior," [40] and in his introduction to *The Unadjusted Girl,* by W. I. Thomas, an early symbolic interactionist, Michael Parenti writes: "An understanding of a situation as reached by the disinterested investigator is . . . never complete until he appreciates the meanings experienced by the participants themselves." [41] As in phenomenology, the interest is in *meaning,* the meaning to the

participants in a situation as appreciated by the disinterested observer. Symbolic interactionists claim that for human beings there is always a
stage of examination or deliberation before any self-determined or conscious act.
W. I. Thomas, an important founder of this school of thought, has termed the
outcome of this deliberation "definition of the situation." The definition creates
the action for, Thomas wrote, "If men define situations as real, they are real in
their consequences." [42] Definition of the situation can be seen to parallel interpretation in the Weberian sense.

Among the early contributors to symbolic interaction theory are Charles Horton Cooley, John Dewey, William James, George Herbert Mead, W. I.
Thomas, and many others. Some of these thinkers knew, and were known by,
the European phenomenologists, the work of each adding insights to that of the
others.

George Herbert Mead (1863–1931)

Mead, the son of a clergyman, was born in Massachusetts. His family moved
to Oberlin, Ohio, in 1870, where Mead was later to do his undergraduate
work. He was a graduate student at Harvard, during the time when Josiah
Royce and William James were on the philosophy faculty, and in Berlin. From
1891 until 1893 he taught in the philosophy department at the University of
Michigan, where John Dewey and Charles Horton Cooley were among his colleagues. He followed Dewey to the University of Chicago in 1893 and remained
there until his death in 1931.

Interestingly, Mead wrote no books during his lifetime, although he did
publish a number of articles. He was, however, a brilliant and popular lecturer
with a large following of dedicated students, some of whom, after his death,
gathered together his lecture notes and published them in four volumes. [43]

He refined and developed the ideas of several thinkers, including Wilhelm
Wundt, William James, and Charles Horton Cooley, into a theory of the development of the *self*. He saw the self as a social product, not to be considered in
isolation but in interaction. For Mead, as for other symbolic interactionists, the
self in interaction is the central focus of a study of human beings.

The self, which is considered a uniquely human characteristic, is seen by
Mead as not present at birth but as developing in each individual through the
process of social experience and social communication. The self is a *process*,
which continues to develop throughout one's life. This notion of the fluidity of
the self comes from William James (1842–1910), who recognized that our con-

sciousness today is not the same as our consciousness yesterday, yet yesterday's experiences are part of today's experiences. We know that our selves change; we are able to discern that what we were, we are no longer. The subjective "I" can stand back, as it were, and view the "me" as an object.[44] The aspect of the self termed the "me" consists of the ways we see ourselves and the ways others see us. It is also known as the "social self," or the "looking-glass self," a term derived from Cooley (1864–1929); in this imagery we see ourselves reflected in the eyes of others, as in a looking glass, and so perceive ourselves as others see us. Sometimes the view another has of us can be seen directly—it is clear that the other approves or disapproves of the way we look, or of what we say—but it is frequently a subtle exchange, a covert sensing of others' opinions.

Also from Cooley comes the notion that different others see a person in different ways, yet these "imaginations people have of one another are the *solid facts* of society." [45] The very structure of our social life depends upon interpretation, which, paradoxically, appears to vary. Although definitions do differ, the opinions of certain *significant others*—a term contributed by the psychologist Harry Stack Sullivan but now used in most modern discussions of symbolic interaction—weigh more heavily in some areas of life than in others. For instance, given conflicting expectations of behavior, a man is more likely to be concerned about his wife's opinion of him than about the view of, say, a neighbor. Perhaps the "me" element of the self is better regarded as an indeterminate number of "me's" from which the "I" selects the one which is most suitable or proper in the situation. The "I," the impulsive, creative aspect of the self, untrammeled by others' expectations, is in constant interaction with the "me(s)"; the self is constantly reflecting.

The self arises and develops through *taking the attitude of the other,* or *taking the role of the other,* toward oneself. This means interpreting gestures, facial expressions, and statements of the other as though one were in his place, imagining how one appears to him. Rather than taking the attitude of a *significant other* towards our action, we might take the attitude of the *generalized other,* this attitude being the one which prevails in the society, that which we perceive as socially proper. We take the attitude of the generalized other when we ask "What would people think?"

The generalized other can be seen as the community exerting control over the individuals who constitute it. Further, it is not enough, according to Mead, for the individual to take the attitude of others toward *himself;* he must also be able to take their attitudes toward various aspects of their shared social activity for the self to develop to its full potential and for the individual to become a fully social being. Put differently, the complex processes of human society are possible only insofar as the individual is able to take the attitudes of all who are involved in these processes and is able to direct his behavior accordingly.

In order to take the role of the other, we use gestures and symbols but, more importantly, we use *significant symbols:* gestures or words which "implicitly arouse in an individual making them the same response which they explicitly arouse, or are supposed to arouse, in the individuals to whom they are addressed." [46] It is in the use of language that Mead saw human social life as differing totally from that of animals and social insects, in that the responses these creatures make toward each other are instinctive and automatic, involving no conscious reflection. Animals cannot *take the role of the other.* This ability comes only with the use of significant symbols—mutually understood or parallel gestures.

A self can be developed only in a creature who can see himself as an object, something possible only by taking the role of the other toward oneself. Further, in taking the role, or the perspective, of others, in identifying with them, shared meanings and common understandings and expectations are learned and reinforced. It is upon these shared meanings that society, in the sense of a cooperating group, is based. This is not to say, of course, that all values are shared. Society is formed by joint actions but these actions may advantage some more than others; they may be based on compromise or unequal power, or on sheer necessity. Society is held together by workable relations.

Mead sees self and mind developing together. Mind manifests itself only when the elements of the self are interacting, using significant symbols. Mind is reflective, abstract thinking. It is social in origin and arises only when the individual can become an object to himself, can become *self-conscious,* can direct his own action through deliberation. Mind, says Mead, is symbolic behavior.

Herbert Blumer (1900–   )

Perhaps the most devoted and voluble proponent of the symbolic interaction theory stemming from Mead's concepts and formulations is Herbert Blumer, who was a member of the sociology faculty at the University of Chicago from 1927 to 1952 and is presently at the University of California at Berkeley, where he has been since leaving Chicago.

In a number of important articles and a major book, Blumer has attempted both to clarify Mead's symbolic interaction theory and to develop research methods for use with this approach.[47] For Blumer, symbolic interaction rests on three simple premises:

1. Human beings act toward things on the basis of the meanings the things have for them.
2. The meaning of such things is derived from the social interaction that one has with one's fellows.
3. These meanings are handled in, and modified through, an interpretive process used by the person dealing with the things he encounters.

These interpretive processes clearly rest on all the foregoing Meadian concepts, including those of the "I" and the "me", and the self as continually developing in interaction with others.

Mead had identified two forms of social interaction: nonsymbolic as well as symbolic. In the former, actors respond directly toward others' gestures and symbols, without interpretation. This may be seen as mere stimulus and response. In symbolic interaction actors not only respond to each others' symbols and gestures and act according to the interpreted meaning, they also convey indications to the others in the interaction as to how they should act. Because of symbolic interaction, human group life becomes an ongoing process in which actors continually fit their lines of action to others' actions.

How does Blumer propose that this symbolic interaction be studied? How can a researcher examine a human being taking account of what others in a situation are about to do and the ways that person "fits his lines of action to others?"

Instead of the terms "ideal types" or "social science constructs," Blumer writes of "devising images of the empirical world" and of testing these images through *"exacting scrutiny of the empirical world"* (my emphasis).[48] Most scientists, he says, have no *personal* experience of what they study. The richness of the exchanges, the complexity of the interlaced activities of groups of people as they relate to each other, the confusions and misunderstandings that arise and become confounded by further misunderstanding—in short, the world of everyday experience, of ongoing group life—are neither familiar to most scholars nor is there any realization by them that they are missing anything. Proper research procedures, he taunts, do not encourage firsthand acquaintance with the sphere of life under study. The predominant procedure is to take one's premises about the nature of the world for granted, without examining those premises.

Instead, Blumer proposes that the researcher must get close to ongoing social life, must lift the veils covering it and dig deep within it. This is a tough job, which must be done carefully and honestly. It requires a creative yet disciplined imagination, resourcefulness, flexibility, and a constant readiness to test and recast our views and images of the area.[49] He provides no rigid set of techniques with which to explore a hitherto unknown sphere of social life. Any method by which one learns about an area is acceptable: direct observation, field study, interviewing, conversing, consulting public records, the use of life histories, letters, diaries, participant observation, arranging group discussions, or counting things, if this seems worthwhile. Informed people who are part of the group also should be encouraged to share their knowledge. Images must be constantly tested and revised.

Thorough exploration of the area is followed by scientific analysis involving the discerning of elements and the isolating of relationships between them. An "element" might be leadership or integration. These concepts should not be defined in advance of careful exploration of the area and inspection of the data.

Symbolic interaction, according to Blumer, is a down-to-earth approach. Its interest is in the natural world and its studies are conducted within that natural world. Study must be *direct,* not through working with a preset model derived from a few scattered observations. The task of symbolic interaction is to discover what is going on in social life. To take the notion of "self," for instance, and attempt to measure or analyze it by the use of scales or similar techniques is, for Blumer, nonsensical and irrelevant to symbolic interactionists, whose task is the study of the relationships and actions between and among people.[50]

If, as in the social interactionist position, the social action of an actor is constructed by himself, then that action must be seen from his point of view. The researcher must see the situation as it is seen by the actor, observing what the actor takes into account, how he interprets it, noting the alternatives that are mapped out in advance, and attempting to follow the interpretation that led to the selection and execution of one of those alternative acts. The formation of social action, says Blumer, depends upon the situation and its interpretations.

Some variations of Meadian symbolic interaction theory have developed over the years, including the role theory of Ralph Turner, Tamotsu Shibutani, Arnold Rose, and others; the labeling theory of Howard Becker; and the neo-symbolic-interaction of Erving Goffman, George G. McCall and J. L. Simmons, and Lyman and Scott. The works of all of these can be seen to fit into more than one such category.

Role theory stems from W. I. Thomas's dictum that "people tend to play the roles assigned to them." [51] They play roles by living up to the expectations others have of them. Mirra Komarovsky's finding that young college women often pretend to be less intelligent than they really are when out on a date, and deliberately play to lose when competing in games with young men, nicely indicates the pressures to conform to the general expectation that men will appear superior in male-female relationships. [52] It also demonstrates the conflicting role expectations prevailing in many situations. While a woman is expected by her parents to make excellent grades in college, the generalized other—and that, paradoxically, includes her parents—expects her to "catch a man" while in college and encourages her to achieve this goal by allowing her men friends to believe in their superiority. Lest this is thought to be an old-fashioned set of expectations in these liberated times, recent studies of college students provide evidence that sex-role stereotypes are not changing with remarkable speed. At least half the young women in recent samples pretended on dates to be less intelligent than they really are. [53]

Among the significant others particularly important for the development, or change, of the self are, of course, parents, especially during infancy; parents and teachers during childhood; and peers, parents, and teachers during adolescence. As one moves along the time-track of life, different others acquire important significance. Significant others are not necessarily consociates, relating on a face-to-face basis. They may be writers or philosophers living on the other side of the world whose work inspires one to live up to certain standards, or achieve certain ends. Such a person may even be long dead, but still be of great significance in directing one's self and one's endeavors.

Robert Rosenthal and Lenore Jacobson's classroom study may be seen to illustrate the effect upon the self-consciousness or self-concept of young children by the expectations of teachers—by the vision of themselves reflected in the "looking glass." [54] The study was designed to test the proposition that "those children from whom the teacher expected greater intellectual growth would show such greater growth." At the beginning of the school year, teachers were led to believe that certain of their pupils had very great potential, shown by their scores on nonverbal tests, and would demonstrate considerable intellectual advancement in the coming months. The children designated potential "spurters" were, in fact, chosen by means of a table of random numbers. The experimental treatment of the children involved no more than giving their names to their teachers; the differences between these children and others in the classroom were entirely in the minds of the teachers.

The results indicated strongly that the children expected by their teachers to make greater intellectual gains did show such gains, relative to other children, even though the gains were greater in grades one and two than in grades three through six. Further, when the teachers were asked at the end of the academic year to describe the classroom behavior of the children, the "experimental children" were described as being happier, more interesting, more curious than the other children. They were also seen as more appealing, better adjusted, and as having a better chance of being successful in later life.

Although the research design has been criticized for, among other things, the limitations that seem to accompany any single-school study,[55] Rosenthal and Jacobson's study appears to support the notion that people tend to play the roles assigned to them. The researchers were not able to offer a clear explanation of their results. Teachers insisted that they had spent no more time with the selected children than with the others. Yet, perhaps through the teachers' tones of voice, nuances, inflections, and facial expressions, the children came to perceive themselves as special, and responded accordingly.

For symbolic interactionists, of course, it is the opinions of significant others that are important to the development of self-concept. In the Rosenthal and Jacobson study, it was among the first and second graders that the effects were greatest. Any mother knows how much "teacher" means to a beginning school child. "My teachers says . . ." is a phrase that precedes many of the child's statements in his early years in school. Later, however, this appears to change. A study by Joseph Kahl indicates that while lower-middle-class boys of sufficient intelligence to cope with college work all attained similar levels of scholarship in the earlier grades, it was the parents whose attitudes most influenced their level of scholarship in the later grades. The parents by that time had become the more significant others.[56]

Another classroom exercise that produced startling results was conducted by Jane Elliott, a teacher who, in attempting to show children the nature of prejudice, "discriminated against" first blue-eyed children and then brown-eyed children by praising the "favored" group and highlighting the weaknesses of the shunned group. The outcome in each case was for the discredited children to become listless, withdrawn, unhappy, and to perform their lessons badly, demonstrating that when the role assigned to one is that of a "person of little worth," the chances are that one will perform to expectation.[57]

The notion of the looking-glass self and the dictum that people tend to play the roles assigned to them appear to be the underlying principles of Helen

Andelin's advice to women who wish to strengthen their marriages. Her book, *Fascinating Womanhood,* has sold more than half a million copies; courses using her methods attract enthusiastic classes wherever they are taught. For Andelin, the cornerstone of a woman's happiness with her husband is to be loved. If she obeys the laws upon which love is based, if she plays her role correctly, she can kindle—or rekindle—her husband's desire to adore and cherish her.[58]

The secret of success lies in treating her husband as though he were a king. "Make Him No. 1." The natural role of man, Andelin says, is to be the guide, protector, and provider for his wife and children; it is his God-given right. He is captain of the ship. A woman must not deprive her husband of his rightfully superior position. If a wife *is* capable of painting the house, repairing the roof, or tuning up the engine of the car, she must refrain from doing these things, for "a man cannot derive any joy or satisfaction from protecting a woman who can obviously do very well without him." [59] Be femininely dependent and helpless, she suggests. Show that you need the assistance of your strong, masculine husband.

While her advice may seem demeaning and degrading to many women of average intelligence, the reasoning behind it is clear. If one treats a person as though he is wonderful, strong, kind, lovable, worthy, and in possession of leadership qualities, there is a fair chance that his behavior will come to approximate that of a man who is wonderful, kind, lovable, and all the rest. For the woman trapped in a union with a husband who ignores her, or mistreats her, this may seem a viable solution.

It is notable that one does not have to believe deeply in the "reflection" one beams to the other for that person to receive it and respond to it. In a story reported by John Kinch, several male college students took turns in dating the least popular and, as was generally agreed by the men involved, the most unattractive and sloppily dressed woman student on the campus. So repelled were the men at the prospect of dating her that they drew lots, the winner/loser being the first to take her out. The plan was to treat her as though she were a highly exciting and desirable woman. After only a few dates, the woman began to take an interest in her appearance, dressed well, and in fact become an attractive and lively person. The men who were placed at the end of the dating list found themselves eager to date her—but the young woman had little free time, having become one of the most popular women on the campus.[60]

Labeling theory is closely related to role theory, for if people tend to play the roles assigned to them, then, labeling theorists would say, the assigning of a role, the "labeling" of one person by another, has consequences. It is the act of labeling that should be studied. The questions to be asked are "Who labels whom, and why?"

From this point of view, what is commonly termed "deviance" is not a quality of the act a person commits, but a consequence of the application by others of sanctions to an "offender." The same act may be labeled deviant in one situation but not in another. Whether an act is termed "deviant" rather than, perhaps, "a prank" may depend upon the characteristics of the person committing it. A deviant is a person to whom that label has been successfully applied.[61] Once labeled "deviant," or "crazy," or "stupid," a person may have few options of behavior. The youth with a "criminal" record may be unable to find employment and so may be forced to turn to crime; sooner or later, he defines himself as a criminal.

Role expectations shift from setting to setting. In familiar situations most people are unaware that they are playing roles, hiding behind masks. Erving Goffman exposes the "rituals" of everyday behavior; the ways in which each person attempts to manage impressions, to present himself in acceptable ways.

Erving Goffman (1922–   )

Goffman, born in Canada, earned his doctorate at the University of Chicago in 1953. He joined the sociology department at the University of California at Berkeley in 1958, remaining there until 1970, when he moved to the University of Pennsylvania.

Probably the best-known and most prolific modern theorist in the interactionist tradition, Goffman examines in witty and sometimes biting style the minute details of everyday, face-to-face encounters. He analyzes the embarrassment and confusion arising from misinterpretations in definitions of situations and the ways in which actors strive to save face, to salvage the remnants of their dignity.

Goffman's is a dramaturgical approach, interpreting actors' behavior as though they were performing in a theater. Although, Goffman says, all the world is not a stage, all the world is like a stage, and we do strut and fret our hour on it.[62] He attends to the dramaturgical problems of presenting one's performance to an audience. Within this frame, it might be said that the actor is viewed as active subject, more as "I" than as "me." The actor is observed as projecting his image, as directing the shaping of the "character" the audience is to perceive. An audience attributes character to an actor on the basis of information known about him. The more information given, the easier it is to ascribe roles to others; when we have little information it becomes a problem to determine a person's meaning. Throughout Goffman's work one finds a concern with information: information *given,* information *given off,* and information *flow.* Information is *given* through speech; a person tells what he wants others to know. Information is *given off* through unwitting gesture, by the cockney undertone to the Oxford accent, by the light perspiration gleaming on the brow, by the nervous tic, the posture or the tone of voice; information is given off by the hint of liquor on the breath, the choice of clothing and jewelry, and in myriad other clues to which the actor must attend if his performance is to be credible. Information *flows* from actor to audience—and back to the actor as reflected image. From this reflection, the actor assesses how well, or badly, he is playing his part, adjusting his actions accordingly.

Goffman demonstrates that people in everyday life are often fully aware of the need to stage-manage their actions, as do Lyman and Scott, whose view of man appears to be of a calculating creature, using what he knows about interaction to maximize his chances of gain. The model for this man is Machiavelli, who knows how to make others believe in illusions, in carefully calculated performances; who knows how to don the mask of respectability, who is continuously aware of the proprieties of behavior in public places.[63]

The cost of failure to observe the proprieties can range from the endurance of minor embarrassment, through ostracism, to incarceration in an asylum or death in the electric chair. While paying attention to the individual actor striving to perform plausibly in the role called for by the setting and the script, Goffman is careful to include surrounding others as participants in the drama. The drama company comprises a troupe of players, a team, which, through collusion, can either support and sustain the actor in his part—or can destroy him.

For Goffman, though, as for all whose work follows the symbolic interactionist tradition, the study of social action primarily concerns the point of view of the actor. The researcher must see what the actor perceives, interprets, and judges and follow the actor's line of conduct as the actor organizes it. Like phenomenology, symbolic interaction is concerned with the actor's meaning. Meanings, as social products, are understood within social settings. The situation under examination must be thoroughly explored and analyzed in terms of the social and cultural expectations of proprieties. Only then can an understanding be gained of the ways actors perceive each other's acts, and the manner in which each fits his line of action to the actions of others.

Ethnomethodology

Ethnomethodology is the most recent phenomenologically based sociology. As far as is known, the term itself first appeared publicly in Harold Garfinkel's book *Studies in Ethnomethodology,* published in 1967, although discussion of its approach and method had appeared in the professional literature for a few years before that.[64] As it is so new, relative to other sociologies, ethnomethodology appears to be shifting rapidly; Garfinkel himself has changed his thinking since the mid-1960s. His ideas are still developing. Others, including some of Garfinkel's former students, are developing ethnomethodology along lines very different from Garfinkel's own earlier formulations.

Harold Garfinkel (1917–   )

Garfinkel was born in Newark, New Jersey. His undergraduate work was at Newark, and he earned his doctorate from Harvard in 1952 with a dissertation entitled *The Perception of the Other: A Study in Social Order.* He taught at Princeton and at Ohio State University before joining the faculty of sociology at the University of California, Los Angeles, in 1954.

The term "ethnomethodology" has been translated as referring to "the study of the procedures (methodology) used by everyday man (ethnics) in his effort to cope meaningfully with his world." [65] That this is a "translation" is evidence of the difficulty of the language used by ethnomethodologists for those who are not "insiders." Garfinkel's own definition—"I use the term 'ethnomethodology' to refer to the investigation of the rational properties of indexical expressions and other practical actions as contingent ongoing accomplishments of organized artful practices of everyday life"—[66] contains terms that are themselves in need of translation:

> The properties of indexical expressions and indexical actions are ordered properties. These consist of organizationally demonstrable sense, or facticity, or methodic use, or agreement among "cultural colleagues." Their ordered properties consist of organizationally demonstrable rational properties of indexical expressions and indexical actions. Those ordered properties are ongoing achievements of the concerted commonplace activities of the investigators. The demonstrable rationality of indexical expressions and indexical actions retains over the course of its

managed production by members the character of ordinary, familiar, routinized, practical circumstances. . . .[67]

This clarification is hardly helpful. Ethnomethodologists, though, defend the use of a special terminology in that the language of everyday life, with its taken-for-granted meanings, renders it difficult for the human being as scientist to make the leap from the first order constructs of the actor to the second order constructs of social science. Some also add, with some impatience, that the language of scientists does not have to be comprehensible to the layman or even to those outside a particular specialty. Why should not sociology as a science have its own terms, just as does nuclear physics, or microbiology?

What, then, is ethnomethodology? In its earliest formulations, its major concern was with bringing into focus the "background expectancies" of situations which make interaction possible, which make of social reality an ongoing accomplishment—those expectancies which are so much taken for granted that they are scarcely perceived by the participants. People *do* things; they get along, more or less well, with other people; they perform their jobs, they shop, they drive, they study, they cook and eat. People *do* hundreds of things. Any and all of these ordinary, everyday activities are treated by ethnomethodologists as important in their own right. They are practical accomplishments which are deserving of the same kind of attention by scientists as are much more extraordinary phenomena.

Ethnomethodology asks *"How* do people *do* things?" How do they accomplish tasks and how do they make their accomplishments known to others as well as to themselves. How do they *account* for what they do? And how does the very accounting—or the methods they use for making their activities visible as rational, commonplace, everyday activities—feed back into the situation to make the activity *real* for the interactants?

The constitution of taken-for-granted, normal background expectancies has been explored and illustrated in quasi experimentation that has become known as "garfinkeling." In ordinary, everyday activities, people assume that others in the situation will share the same expectancies and definitions of the situation. We "trust" that actions will proceed in familiar ways: "How are you?" we ask, expecting the other to respond, "Fine, thanks, and you?" or something of the sort. By violating these expectations, by removing the taken-for-granted, one can cause consternation, confusion, bewilderment, anxiety, shame or guilt, or indignation. The production of this kind of disorganization, and the attempts made by people to "normalize" the situation, tells something about the way the structures of everyday activities are ordinarily produced and maintained.

A nice illustration of the fury generated by the violation of a supposedly shared definition is in Pinter's play *The Dumb Waiter:*

BEN: Go and light it.

GUS: Light what?

BEN: The kettle.

GUS: You mean the gas.

BEN: Who does?

GUS: You do.

BEN (*his eyes narrowing*): What do you mean, I mean the gas?

GUS: Well that's what you mean, don't you? The gas.

BEN (*powerfully*): If I say go and light the kettle I mean go and light the kettle.

GUS: How can you light a kettle?

BEN: It's a figure of speech! Light the kettle. It's a figure of speech!

GUS: I've never heard it.

BEN: Light the kettle! It's common usage!

GUS: I think you've got it wrong.

BEN (*menacing*): What do you mean?

GUS: They say put on the kettle.

BEN (*taut*): Who says?

They stare at each other, breathing hard.

(*Deliberately*) I have never in all my life heard anyone say put on the kettle.

GUS: I bet my mother used to say it. . . .

BEN (*vehemently*): Nobody says light the gas! What does the gas light?

GUS: What does the gas —?

BEN (*grabbing him with two hands by the throat, at arm's length*): THE KETTLE, YOU FOOL! [68]

This particular example, besides demonstrating the anger caused by violation of the expectation that another will understand an ordinary request, also reveals the way people use *glosses*. These are much abbreviated terms or phrases which convey meaning and yet gloss over the details of the activity or object intended. "Light the kettle!" or even "Put on the kettle!" is a gloss for "Go into the kitchen, take the kettle from the stove, take it to the sink, fill it with water, take it back to the stove, strike a match, turn on the gas tap, light the gas jet, put the kettle over the flame, wait until the water in the kettle boils, turn the flame down, pour the water into the prepared teapot. . . ." Glossing is one of the methods used in the accomplishment of practical activities. The mastery of language—very much taken for granted—is throughout and without a relief a practical, situated accomplishment.[69]

For ethnomethodologists, actors' (or members') accomplishments are *situated activities*. They are achieved in situations and must be studied in the situations which are, themselves, ongoing, practical accomplishments. The practices, or methods, actors use to keep them going, to make them real, are the subject matter for study by ethnomethodologists. To study this action-in-context as a practical accomplishment, the ethnomethodologist, Garfinkel writes, must treat the rational properties of practical activities as "anthropologically strange." [70] The researcher must ask how the familiar commonplace activity is recognizable as familiar, commonplace activity. Garfinkel uses the term *reflexivity* to describe the ways in which the very acceptance of the usage of a familiar term, or rule, by being understood as intended, *reinforces* that term or rule's familiarity and further assures the actors of its reality and propriety.

Norms, rules, instructions—the taken-for-granted guidelines by which people direct their everyday activities—are seen by ethnomethodologists as essentially vague. The ways in which they are to be used are negotiated and renegotiated from situation to situation. They have what Garfinkel terms an "et cetera" property. There are always some people to whom the rules do not apply; there are always some circumstances in which the norms are unclear. Although the sign in the theater says "No Smoking," the actors on the stage are smoking; although the young man on the college campus no longer holds doors open for women students, he still performs this service for his mother's friends. This means that members of society are constantly engaged in creating and maintaining their world, in determining, in the light of present practical circumstance, what the rule "really" means; they do this with the cooperation of others. Guidelines, norms, rules—meanings themselves—have to be discerned and forged anew in each situation. Rules, or norms, or terms, or explanations are seen by ethnomethodologists as having *indexicality;* they have meaning in a particular situation but this meaning may not be the same in another situation.

The concern of ethnomethodologists, then, is with the methods people use to carry out the activities of everyday life and the practices by which they convey to others that these actions are rational—the ways in which actors continually account for what they do and so establish for themselves that these actions are, indeed, rational. People *do* things by talking about them.

Since the late 1960s Garfinkel's interest appears to be directed more to the interpreting and accounting practices of actors than to the explication of background expectancies. It is the *accounting,* the continual "storytelling," that shapes the social world, that constantly defines and redefines reality.

The programs current in ethnomethodological circles are probably as numerous as the practitioners, although it is possible to group ethnomethologists together in ways that are not entirely arbitrary.[71] Among those whose work might be considered ethnomethodological are Egon Bittner, Alan Blum, Aaron Cicourel, Lindsay Churchill, Peter McHugh, Melvin Pollner, Edward Rose, Harvey Sacks, Emanuel Schegloff, Dorothy Smith, David Sudnow, Roy Turner, D. Lawrence Wieder, Thomas Wilson, and Don Zimmerman. It would be safe to say that they are all interested in studying language and language usage, although their methods of study vary considerably.[72]

How does a researcher discover background expectancies, or learn how people decide which rules are operable in given situations? What are the methods by which ethnomethodologists can observe the construction and maintenance of reality? How, in fact, does one *do* ethnomethodology?

Garfinkel is emphatic that one cannot learn how to do it from descriptions of what it is. It is not particularly useful to keep reading and rereading Schutz, he says. We should not be neglecting *the world of everyday life,* about which we keep theorizing. There is too much writing *about* ethnomethodology. "We are taking in each other's intellectual wash." Instead, we should be learning on a day-to-day basis. To know what ethnomethodology is, you must *do* it. "The stuff is learned in the streets." [73]

For most of us, this is still not guidance enough. If we turn to reported studies we find a considerable array of methods, including observation of all kinds, filming, the use of tape recordings and transcripts for language analysis, the examination of letters and other documents, field work, participation, and more. What the researcher, as ethnomethodologist, must do on entering study settings is to suspend all notions that situations are rule-governed. Instead, ask what role norms play; do not settle the question in advance of thorough investigation. Ask how norms appear in what people say about what they are doing and why they are doing it—in their accounts. Look for the ways in which these accounts reflexively give order to the activities of the members of the settings.[74] The topics for study are infinite. Emanuel Schegloff and Harvey Sacks, for instance, have made a detailed study of the ways conversations are closed, the ways leave is taken of a gathering. Sacks, Schegloff, and Gail Jefferson have analyzed "turn-taking" in conversation. Other ethnomethodologists have studied action from within various kinds of organizations: hospitals, prisons, law courts, psychiatrists' offices, and so on.[75] An endless variety of settings offer possibilities for ethnomethodological research.

Ethnomethodology is for the intellectually curious. Its proponents do not claim that ethnomethodological studies are in search of humanistic arguments, nor are they directed to formulating or arguing correctives. It is similar in this regard to the sociology of the absurd, which does not seek meliorative remedies; it, too, does not claim to offer any solutions to societal problems. These approaches have as their aim the discovery of the methods by which the actor makes sense of his world, creates order where none is inherent, and organizes his routine activities. It cannot be overlooked, however, especially by ethnomethodologists, that the reports of social scientists are themselves reflexive and have effects upon the society from which they are derived.

The common strands stringing the creative sociologies together are that these sociologies all have an image of human beings as creating reality in interaction with others. They all call into question the deterministic notion that the "solid structures" of society act as forces on the individual, deciding his fate. They all use methods of study that are different from the natural-science methods of positivistic sociology. As has been hinted, however, although the similarities among them have been emphasized, these are distinct and separate ways of studying social phenomena. They are not the same. In the following chapter, the distinctions among them will be examined.

The river flows onward
lively,
turbulent.
Streams diverging,
Streams converging
Over the rocks . . .

—SEMUS

CHAPTER TWO

Distinctions Among, Between, and Within the Creative Sociologies

ONE EVENING, during my first visit to Los Angeles, I was taken by a friend for a drive through the city. Over on the west side we passed the massive Mormon temple, set high off the road on a hill, the huge angel atop his steeple dazzlingly floodlit. We soon drove by a temple adorned with an oversized Menorah and, further along, past an important Catholic church, bearing an enormous cross brightly lighted from within. My friend, an astute Los Angeleno, smiled and remarked, "The more we stress our differences, the more we emphasize our similarities."

Let us investigate the differences claimed among, between, and within the creative sociologies in an attempt to see whether these differences are more of degree than of kind. Among the creative sociologists are some who are adamant that their approach is not only radically different from that of "conventional" sociology, but that it is also different from other creative sociologies. Some ethnomethodologists, in particular, insist that theirs is an entirely new approach to the study of social life, while other sociologists are not convinced that ethnomethodology is as radical as it claims. Both sides of this debate will be presented, as well as some indications of the differences within ethnomethodology itself.

Some Distinctions Between Pairs of Creative Sociologies

Existentialism and Phenomenology

"One of the embarrassments of contemporary phenomenology is that it is inextricably caught up in the much broader cultural movement called 'existentialism.' " [1] So begins one discussion of the differences between these two approaches. There has undeniably been a convergence of these two movements—in France they became almost synonymous—yet phenomenological purists continue to claim that phenomenology is a rigorous philosophical method, to which the fad of existentialism owes whatever genuine philosophy it may contain, and that existentialism can only "contaminate" phenomenology by its lack of scientific rigor. At the other extreme, there are those who see phenomenology as a necessary first step to existentialism. It has been said that whereas phenomenology remains situational in analysis, the existential sociologists search for a synthesis of the situational and the broader, social-cultural ideas. [2]

In his presentation of the steps of the epochē, or reduction, John Wild writes that what distinguishes phenomenology from "what is commonly known as *existentialism*" is that existentialism abandons the search for meaning too easily and too soon by performing only one step of the epochē. [3] The first epochē lies in the capacity to play the role of the other, an art closely related to that of the actor. To understand the ceremonies of a primitive tribe or the problems of another person, to write a biography, or even to understand my own past, I must bracket my present attitude, but this *is* only the first step. Much more remains to be revealed than the world of an historical person, or a past culture, as it was actually understood and lived. The second epochē leads the phenomenologist to higher levels of meaning that go beyond the given facts, yet take account of them, to consider such topics as time, history, freedom, death—matters which are not relative to any particular group or individual but which transcend individuals' special versions of the world. This is a somewhat different view from that which sees existentialism as seeking a synthesis of situational and trans-situational meaning, and phenomenology as situational analysis!

Similar contradictions are found in the debate between Edward Tiryakian and Peter Berger. [4] While Tiryakian links phenomenology and existentialism together as a single sociological approach, a radical description of social reality searching for the *roots* of social existence (seeking the multilayered meanings of social reality by uncovering the surface institutional nature of the everyday world concealed from the public view), Berger insists that the two are quite different developments, linked only in the earlier writings of Heidegger and Sartre. Kierkegaard, he says, would probably have been as little interested in phenomenology as Husserl was in existentialism. Yet Kierkegaard's work on religion was clearly phenomenological in its concern with the understanding of religion in relation to the consciousness of the thinker of the thought,[5] and it is further clear that others besides Tiryakian have linked phenomenology and existentialism in ways pertinent to sociology—Maurice Natanson, Herbert Spiegelberg, and Merleau-Ponty, to mention only a few. This does not mean that the two are *identical* and have the same set of preoccupations, but there exists a striking complementarity between phenomenology and existentialism, a complementarity that outweighs the incompatibilities in their paired use as a sociological perspective.

Phenomenology and Symbolic Interaction

Perhaps the differences between phenomenology and symbolic interaction are of more consequence to sociology than are those between existentialism and phenomenology. Indeed, the emphasis on the very concept of "role" by symbolic interactionists is called into question by phenomenologists. Roles are the representations of the various "me's"—the social self, or social selves. Role is behavior in a particular "part," objectively viewed by self and others. Symbolic interactionists generally consider roles to be imposed by the expectations of others. Phenomenologists, however, emphasize the importance of subjectivity, of the "I" aspect of the self. Their challenge to the legitimacy of the role concept is founded upon the requirement of the epochē, of bracketing, of the suspension of belief by the scientists in the reality of the taken-for-granted world. Phenomenology requires, in effect, suspension of belief in the concept of role in order to understand social life as it is presented to and perceived by those we study, rather than embarking upon research with such presuppositions unquestioned. As symbolic interaction aims to understand by taking the role of the other, attempting to experience the subject's experience, it may be that the criticism Wild leveled against existentialists is more properly applied to symbolic interactionists. They appear to perform only the first epochē, at the role-taking level.

One might ask, too, whether people do really sort their various roles, segments of their selves, into compartments, bringing out the role called for by each situation and, if they do this, whether they "believe in" the role they play. Do they "become" it in order to play it, or do they recognize that they are acting? The phenomenological alternative to role theory (which claims the validity of *role* as the primary organizer of social experience) is that the subjective self possesses a set of attributes which does not vary with the actions the person takes. One sometimes hears others described as "having a strong sense of self." It is possible that such persons are aware of playing roles without altering the presentation of who they are in the process. This, says Jacqueline Johnson, is a different view from that usually presented in the sociological literature.[6] She suggests that the dramaturgical model is superficial in its focus on the external behavioral expectations, on the objective manifestations of role and self. The phenomenological perspective proposes exploring more than is presented here and now. It may involve an attempt to understand an individual's past, to perceive something of the stock of knowledge brought into the situation. Schutz has made it clear that those of the past and the future, as well as those in our immediate present, are important to our perception and our intention.

Johnson presents several examples, drawn from literary work as well as from "real life," of women who refuse to follow societal role expectations—women who have, or have had, a strong "sense of self" which has brought them to public notice. Emma Goldman, the feminist anarchist, was one such woman. Another example of strong sense of self which springs to mind is that of the one small boy in Jane Elliott's third grade class who refused to accept discriminatory statements and actions and who remained in firm possession of self throughout the exercise.[7] Most of the other children appeared both to accept totally and to play with conviction the roles of discriminator and discriminated-against. Whether these are examples of truly remarkable or exceptional people with, perhaps, the majority of persons being more "me" than "I" is worthy of study.

A further distinction between phenomenology and symbolic interaction concerns the subject matter of the two perspectives. Helmut Wagner notes that symbolic interaction stresses the *means* of communication, while sociologists of understanding, or phenomenologists, are more interested in discovering the *content* of meaning, intention and volition.[8] Weber, as a phenomenological thinker, emphasized the substantive meaning of interactional exchange; Mead, a symbolic interactionist, accented its form, the vehicle of its expression.

Between these two approaches, then, substantial distinctions do seem to emerge. In the first place, phenomenologists call into question the imposition of presuppositions, such as the concept of role as an organizer of experience, upon that which is studied; secondly, the subject matter for study is different in each case.

Phenomenology and Ethnomethodology

Because ethnomethodology is largely a phenomenological approach, the distinctions are, perhaps, less clear than those between other perspectives. In his book on theory groups in sociology, Nicholas Mullins throws the phenomenologists in with the ethnomethodologists as a "theory group." [9] Alfred Schutz, who combined the philosophical interests of Husserl with the Weberian notion of *Verstehen,* has influenced Berger, Tiryakian, Natanson, and Wagner—none of whom would consider himself an ethnomethodologist—as well as Arlene Daniels, Donald Ball, and Jack Douglas. Schutz's ideas, posits Mullins, are necessary but not sufficient to create ethnomethodology, which has a mixed bag of forebears that includes Schutz along with linguistic philosophers, among them Ludwig Wittgenstein and John L. Austin, such cognitive anthropologists as H. Conklin, Charles Frake, and Dell Hymes, and existentialists.

Two ethnomethodologists, Don Zimmerman and Thomas Wilson, in distinguishing ethnomethodology from phenomenology, say that the two approaches are mutually compatible and interdependent in that each raises significant problems and provides important insights for the other. For ethnomethodologists, meanings may be acknowledged as essential features of social objects, but they are not what ethnomethodology studies. Whereas phenomenology is interested in the meaning structure as known by the members of the society (the *content* of meaning for the actors, the description of the subjects' reality as it appears to them), ethnomethodology is concerned with the *procedures* by which meaning structures are *made* meaningful and sustained as meaningful.[10] Ethnomethodology is the study of indexicality, reflexivity, glóssing, and so on as phenomena in their own right, as procedures by means of which people make available and sustain, for themselves and for others, the nature of social reality. Meanings display indexicality, reflexivity, and the rest, regardless of the *content* of the meaning.

The phenomenologist George Psathas adds that ethnomethodology is not just phenomenological philosophy in new guise. The difference he sees between the two lies in the bracketing procedures of each. Ethnomethodologists suspend belief in society as an objective reality, he says, *except* as it appears and is accomplished in and through the everyday activities of the members themselves.

Society is not denied in this epochē. Society is discovered and accomplished by the members' activities. It is these very activities and practices, by which people produce society and make it real, understandable, and accountable, that are looked at by ethnomethodologists. Where ethnomethodology's topics are members' practices and activities in the everyday world, says Psathas, phenomenological philosophy would bracket these and look for their foundations as well. The epochē of the ethnomethodologists is of more limited scope than that of phenomenological philosophy.[11]

As can be seen, although much ethnomethodology is a form of phenomenology, the differences between them involve both subject matter and method. Phenomenology studies the *content* of meaning structures; ethnomethodology looks at members' *practices* for constructing and maintaining meaning; the scope of the epochē is narrower in ethnomethodology than in phenomenology.

Symbolic Interaction and Ethnomethodology

There can be little argument that both symbolic interaction and ethnomethodology are phenomenologically informed, if "phenomenological" is defined in terms of the meaning that an act has for the actor himself. Yet it is against symbolic interaction that ethnomethodologists appear to have launched their most sustained attacks in rejecting comparison with other kinds of sociology.

The differences between two, particularly through the eyes of ethnomethodologists although others have joined the examination, may be seen as matters of scope, of method, of theory, of subject matter, and of the confusion of "topic" and "resource" in the research activity.

The *scope* of symbolic interaction research is theoretically broad. While the situation, the episode, the encounter between two or among a few provides the research setting for most studies, symbolic interactionists claim to be able to make the leap from small interactions to society. They declare their intention to look upon society as if it were an interactional network tied together by symbolic communication.[12] The activities of any collectivity—a family, a gang, a large industrial corporation, a political party—are formed through processes of interaction and interpretation. Whole mass societies, in theory at least, can be analyzed from the symbolic interaction perspective.

Ethnomethodologists, on the other hand, make no claim to answer the question, "How is social order possible?" if by "social order" is meant the tie between micro-relationships and some social structure "out there." The social order which interests them is that which appears to individuals in their daily lives. Rules and norms are of interest to ethnomethodologists but not as *resources* to be uncritically accepted by the investigator as existing and as explaining the shaping and maintaining of social order. Rather, they become topics for study. The assumption that order exists, that rules and norms provide order, is bracketed. The interest of ethnomethodologists is in uncovering taken-for-granteds of this kind and examining the ways, the *processes,* by which human beings go about the task of explaining order in the world in which they live. Rules, as such, do not provide order, but the *use* of rules provides a sense and *appearance* of order. [13]

The *methods* used by ethnomethodologists to discover how people define and present their actions as rational to others—how they define their world as orderly—include listening to talk, to accounts that persons make of their actions; watching the ways that records are kept and decisions are made; observing the manner in which "background expectancies" are invoked or used as a scheme of interpretation, the manner in which records became transformed by manipulation of background expectancies to make accounts convincing for all practical purposes; and noting the ways in which an individual reconciles the image of himself as a trusted person with his act of trust violation—such as suicide—by means of verbalization. [14]

W. I. Thomas in the 1920s and Herbert Blumer a generation later made clear statements about the nature of symbolic interaction and the types of methodology suited to study within this framework. [15] The study of action has to be made from the position of the actor. The scientific observer arrives at meanings beyond those held by participants but can comprehend them fully only by understanding the "realities" as defined both by and for the actors. Human beings construct their lines of action in terms of their own definitions of the situation; they make choices on the basis of their perceptions, interpretations, and judgments. To understand such actions fully, Blumer insists that the researcher has to see the operating situation as the actor sees it, perceive objects as the actor perceives them, ascertain their meanings in terms of the meanings they have for the actor, and follow the actor's line of conduct as the actor organizes it. In short, one has to take the role of the actor and see his world from his standpoint.

The basic symbolic interaction methods are participant observation and the collection and examination of life histories, although many other methods are used. From the symbolic interactionist point of view, the best way to understand a process is to become part of it.[16]

Where the symbolic interactionist immerses himself in the world he studies, the ethnomethodologist, if he is to take note of the taken-for-granted rules that guide the behavior of the members of the world of study, must maintain sufficient distance to avoid taking these rules for granted, himself.

Another sharp distinction between symbolic interaction and ethnomethodology is in their approaches to language. Ethnomethodologists study *what is said* as an important guide to that which they wish to study, that is the achievement of the *appearance* of order, the sense of order. They use accounts, both verbal and written, as their major source of data. Yet, although Mead claimed that it is the use of language, especially of significant symbols, that distinguishes humans from other animals, symbolic interactionists rarely appear to study language, as such, relative to the numerous linguistic analyses of the ethnomethodologists. Goffman, for instance, demonstrates a much keener interest in information given *off*, in gesture, expression, stance, and so on, than in what is actually said. Symbolic interactionists appear to take seriously the maxim that it is in what we do *not* hear that the important message is conveyed. Again, the differences in data for examination can be referred back to the aims of each of these perspectives. Ethnomethodologists are not concerned with "what is *really* going on" in a situation. Their purpose is to discover the practices by which what *appears* to be going on is made to appear so by the participants.

Finally, one of the distinctions which ethnomethodologists make between themselves and other sociologists, particularly symbolic interactionists, is that the others confuse "topic" and "resource" in their research. This argument revolves around the manner in which conventional sociologists, among which symbolic interactionists are included, define their problems, collect their data, explain what happens—all involving them in the use of a vocabulary which they assume they share with those they use as informants or collaborators. This assumption of shared meaning is simply taken for granted, remaining unexamined. For this reason, ethnomethodologists claim that sociology does not attain a significantly higher level of theoretical awareness than that possessed by the ordinary person in everyday life.

Perhaps the clearest example in the literature of this confusion of topic and resource is that given by Melvin Pollner regarding Becker's labeling theory—a variation of symbolic interaction.[17] Ethnomethodology, says Pollner, does not just take things for granted; it looks for *process* through which perceived stable features of social settings are continually created and sustained. Even though labeling theorists appear to be concerned with the same endeavor, they still take for granted what other members of the society take for granted. Becker says, for instance, that "deviance is what is labeled such," [18] yet he still implies that a deviant act is an act that is *generally* conceived of as wrong or immoral, that act then being punished by the community. Instead of treating the latter, taken-for-granted, view of deviance as a *topic* for research, as problematic, it is used as a resource, or tool, to aid in explanation. This becomes apparent in the matrix Becker uses to illustrate reactions to "deviant acts":

	Obedient behavior	*Rule-breaking behavior*
Perceived as deviant	Falsely accused	Pure deviant
Not perceived as deviant	Conforming	Secret deviant

The model Becker provides is that used by the everyday person, the judge, or the legal system in general. An ethnomethodological matrix, then, would appear as follows:

Perceived as deviant	Deviant
Not perceived as deviant	Not deviant

Instead of using the norm, the rule, or the law, as a *topic,* to be examined in its own right in terms of the ways it is invoked to produce "deviance," Becker has used it as a *resource,* a taken-for-granted, background expectancy.

The problems in taking roles, norms, and rules for granted, and using them to "explain" social organization and social order are more than apparent when these rules are invoked and adhered to very closely. Under such circumstances, instead of "perfect order" prevailing, "order" breaks down completely! British trade unions' threats to "work to rule" are sufficient to start negotiation procedures immediately, for if the rule book is followed, chaos must ensue. When railway employees "work to rule," few trains appear upon the tracks, and in a recent discussion regarding possible strike action by post office workers, a union representative indicated that by a careful following of the rules, mail services could be brought to a complete halt within days. The rules stipulate, for instance, the proper positioning of stamps on envelopes, the range of envelope sizes which may pass through the mails, and so on. It is not difficult to imagine the results if post office workers followed the rules by carefully measuring each piece of mail and checking it for the exact positioning of stamps.

Most organizations devise and distribute rule books, yet they are only rarely read, the rules being followed loosely, if at all. The occasions on which rules are sought and invoked are usually those on which there is a need to establish the propriety, and the method, of, perhaps, promoting—or firing—an employee. In such cases, the rules become convenient legitimations. It is clear, then, why ethnomethodologists maintain that rules are important *topics* for study, rather than established "facts" which order and organize social life.

The differences between symbolic interaction and ethnomethodology appear to be considerable, especially from the ethnomethodological standpoint. There are differences of scope, of theory, of method, and of substantive interest. Attempts to synthesize these two perspectives have met with strong resistance by ethnomethodologists.[19]

Some Differences Within Creative Sociologies

Distinctions Within Symbolic Interaction

One tends to forget that symbolic interactionists were once sociology's "rebels," so established and accepted are they now. Theirs was a revolt against the increasing use of the methods of the natural sciences for the study of society. The approach was, and still is, termed "social psychology," but this is very different from the experimental social psychology found in psychology departments. Several variations of symbolic interaction have already been presented: Becker's labeling theory, Goffman's dramaturgical perspective, and the role theory of Shibutani, among others. All of these adhere fairly closely to the Meadian-Thomasian-Blumerian school of symbolic interaction but, although this is probably the more influential of the approaches, there is another, separate strain of symbolic interaction whose emphasis and research methods differ from those of the "creative" symbolic interactionists.[20]

The University of Chicago, where Mead lectured for most of his teaching career, was the main training center for symbolic interaction, but a second center was established in the late 1940s by Manford Kuhn, at the State University of

Iowa. In contrast to Blumer, who insists that the concepts of symbolic interaction are "sensitizing concepts" that cannot be "operationalized" (that is, defined in such a way that they can be measured),[21] Kuhn holds that the methods of the natural sciences can be used to discover and "explain" concepts such as "self" and "social act." Implicit in this stance is the assumption that the self is "structure" as well as process, that the attributes composing the "self" constitute a firm, definable core. Kuhn developed a widely used test, the Twenty Statements Test (TST), also known as the "Who Am I?" Test, in his attempts to convert vague concepts into research variables. For research purposes, Kuhn defines the self "as answers which an individual gives to the question which he directs to himself, 'Who am I?' or to the question another directs to him, such as 'What kind of person are you?' 'Who are you?' etc." [22] The answers given represent a definition of the self of the respondent, a self which is considered to determine the person's actions.

The major theoretical difference between the two schools appears to be that, from the positivist-structuralist perspective, meaning is determined by external factors, mainly through processes of childhood socialization that inculcate sets of meanings from which the person draws thereafter, as the situation demands. The nonpositivists, the Meadian-Thomasian-Blumerians, see meanings emerging from interactions in social settings; while socialization processes, cultural background, and other factors are important to interpretation, they do not determine meanings.[23] The nonpositivists hold firm to their view that human beings are rational and practical, and essentially in control of their actions—this, of course, is the legacy of their pragmatist ancestry. They see human beings as able to view themselves objectively and to change their lines of action as necessary.

Even among nonpositivist symbolic interactionists, however, the question of self as structure or as process, or as both, seems to be troublesome. Thomas said, "If men define situations as real, they are real in their consequences," but he also wrote, "There is always a rivalry between the spontaneous definitions of the situation made by the member of an organized society and the definitions which his society has provided for him." [24] This ambivalence is reflected in the different emphases placed on the "me" or "I" aspects of self by different writers. Some stress the ability of the "I" to stand aloof, as it were, as it controls the presentation of "me's"; others see society as imposing upon and tightly constraining the choices open to the individual. There is a divergence between those who see people as "making" roles and those who see them as "taking" roles.

The Iowa group of symbolic interactionists, as well as another, smaller group at Minnesota, under the direction of Arnold M. Rose, failed to develop large followings of students. It therefore seems likely that the Blumerians, or the Chicago school of symbolic interaction, will remain the most important, although some of the structural ideas of the Iowa school may converge with those of the Blumerians.

Distinctions Within Ethnomethodology

Any developing theoretical or methodological approach changes as its practitioners apply their ideas, share them with each other, revise them, state them and restate them, find them perhaps inadequate, and begin again on a slightly different tack. Ethnomethodology is no exception to this, some of its earlier statements being already outmoded, superceded by reconsiderations. Not only has Harold Garfinkel, the founder of ethnomethodology, changed his own ideas somewhat over the past ten years, but some of his students and colleagues have also moved in intellectual directions different from his.

The University of California at Los Angeles was the first training center for ethnomethodology but more can now be found at other University of California campuses. One center is at Santa Barbara, another at San Diego, where Aaron Cicourel, who is probably as influential a leader in the field as is Garfinkel, is the central person, and at Irvine, where the late Harvey Sacks, an important ethnomethodologist, was on the faculty. Other ethnomethodologists are to be found on the faculties of colleges and universities on the east coast, in Canada, and in Britain. As ethnomethodology develops, differences within the field are becoming apparent, although there are indications—the establishment of an annual meeting of ethnomethodologists and phenomenologists—that a keen willingness exists to share and discuss ideas.

As all ethnomethodologists are interested in language, it would be safe to say that the differences among them lie in the types of language analysis they conduct, and in the purposes of that analysis. Ethnomethodology is not only phenomenologically based, but it also owes much to the linguistic philosophies of Wittgenstein and Austin, and to the generative linguists, such as Noam Chomsky. The differences in analysis depend to some extent on the balancing of these influences.

Garfinkel, whose work is, perhaps, as Schutzian as any of the ethnomethodologists, studies what people say, the accounts they give, in order to see how the structure of the situation—the substantive features—is produced and maintained, the manner in which it comes to "make sense" for the participants. People, Garfinkel indicates, make a situation "sensible" for themselves and for others by telling about it. This making of sense is a practical accomplishment *within* a situation and it is the *procedures* of this sense-making, this telling, which Garfinkel studies. His quasi experiments, in which he deliberately set up or disrupted the flow of interactional activities, were designed as demonstrations of the practices used by persons to restructure "sensibleness" into the scene. Garfinkel appears to have moved away from contrived situations to the study of naturally occurring interactions but his concern appears to remain with contextually tied, formal properties of accounts, such as indexicality and reflexivity.

Others, including Sacks, Schegloff, Jefferson, and Speier, are also preoccupied with situations as ongoing constructions, produced and reinforced by ordinary practices, but their empirical studies are directed toward specific features of conversational exchanges. Sacks, for instance, demonstrates an interest in the way pauses are used in giving a string of numbers, or in spelling a name. In giving the number 1236, for example, one might say "twelve, thirty-six," or "one, two, three, six," or, less likely, "twelve, three, six," but it would be unusual, even "wrong" to say "one, twenty-three, six." [25] A very long paper by Sacks, Schegloff, and Jefferson deals entirely with turn-taking in conversations, while an article by Matthew Speier attends to some of the basic features of conversational exchanges, such as the effects of different numbers of participants on the ordering of conversation; turn-taking; and some of the technical problems of conversational analysis itself, such as how to categorize speakers. [26]

One might ask whether detailed conversational examination of this kind is not in the field of linguistics rather than in sociology, and it is true that these analysts have close ties with linguists, frequently publishing their findings in language journals. These researchers, however, claim that the disciplinary motivation for their work is sociological. [27] Speier treats conversational exchanges as "socially organized sets of speech events," indicating that "cultural competence in using conversational procedures . . . provides a procedural basis for the ongoing organization of that culture." The study of the procedures used in conversational exchanges, then, provides "a powerful clue to the nature of social organization." [28]

A somewhat different emphasis is found in the work of Aaron Cicourel, which he terms "cognitive sociology." [29] As with all ethnomethodologists, his interest is in language and meaning in social interaction, but he expands "language" to include kinds of communication other than speech. He studies, for instance, the manual sign language and finger spelling of the deaf, his concern here being with the interpretive procedures in interaction that exist even without the use of talk. That deaf mutes as well as those equipped with language capabilities can create meaning, can understand and be understood, indicates, among other things, that the ability to "make sense" is not dependent upon the possession of language but probably exists prior to language acquisition, making language acquisition possible. We can see, for instance, that when an infant says "Daddy, car!" he means a great deal more than he can say with his limited vocabulary and knowledge of sentence structure. The child knows what he means; others must interpret as best they can.

In Cicourel's work, as in the work of several other ethnomethodologists, we find attention directed to procedures or interpretive rules that appear to be used in *all* situations, regardless of the content of meaning. The notion of *invariance* enters our discussion because it is the seeming paradox between Garfinkel's insistence upon the *indexicality* of meanings and this concept of *invariance* that appears to be a stumbling block for many outsiders in understanding ethnomethodology.[30] Indexicality indicates that meanings are tied to situations; invariance indicates that procedures are *trans*situational and universal. How do ethnomethodologists reconcile the two?

Most ethnomethodologists agree that the *content* of meaning is situational, that meaning is generated in a situation and is reflexively reinforced in accounts, or talk. The *procedures* by which that meaning is made visible, however, the *practices* by which structures of meaning are made to appear real within a situation are the same *across* situations. Those whose research does not deal with the content of meaning are not concerned with indexicality. Sacks, Schegloff, and Jefferson, for instance, claim that turn-taking is part of any and all conversations and, in fact, is not limited to conversation. Turn-taking can be found in such other kinds of interaction as interviews, trials, therapy sessions, and the like. There is a universality to turn-taking; it is not tied to context.

Zimmerman and Pollner appear to handle the indexicality-invariance paradox by expanding upon Schutz's concept of "stock of knowledge." Each individual possesses a stock of knowledge that he or she brings to a situation. This stock of knowledge is not a shared, intersubjective body (or "corpus") of knowledge.

Somehow, each participant, with his or her individual stock of knowledge comes to share an "occasioned corpus," that is, a body of knowledge which is assembled in and from the situation and which is unique to that situation. This occasioned corpus of knowledge is indexical, but the "family of practices" used to make the situation understandable presumably transcends the situation. It is these practices that are invariant.[31] Zimmerman and Pollner term as *methodography* the research vehicle with which to search for the invariant practices which make features of settings observable.[32]

The interests of some other ethnomethodologists appear to remain tied to context, so that the notion of invariance does not enter into their discussions. Peter McHugh, for instance, devotes an entire book to "defining the situation," his main focus in that work apparently being upon what Zimmerman and Pollner term the "occasioned corpus," its content and its meaning for the participants in the situation. His major guide in this enterprise seems to be Schutz rather than the linguistic philosophers.[33]

The distinctions within ethnomethodology, then, appear to stem largely from differences in theoretical emphases. The descriptions of the various kinds of work done by ethnomethodologists, though, should not be considered complete, for to name an ethnomethodologist and define *this* as what he or she does is to oversimplify. Most practitioners do more than one kind of analysis, and the interests of different ethnomethodologists frequently overlap. It should also be remembered that even the most recently appearing articles were probably written a year or two prior to publication. In the time lapse, ideas and directions change, especially in a developing perspective. The river flows onward. . . .

The Eclectic Creative Sociologies: The Sociology of Knowledge and the Sociology of the Absurd

The Sociology of Knowledge

The sociology of knowledge presented by Berger and Luckmann has been described as essentially the Schutzian synthesis of Husserl and Weber "with large dollops of Durkheim."[34] While they are concerned with the ways individuals create, or construct, reality, Berger and Luckmann also stress the manner in which the society into which the individual is born constrains and constricts the types of reality that may be created. Their approach appears to smack considerably more of social determinism than do other phenomenological approaches. Berger and Luckmann conceive of a taken-for-granted *shared core universe,* whereas Schutz saw individuals as each possessing a stock of knowledge different from that of others. For Berger and Luckmann, this shared core universe is internalized in the process of socialization.[35] The internalized aspects of society or, one might say, the "me" aspects of the individual self, are much better explained in their theory than is the "I," or autonomous self.

In *The Sacred Canopy,* a work in the sociology of religion that he cast within the theoretical framework of *The Social Construction of Reality,* Berger sees alienation as the result of the loss to consciousness of the dialectical relationship between the individual and his world. The individual "forgets" that his world was, and continues to be, co-produced by himself. The actor becomes only that which is acted upon. Yet this very alienation serves to maintain the firm structure of the social-cultural world because it seemingly minimizes the choices needed for the human enterprise of world-building. It replaces choice with fictitious necessity, just as does "inauthenticity" or "bad faith," to use existentialist terms. Bad faith, explains Berger, is that form of false consciousness in which the dialectic between the socialized self and the total self is lost to consciousness. Instead of a continuous reflection between the "I" and the "me," the individual totally identifies himself with the internalized roles of his socially assigned identity. Once the false unity of self is established, Berger writes, and as long as it remains plausible, it is likely to be a source of inner strength. Ambivalences are removed. There is no hesitation between alternative possibilities of conduct. The individual "knows who he is"—a most comfortable condition. The essence of all alienation, Berger goes on, is the imposition of a fictitious inexorability upon the humanly constructed world. Men live by the world they made themselves as though they were fated to do so by powers quite independent of their own world-constructing enterprises.[36]

Despite this warning with which Berger directs our attention toward the possible manipulation of man by society, in Berger and Luckmann's model, the existing reality seems to be of a static world in which each newcomer adjusts to expectations rather than balks against them. While in their theory reality—resting on the three processes of externalization, internalization, and institutionalization—is the creation of human beings, only internalization and institutionalization appear fully plausible within their framework.[37] Their emphasis is on conformity to what has already been constructed rather than on individual creativity or innovation.

Another way in which Berger and Luckmann's work differs from that of some other creative sociologists is in its scope. The focus of phenomenologists, symbolic interactionists, and ethnomethodologists is predominantly situational or microsocial. Berger and Luckmann's theory is macroscopic, dealing with overarching symbolic universes in society, social structures which impinge upon, or serve to deny, the freedom of individuals.

The Sociology of the Absurd

Drawing from all the creative sociologies introduced in this book, Lyman and Scott offer a synthesized sociology of the absurd. In so doing, they underplay, if not deny, the differences between and among the several approaches. Theirs is a situational approach: Life is a sequence of episodes. In this, they owe much to the dramaturgical work of Erving Goffman. They use a "game" model of society when they find it useful for illustration, labeling theory, neo-symbolic interaction, and the linguistic approach of ethnomethodology, among others. They are meticulous in acknowledging intellectual debts to Husserl, Schutz, Merleau-Ponty, Cooley, Simmel, Mead, and dozens of other thinkers, both contemporary and historical. Because of the diversity of sources of inspiration, occasional contradictions are to be found in their writing. On the one hand, they see actors as giving meaning to situations, meaning which is not totally determined by characteristics such as class, race, caste, and so on. On the other hand, they distinguish between the "star performers" who, because of their positions of power, may exercise *virtu*—integrity, composure, gallantry, and valor—and those for whom life presents few opportunities. "Such people are the oppressed, the downtrodden, the people who walk in despair. . . . They have their entrances and their exits, but these are determined and involuntary. . . ."[38] On the whole, such contradictions are few, considering the somewhat different assumptions underlying the numerous perspectives that are freely blended to create the sociology of the absurd.

Creative Sociology—Old or New?

During the past few years, a lively debate has developed, both in the United States and abroad, over the "novelty" of the creative sociologies. Some ethnomethodologists claim to present an entirely new paradigm, one that will shift sociology from its present course.

The notion of "paradigm shift" comes from Thomas Kuhn's work *The Structure of Scientific Revolutions.* This book burst into prominence in 1962; it has run into many printings and has totally reoriented the thinking of many scientists about the nature of theoretical development. Kuhn maintains that science has developed not by a careful piling up of information, brick upon brick, although sciences do amass information while working within a particular framework, but by a series of radical shifts in perspective. These changes are made by the reconstruction of previous theory and the reevaluation of prior fact—an intrinsically revolutionary process.

In the first edition of his book, Kuhn was concerned primarily with physical science, the more obvious "revolutions" in the physical sciences being the Copernican, the Newtonian, and the Einsteinian revolutions. An example of a paradigm shift within a particular field is that of physical optics. Today, physics textbooks tell the student that light is photons, which exhibit some characteristics of waves and some of particles. Research proceeds accordingly. This characteristic of light, though, is scarcely half a century old, developed by Max Planck and Einstein early in this century. Before that time, textbooks taught that light was transverse waves, a paradigm derived from Young and Fresnel in the early nineteenth century. During the eighteenth century, the paradigm for the field was that provided by Newton's *Optiks,* which taught that light was particles. This, says Kuhn, is the usual development pattern of a *mature* science. Before a science reaches maturity, many paradigms hold sway at the same time; it is at the preparadigmatic stage.

Kuhn did not initially address himself to the social and behavioral sciences, intimating that the social sciences are in a preparadigmatic stage and are not, therefore, "science." This has not prevented sociologists from examining their own field in terms of paradigm shifts; several books are presently available that discuss sociology in the light of Kuhn's insights regarding the development of science.[39]

Can the creative sociologies, especially ethnomethodology, be seen as constituting a radical paradigm? Let us examine the opinions of those on both sides of this issue.[40]

Consider first the work of Erving Goffman. Randall Collins and Michael Makowsky see it as presenting a radically new way of viewing society, a revolutionary way.[41] In seeing society as theater, as drama in which in each social interaction human actors create meanings for themselves and for each other, insights are produced that throw new light on the sociological theory that has previously guided research. If reality is constructed by persons interacting with each other, then such matters as crime, delinquency, and deviance are socially constructed. Collins and Makowsky point to the labeling theory which, as we have already seen, has developed both from Goffman's work and from those whose ideas have informed Goffman's writings. Such a new sociological perspective calls into question the methods previously used to study social phenomena. To correlate delinquent acts with broken homes or with skin color no longer makes sense unless account is taken of the manner in which some people, of particular age and sex, in certain residential areas, are more likely to be charged with unlawful acts than are others. Once labeled, such people are unlikely to be able to escape the effects of their "criminal" records. The sociological question thus becomes one of "Who labels whom?" rather than "Why did he do it?"

Stanislav Andreski, on the other hand, indicates that nothing new has happened in the social sciences for a very long time—not since Herbert Spencer (1820–1903), in fact—although several new fads have come to the surface.[42] Among these "new fads" he includes phenomenology, ethnomethodology, existential sociology, and the sociology of the absurd, all of which, he maintains, do no more than what sociologists of the old Chicago School, like Robert Park, Ernest Burgess, and W. I. Thomas, were occupying themselves with in the early decades of this century. Then, writes Andreski, sociologists were studying "informal social relations." This is no different, he suggests, from the description which Tiryakian gives of existential phenomenology as seeking "to elucidate the existential nature of social structures by uncovering the surface phenomena of the everyday accepted world; by probing the subterranean, noninstitutional social depths concealed from public gaze, by interpreting the dialectic between the institutional and noninstitutional." [43] We can appreciate the magnitude of the progress accomplished since Park, Burgess, and Thomas were at Chicago when we realize, Andreski writes bitingly, that they "did not even suspect that what they were doing was ethnomethodological, existential phenomenology."

In response to Andreski, some creative sociologists do not hesitate to acknowledge the debt they owe to sociologists of the past. The work of Lyman and Scott, for instance, is so heavily laced with proper appreciation to such persons that, although theirs may be a unique and lively synthesis, their approach clearly draws deeply from already existing ideas.

John Goldthorpe, a British sociologist, addresses himself to what he terms "the ethnomethodologists' claim to have made, or at least to have made imminent, a revolution in sociology," and concludes that ethnomethodology is not as novel an approach as some of its exponents would seem to think, "being, in fact, but a modern variation on what is a very old theme." [44] This is in no way intended to deny the value of the ethnomethodological position in furthering understanding but merely to question its revolutionary claims. Goldthorpe writes that ethnomethodologists do not substantiate their claim that they differ radically from the several varieties of traditional sociology, but demonstrate, rather, that ethnomethodological inquiry is incomplete in itself and not intellectually viable in isolation from other, more traditional concerns. To support his view, Goldthorpe suggests first that the criticisms of "positivistic" methods and technical shortcomings, and of logical weaknesses ethnomethodologists find in conventional sociology, are of a kind that have already been expressed by conventional sociologists themselves. Second, Zimmerman and Pollner's criticism of the systematic confounding of "topic" and "resource" by conventional sociologists may ultimately be leveled against ethnomethodologists themselves. [45] In this confounding of topic and resource, ethnomethodologists claim that conventional sociology does not attain any significantly higher level of theoretical awareness than that possessed by lay members; sociology remains a "folk" discipline and, as such, must be "deprived of any prospect or hope of making fundamental structures of folk activity a phenomenon." [46] This may be so, says Goldthorpe, but this is not to deny that, although information so derived by the sociologist is qualitatively similar to that available to the actor in everyday life, such information may be greater and more reliable than that available to lay members. Further, Zimmerman and Pollner do not address the question of whether *any* kind of sociology, ethnomethodology included, can ever entirely escape dependence on commonplace meanings and understandings. The statement regarding the confounding of topic and resource comes down to a criticism of complacency by sociologists regarding what they take for granted; it indicates an important new area for sociological inquiry, but it does not provide anything like a basis for promulgating a sociological revolution.

A more consequential argument by ethnomethodologists, suggests Goldthorpe, is that deductive explanations cannot be pursued because literal description of social interaction is not possible. Social interaction is regarded as an interpretive process, the descriptions of social interaction by sociologists similarly being interpretive descriptions, not literal ones. Such interpretation may be indefinitely revised as situations change, just as history is revised by new generations of historians, whose values and viewpoints are colored by the spirit of their own times. Yet, questions Goldthorpe, are *all* norms and roles always unspecific and subject to differential interpretations? May *nothing* ever be taken for granted? Here, says Goldthorpe, the lack of consensus among creative sociologists, indeed among ethnomethodologists themselves, becomes apparent. While Garfinkel emphasizes the "awesome indexicality" which characterizes interaction—that meanings are situationally dependent—lack of consistency in the arguments of ethnomethodologists renders it difficult to assess their stance.[47] Further, at some points, Goldthorpe goes on, ethnomethodologists write as if they accept a straightforward duality: The physical world is "out there" and real, the world of mental states is "in here" and real, but the social world does not exist independently of the social meanings that members use to account for it and, hence, to constitute it; social structure has no identity independent of members' everyday sense of it.[48] At other points, ethnomethodology argues for the objective character of the social world which members apprehend, explain, define, perceive, externalize, and objectify through the mode of natural language.

A final criticism by Goldthorpe considers the central concern of ethnomethodology: social action. "Central," he suggests, is not the same as "total." While study of actors in interaction in a situation is of value, to disregard, or take the stance of "indifference" toward such matters as the ecological, demographic, technical, economic, and political conditions that may be relevant either as constraints or as facilities on interaction—for example, whether or not interaction is possible, who participates in it—is to have less than a complete understanding. Such a complete understanding lies beyond the scope of the methods of inquiry and conceptualization of lay members in everyday life, and the study of members' constructs to the exclusion of other kinds of inquiry provides for an incomplete sociology.

Doug Benson, in his rejoinder to Goldthorpe, agrees that the positions taken by ethnomethodologists on certain issues are divergent; ethnomethodology is by no means monolithic in structure. He points out, however, that to fault ethnomethodology because of its "congruence theory"—that a member's "constructed object" is held to be identical with the "real concrete object" and nothing "lies behind" the member's construction of the world—is to misunderstand the nature of the ethnomethodological enterprise.[49] From the ethnomethodological viewpoint, it makes no sense to inquire about "extrasituational" constants guiding and limiting members' activities except when these "external" elements are perceived as "facts-in-the-world" by members in the situation. Ethnomethodologists hold that the topic of interest is the *member's* view of what is going on and that the sociologist who looks for what is *really* going on is assuming that, somehow, the sociologist's view of what is going on is not also constrained by his intersubjective world, both as a sociologist and as a lay member. He adds that to see ethnomethodology as merely a deviationist position in sociology or as one which seeks to repair or modify conventional sociology is to misconceive its central policies. Further, its policy statements are not enough to establish the "paradigm" status of ethnomethodology; one must turn to the increasingly available body of ethnomethodological studies to discover the findings *"which could not have been imagined by lay members"* (emphasis added).

Goldthorpe snaps back that Benson does little but concede Goldthorpe's main point: that the claim ethnomethodologists make that they have made possible a "revolution" in sociology is without secure foundation.[50] If an examination of what Benson considers "a selective reading" of the literature of ethnomethodology reveals important differences of position among ethnomethodologists, a more comprehensive review would presumably reveal yet greater philosophical, methodological, and theoretical disarray. Further, says Goldthorpe, while one must agree with Benson that ethnomethodology is best defined by demonstration that "it is capable of yielding findings which could not have been imagined by lay members," he does not provide the criteria by which a "finding" of ethnomethodology should be accepted as such. If, from the ethnomethodological standpoint, nothing "lies behind" the member's construction of the world and his interpretive procedures for making sense of that world, what is the status of just those findings which could not have been imagined by lay members?

Another theorist who fails to see ethnomethodology as a new approach is Bauman. On the contrary, he regards it as a consistent version of positivism. He suggests that in their reluctance to admit any concealed "hard core" of reality, no rupture between ethnomethodological and positivistic ventures can be spotted: "they crumble events into multitudes of essentially non-generalizable, endemically individual experiences."[51] Bauman indicates that many ethnomethodologists profess a faith which is even more uncompromising than positivistic statements, which admit at least the ultimate authority of the event:

> The social world is nothing but the "ongoing practical accomplishment" of the members, according to Garfinkel and Sacks (1970); events are nothing but "occasioned corpuses," according to Zimmerman and Pollner (1970); "Members can

be said to be programming each other's actions as the scene unfolds" says Cicourel (1970); and the basically contingent social reality develops freely as a series of bargains negotiated and struck by the members—a chain of events analyzable at best in terms of games theory. As positivists, the ethnomethodologists stoutly refuse to admit as epistemologically relevant any fixity, toughness or inflexibility in the social world. The only end we can achieve when engaging in sociological inquiry is to say, with some degree of certainty: that is what, so far, the events looked like. But that is precisely the task placed before science by the positivistic venture.[52]

On the other hand, Mullins, in his expansion of Kuhn's concept of paradigmatic revolutions to sociology, includes both ethnomethodology and symbolic interactionism as distinct paradigms in sociology.[53] While Mullins tends to dismiss symbolic interaction as so far disappointing its promise in its relative lack of publications of an empirical nature, he sees ethnomethodology's attempt to understand the accounting procedures by which members produce and sustain a sense of social structure as constituting a "radical break" from standard American sociology. Mullins is well aware of the splits, existing and potential, within ethnomethodology. He sees both an East-West split and potential splits within the West Coast group between the conversational analysts, including Sacks, David Sudnow, and Schegloff, and the language acquisition and rule-using analysts, including Cicourel and his students.

Coulter, too, while acknowledging that ethnomethodology does not denote a homogeneous school of thought, feels that in the addressing of analytic issues by generating observations of the practical methods of people's everyday activities and reasoning, it "may well be the most significant development in sociological thinking in recent years."[54] He feels that the ethnomethodologists' view—that the properties of members' sense-assembly and order-assembly procedures in practical reasoning are investigable as topics in their own right—represents a real advance in the study of language and the conceptualization of meaning, much more far-reaching than previous sociolinguistic approaches.

Finally, it is in the notion of "invariance" that Paul Attewell sees the justification for new paradigm status for ethnomethodology.[55] To study invariance, Attewell says, is to aim for one-hundred-percent nonstatistical laws. This is not just studying probability, nor is it determining absolute regularities for limited populations. Invariance applies to all people in all settings. No other sociology would make this claim.

Is it possible, on the basis of the fairly representative sample of views presented here, to answer the question "Creative sociology: old or new?" Do the spokesmen for each side provide enough evidence upon which to decide whether or not new paradigm status is justified? If a group of theorists claims to have developed a revolutionary new paradigm which will replace existing paradigms, then the burden of proof rests on them. It seems to me that, so far, they have not provided support which makes it possible to accept their claim.

It must be admitted that the difficulty of deciding the issue is confounded by the inclusion of several sociologies under the one blanket term, yet the focus on these approaches separately still does not allow an answer. Ethnomethodologists, for instance, agree with their critics that theirs is not a unified approach. Different assumptions underlie different ethnomethodological enterprises, as has been seen from the discussion throughout this chapter. While much ethnomethodology is phenomenologically informed, some is not. The splits and rifts continue to develop; the field changes as one tries to examine it; it shifts and moves in different directions. Some of the work being done by ethnomethodologists is objectivistic-positivistic in its methods; other work remains interpretive. At this time, until more convincing evidence is submitted, I would prefer to agree with George Psathas that ethnomethodology, as a distinctive enterprise, supplements rather than supplants all the social sciences, especially sociology.[56]

Let us now turn to some substantive topics, using the creative sociologies as perspectives. In each of the three essays that follow, different creative approaches will be emphasized. First, the drama!

PART TWO
Meanderings

Life
Like flowing water
fills cracks and crannies
more than enough.

—TADEUSZ RÓZEWICZ
Kartoteka (The Card Index)

CHAPTER THREE

"The Drama Is in Us, And We Are the Drama"

PLAYWRIGHTS and novelists are frequently fine sociologists—although they may not acknowledge themselves as such—able to illustrate sociological concepts in familiar, day-to-day situations without the burdensome terminology so many sociologists feel constrained to use in their attempts to appear scientific. Plays and novels of all kinds, then, provide excellent resources upon which students may draw to test their newly acquired sociological perspective and to discover sociological concepts in artistic guises.

Just as the social scientist's philosophical view of the social world shapes the manner in which he or she approaches the study of social phenomena, so does the world-view of a novelist, dramatist, or other artist determine in large measure the style he uses to demonstrate this view. While all dichotomies should be viewed with caution as oversimplifications, dramatists, like sociologists, may be seen either as "positivistic-naturalistic" or as "subjective" in their approach, with, of course, considerable overlapping of types within many of their works.[1] Some, in the novelistic style of Émile Zola, put onto the stage in microscopic detail every characteristic of the actors, every exchange among them, every word and gesture, every item in the background, as though they were practical scientists describing and classifying physical phenomena. Others—the expressionists, symbolists, surrealists, dramatists of the absurd—stress the subjective, that to each individual the world appears as something different and, because it is a construction of the human mind, only vague guidelines need be provided by the dramatist.

The chapter title is a quotation from Luigi Pirandello, *Six Characters in Search of an Author.*

Further, if to be a human being is to be "on the way to something else," [2] a character eludes definitive description because by the time it is described it is becoming something other than it was. "Subjective" playwrights often omit information about a character's past experience, his origins, or his aspirations, for although a person carries with him all his past experiences, they have become distorted so that the "real" and the "imaginary" are inextricably woven together. Tadeusz Rózewicz, the contemporary Polish writer, demonstrates this in his first play, *Kartoteka* (The Card Index), by showing his hero at several different points in his life within the same scene. From moment to moment, he changes. At one moment he is a boy being reprimanded by his parents, at another, he is a middle-aged man in bed with his mistress. That we are different, yet the same, at various stages in the cycle of life does not, however, exhaust the many selves we assume even within each time span. Each is spouse, sibling, parent, child, employee, driver, tennis player, consumer, producer, subordinate, superordinate. We have so many selves, play so many roles, that we struggle for a sense of "true" identity. We can see, for instance, in the character of Archie Bunker in the popular television series "All in the Family," the struggle of the "little man" to make a place in the world, to claim a corner of it as his own, to know exactly who he is. His chair, upon which no one else may sit, helps him to determine and establish his identity—at least in his own home. But no one, not even the dramatist, can describe a character in totality.

The dramaturgical approach to human behavior, which has reached its highest form in the work of Erving Goffman, is not new in sociology. The study of roles grew out of the study of urbanization and dates back, therefore, many decades.

When almost everybody lived in a small town or village and drew sustenance directly from the soil, people generally knew very few others. Perhaps a villager might meet a hundred people in the course of a lifetime. Many readers will remember Lili, in the musical comedy *Carnival,* who sang of the little town from which she had come: "What I liked most about Mira was everybody knew my name." Everybody knew one's name, and everything else about him. One's neighbors knew him from birth to the grave, knew one's parents and grandparents, one's faults, one's strengths. Most of us, in our modern, industrialized urban society see a hundred or more people every day, and we see them not as whole persons but as fragments of their totality of roles. In urban life, most situations between human beings are characterized by presentation of only portions of the personalities concerned. We present segmented selves.

Reference to this in the sociological literature began to appear with industrialization and the move to the cities. Ferdinand Tönnies (1865–1936) used the terms *Gemeinschaft* [community; mutual participation] and *Gesellschaft* [company; business partnership] to refer to the close personal relationship and the impersonal, or businesslike, relationship of the city. A number of other distinctions of this type are to be found: Henry Sumner Maine (1822–1888) provided the terms *status* and *contract*. Among close friends and family members, one is judged on the basis of who one is (status); with that knowledge one may, for instance, borrow or lend money. Among strangers, however, it is wise to have records in writing (contracts) for such transactions. Charles Horton Cooley wrote of *primary* relationships, warm, caring, intimate affinities in which people knew each other as whole persons; the logical partner is *secondary* relationships, not Cooley's own term but one that has been added through the years.

In the city, cooperation is required of people who do not know each other. Persons deal with each other in a series of exchanges. We go to the store to buy a loaf of bread, wait at the check-out stand, pay our money. "Have a nice day!" the checker insists, and we know, and she knows that we know, that she does not care whether we have a nice day or not. She has been trained to say the words in a certain way; she plays a role while dealing with customers in a purely "secondary" relationship. Her responses are, perhaps, even more automatic than if all those involved were characters in a play.

Many writers who discuss the move from primary to secondary relationships, from rural to urban life, do so with a measure of dismay, as a tragedy, as reducing security and happiness and inducing alienation, loneliness, and mental illness. But perhaps life as a "whole person," known to others in totality, may have it drawbacks. It seems that most of us strive for a life that offers both freedom and security, although these appear to be mutually incompatible—more freedom means less security, and more security reduces freedom. Within family and friendship groups, or in a small community, individuals are limited in their actions *because* they know each other so fully. Some actions require more privacy for their performance or completion than is attainable in a closely knit circle. In an urban setting individuals have the opportunity to present only segmented views of themselves and so may be able to be free with regard to aspects of their lives they would have to conceal or repress in their small, close community.

This lack of freedom, the sometimes total power of the small group over the individual, is magnificently illustrated by Samuel Beckett in *Endgame,* in which the two major characters, Hamm and Clov, are locked together in their terrible dependency upon each other. Hamm, the invalid, needs Clov, his companion, for hour-to-hour, day-to-day ministrations: to fetch and to carry, to mop his wounds, to act as butt to his jokes, to serve as victim to his assaults. Clov's need for Hamm is built of habit—his tasks give shape to his existence. Such dependency, while mutual, is seldom equal.

Georg Simmel, a forerunner of many of the creative sociologists of today, maintained that conflict underlies every episode and every relationship. That two people, or a few people, live in very close proximity for protracted periods of time does not necessarily mean that their lives together will be harmonious or that they will understand each other—or even that they will attempt to understand each other's point of view. Simmel saw subordination/superordination as one of the basic "forms" of social relationships, a form that could be found in different guises, different contents, in a variety of situations. Power relationships prevail in human exchanges. Max Weber has defined power as the ability of a person or a group of persons to exert his or their will over another or others, even against opposition. The conflict, the failure to see the other's point of view, the demands, the power of those in primary relationships to impose their will upon others can be seen in style both stark and subtle in such plays as Pinter's seven-page *Night,* in his *Dumb Waiter,* in Beckett's *Endgame,* in Sartre's *No Exit*—a work whose major theme is that we provide a living hell for each other in our day-to-day exchanges with those to whom we are most closely bound—and in perhaps the most striking example in drama of the destructiveness of those in an intimate, primary-group setting, Albee's *Who's Afraid of Virginia Woolf?*

The formulations of the early sociologists, then, in deploring secondary relationships, may be seen as oversimplified or narrow. It does not necessarily require a crowded city for persons to endure isolation. In groups of two, three, thirty, or three hundred, human selves are segmented, and the drama of the subjective school illustrates this fundamental aloneness of the human being and his or her struggle to discover meaning and closeness in a world in which each is seeing through different eyes, each talking past the other.

Both Beckett and Pinter use the pause, the long silence, as a device to illustrate how difficult it is to reach another person, how little we can actually say to each other. Language is devalued by these writers because, even in its excessive use, what is said is not what is meant. Speech frequently conceals what is meant, yet, in the saying, images are conveyed that have undeniable effects. Erving Goffman writes that we *give* information in talk, but that we *give off* much more in unspoken gesture, in adornment or lack of it, in clothing, walk, twitch, or mannerism.[3] Speech is a more or less carefully monitored account of what we wish the other to know about us. It may be belied by a multitude of other indications. Pirandello finds human speech inadequate to overcome the isolation of human existence. In *Six Characters in Search of an Author* the father, in his realization that each views the same occurrence from a different vantage point, that an act of kindness may be interpreted as a threat by one who has known little kindness before, or whose perception is of having been treated cruelly, says:

> Each of us has within him a whole world of things, each man his own special world. And how can we ever come to an understanding if I put in the words I utter the sense and value of things as I see them; while you who listen to me must inevitably translate them according to the conception of things each one of you has within himself. We think we understand each other but we never really do.[4]

The same message is conveyed in even simpler terms on the poster which I have on my study wall:

I KNOW THAT

YOU BELIEVE YOU

UNDERSTAND WHAT

YOU THINK I SAID

BUT

I AM NOT SURE

YOU REALIZE THAT

WHAT YOU HEARD

IS NOT

WHAT I MEANT

The failure to comprehend the other's viewpoint is not because the speech is unclear but because each perceives the world differently. This is marvelously illustrated in the sociological literature by Jessie Bernard, whose examination of marriage reveals that in each marriage there are two marriages: his and hers.[5] Each partner perceives and experiences the same marriage differently, being affected by it and responding to it in a different way. Had she broadened the study to include each parent of the husband and wife, and each child of the marriage, she would undoubtedly have found that the "same" marriage would have appeared different to each who viewed it.

Harold Pinter has written of his reluctance to express himself in any way, knowing that there are dozens of possible aspects of any single statement. No statement is finite. Such a weight of words confronts us every day, he says, and so little is actually said. Much that is important lies unspoken. It is the unspoken that is important in understanding the core of the person rather than the role that is being played here and now. When a torrent of words pours forth, it is in that which we do not hear that the important message is conveyed. "One way of looking at words is that it is a constant strategem to cover nakedness." [6] Ionesco, too, in *The Bald Soprano,* uses language as a tool to hide the characters' isolation. Each uses the cliché or the platitude as a refuge. It is safe, it allows one to be included in the group without the requirement of thought or reflection, and without risk. It is an example of the hollow gestures abounding in all social situations. When they experiment with these ideas, my students find that they can survive entire days using only standardized clichés and trite phrases in their dealings with others. They can pursue their mundane activities saying little more than "Nice day!" "How are you?" "Very well, thanks," "Good to see the sunshine," "We need some rain, though," "Won't be long until Christmas," "Thank goodness, it's Friday." It is acceptable to "say nothing" with one's words—more acceptable than divulging one's "true" feelings or opinions. As Pinter puts it: "Communication is too alarming. To enter into someone's life is too frightening. . . ." [7] In *Waiting for Godot,* after watching Pozzo endure a torment of suffering, for which he apologizes profusely—"Gentlemen, I don't know what came over me. Forgive me. Forget all I said . . . you may be sure there wasn't a word of truth in it"—Beckett's two tramps, in a glorious parody of accepted social niceties, turn to each other with:

VLADIMIR: Charming evening we're having.
ESTRAGON: Unforgettable. [8]

Just as one need not reflect deeply when dealing in trivialities, so the one addressed need not listen. Words are heaped on words. In the first scene of Eugène Ionesco's *Bald Soprano,* Mrs. Smith describes in agonizingly minute detail the most minor aspects of the preparation of the dinner, as though it were of world-shattering importance, while Mr. Smith reads, clicking his tongue conspicuously to punctuate her ramblings. Yet of such trivia, such rambling, is the shape of our everyday life constructed. Ionesco also uses non sequiturs, seemingly meaningless phrases, each character following his own train of thought, as a demonstration of the lack of common ground against which we each struggle to make sense of our world. [9]

How we make sense of the world is the topic of primary interest to subjective dramatists as it is to creative sociologists. Ionesco writes of his belief that life is painful and unbearable, "like a bad dream." [10] And, indeed, at those times when we dare to pause for consideration of the inhumanities being perpetrated upon living beings, of war, crimes, disasters, of death waiting for each of us, the "realities" are incapable of comprehension. Well within living memory, millions of human beings, young and old, men and women, strong and frail, were burned in incinerators by other human beings. More recently we have witnessed the burning alive of human creatures with napalm. We sell bombs, and the aircraft from which they may be dropped, to nations that will use them for the destruction of other peoples, while maintaining that our own economy would suffer if we did not do these things. Those who live in the United States take for granted the enjoyment of personal luxuries of a quality and quantity not dreamed of by the many millions in the world who are dying of starvation, either rapidly or excruciatingly painfully, while we embark on one slimming regimen after another to shake off the results of over-nutrition. How do we reconcile these kinds of inconsistencies? How do we cope with the awareness of their existence without going mad? "Men," says Ionesco, "hide behind their clichés." [11] We mask what we know in our meaningless language so that thinking may be avoided. As Vladimir and Estragon confide to each other:

VLADIMIR: We're in no danger of thinking any more.
ESTRAGON: Then what are we complaining about?
VLADIMIR: Thinking is not the worst.
ESTRAGON: Perhaps not. But at least there's that.
VLADIMIR: That what?
ESTRAGON: That's the idea, let's ask each other questions.
VLADIMIR: What do you mean, at least there's that?
ESTRAGON: That much less misery.
VLADIMIR: True.
ESTRAGON: Well, if we gave thanks for our mercies.
VLADIMIR: What is terrible is to *have* thought.
ESTRAGON: But did that ever happen to us?
VLADIMIR: Where are all those corpses from?
ESTRAGON: These skeletons.
VLADIMIR: Tell me that.
ESTRAGON: True.
VLADIMIR: We must have thought a little.
ESTRAGON: At the very beginning.

VLADIMIR: A charnel house! A charnel house!
ESTRAGON: You don't have to look.
VLADIMIR: You can't help looking.
ESTRAGON: True.
VLADIMIR: Try as one may.
ESTRAGON: I beg your pardon?
VLADIMIR: Try as one may.
ESTRAGON: We should turn resolutely towards Nature.
VLADIMIR: We've tried that.
ESTRAGON: True.
VLADIMIR: Oh it's not the worst, I know.
ESTRAGON: What?
VLADIMIR: To have thought.
ESTRAGON: Obviously.
VLADIMIR: But we could have done without it.[12]

In *Waiting for Godot,* Beckett presents the world as a wasteland; a void from which his characters must wrest some meaning for their existence and some reason for continuing day after day, year after year. "The world is a veil we spin to hide the void." [13] Meaning must be spun by each of us. This "spinning of meaning" closely approximates what phenomenologists and ethnomethodologists refer to as a *sense* of reality as a practical accomplishment of actions in each situation.

In a recent study of automobile workers in four nations, William H. Form found, contrary to previous pronouncements by social scientists about the "alienation" and "isolation" perceived by workers on the assembly line, that most workers are satisfied with their jobs. Above all, their work "provides organizational cement to their lives." [14] The daily routine gives meaning to their existence.

I have implied earlier that habit allows us to get by without thinking, without reflection. In this sense, much of what we do may be seen as something less than human in that it does not require of us the exercise of that which is essentially human. It is automatic, nonsymbolic, requiring no interpretation. Form, in his summary, calls to task those social scientists who bewail the lot of the semiskilled worker as pitiable, dehumanizing, and deadening. They are happy in their work, he says, and that is a matter of empirical, verifiable fact. Social scientists should reconsider. What is it that we are being asked to reconsider? That without the simple, intellectually undemanding task of, perhaps, screwing a given number of headlights into sockets each hour, day after day, year after year, decade after decade, life would lack meaning? Perhaps, as has been pointed out elsewhere, some assembly-line workers are able to tolerate their work because, while performing their tasks, they are able to let their minds wander, to daydream the long hours away, to build elaborate, if unattainable, plans for the future.[15] Yet this would seem to support rather than to provide an alternative to the existentialist-absurdist view of the routine and habitual as a hollow substitute for meaning.

The kind of "meaning" found by the automobile workers in Form's study is demonstrated in all of Beckett's plays; the endless repetition of chores, tasks, statements, night following day, day following night, ending only in death. The recognition that there can be no other kind of life for the characters because they have no larger horizons than their four walls is brilliantly, even humorously, demonstrated in *Endgame*. Beckett tells us in another context: "Habit is the ballast that chains the dog to his vomit. Breathing is habit, Life is habit. Or rather, life is a succession of habits since the individual is a succession of individuals." Habit allows us to replace with the boredom of living the need to think, to acknowledge the void.[16]

We see this attempt to bring some sense of meaning and structure into a world in which none is inherent in *Waiting for Godot*. The day-to-day existence of Beckett's tramps, Vladimir and Estragon, seems to have little rationale. The bare universe provides few guidelines to direct their actions. The two acts of the play differ only slightly. In each, the tramps pass a day that we know is similar to hundreds of others they have passed together. The same trivial pattern of events occurs each day. Estragon sums up their situation: "Nothing happens, nobody comes, nobody goes, it's awful." [17] To provide reason for living, to give meaning to their suffering, they constantly remind each other that they do, in fact, have a purpose. They are waiting for Godot. That Godot will never come is apparent to both of them but not acknowledged, for, without that hope, life would be unbearable. There would be no point in going on, no point in living. In similar ways, most of us make plans, both short-term and long-term, prepare for some future occasion, look forward to a holiday—and frequently acknowledge that it is the *looking forward*, the anticipation, that provides us with a pleasure far more profound than does the event itself, if and when it is attained. In our joyous anticipation, we need not think of the humdrum days as we pass automatically through them, one by one. Further, by the time the event rolls around, it might find us different persons with different notions of how pleasures may be taken.

The days must be filled. Thomas Mann has said: "Time has no division to mark its passage, there is never a thunderstorm or blare of trumpets to announce the beginning of a new month or a new year. Even when a new century begins it is only we mortals who ring bells and fire off pistols." We divide our days in "meaningful". ways. A "Peanuts" cartoon by Charles Schulz shows Snoopy, the beagle, sighing through his day, complaining that life has no meaning, everything seems empty. "I search the skies but I can find no meaning—no meaning." His sighs grow longer and heavier, until along comes Charlie Brown with a bowl of food. "Ah! *Meaning!*" exults Snoopy. Mealtimes provide divisions in the day which would otherwise loom emptily ahead.

Especially does time hang heavy and empty for old people. It must be filled with recreational activities, but these are designed to "pass the time." For many old people, life lacks meaning because the routine of work has ceased, just as Form indicates in his summary—or, for women, the children have grown and gone away. The nest is empty.[18] A middle-aged woman whose children had all left to establish homes of their own told me, "I am glad when the night comes so that I can go to bed and sleep." Shocking? Perhaps. Unusual? Perhaps not. While we are busy, we do not notice time; it "flies" and we wish that we could grasp it and hold it back. We think our days are filled with useful activities, that we are "making progress," working toward some end. The "absurdity" of human beings' existence in the world is that we struggle to find sense when none is inherent, that we are born, live, and die, few of us leaving much impression, that most of our activity is in itself empty, routine, and repetitious.

Time and timelessness, or atemporality, become almost tangible entities in the dramas of the subjectivists, as they are of the Japanese Noh theater. Beckett's plays, especially, embody this element of the Noh and, as Leonard Pronko reminds us in his excellent discussion of Eastern and Western theater the critical reception accorded the Noh troupe at the Théâtre des Nations in Paris was not very different from the way Beckett's plays had been received earlier.[19] The critic for *Le Monde* was thoroughly bored by the Japanese work and wrote of the "torpor, the slowness of the performance, and the insignificance of the subjects."[20] One can well imagine, adds Pronko, his making the same comments after seeing Beckett's plays, for if Beckett's characters, particularly in *Endgame* and the later plays, are turned toward the past, constantly reenacting the incidents of a life already lived, "it is because they, like the Buddhist ghosts of the Noh, are tied to the wheel of life, unable to free themselves from a cycle that has become meaninglessly repetitious." [21]

Martin Esslin, writing on Beckett, adds that the subject of *Waiting for Godot* is not Godot but waiting. It is in the act of waiting, he says, that we experience the flow of time in its purest form. When we wait, we feel the full weight of time itself.[22] Beckett himself points out that there is no escape from the hours and the days. Yesterday has deformed us or been deformed by us; the flow of time, he says, confronts us with the basic problem of being—the problem of the nature of the self, which is in constant flux and is therefore outside our grasp.[23] Pinter says much the same about time: "I feel more and more that the past is not past, that it never was past. It's present . . . and the future is simply going to be the same thing. It'll never end. You carry all the states with you until the end . . . the previous pasts are alive and present." [24]

Arthur Waley speaks of the Noh story as "creeping at its subject warily." Since the action is presented as a memory evoked by a dead man, we get a vision of life, indeed, but painted with the colors of memory, longing or regret. Such a description, suggests Pronko, applies to *Krapp's Last Tape* and *Embers,* in which Beckett's protagonists are ghosts and the action is remembered, as it took place long ago.[25]

Pinter, as indicated earlier, is much concerned with time in his writing and in his thought. A thesis of his short play *Night* is that time warps memory as memory warps time. From the beginning, it is evident that in all the years since the night the couple first met, each of the two characters' imaginations has altered the original sense perception of whatever happened. Not only has time served to spark their imaginations but their imaginations have also perverted the accepted unity of time.[26]

Ionesco, too, acknowledges a debt to the Noh theater. He wrote that Zeami's *Secret Tradition of the Noh* revealed techniques reminiscent of the Greek plays and recommended that it be read by the "closed minds of the West." [27] Part of his stage directions for *The Bald Soprano* read: "Another moment of silence, the clock strikes seven times. Silence. The clock strikes three times. Silence. The clock does not strike." That the clock strikes on its own, when it wants to and as many times as it wants, changes the quality of time. The implication is that time cannot be measured outside personal experience, that it becomes something different for each of us.

These dramas, then, both of the East and of the West, use time as one device

among others to indicate that the reality of existence is subjective; to emphasize, once more, that "existence is the very process whereby the hitherto meaningless takes on meaning." [28]

Meaning, though, cannot be found entirely within ourselves. The uncertainty
of our social identity is eased, symbolic interactionists might say, by social
norms: the expectations of us by others. Each role that we play, each part, has
its required lines and gestures, tone of voice and mannerisms, which we re-
hearse in private before performing in public. The manner in which our playing
is received gives us clues as to its strength of conviction, its credibility. Eti-
quette, manners, the "proper" ways of doing things act as the lubricants of
daily life, allowing us to slip by in routine situations with minimal anxiety,
just as trite phrases provide acceptance into the group without risk. By these
means, we do not have to investigate *who* we are, as long as *what* we are is apparent and acceptable to those with whom we interact. We have our "place,"
we greet and treat each other as "types." We are teacher, or parent, or social
worker, or servant, as the scene demands, and as such we soon learn our parts.
Violate the expectations of these types and our social world collapses along with
the images of ourselves.

"All the world's a stage, and all the men and women merely players. . . . "
At times, Erving Goffman appears to take Shakespeare's lines literally, portray-
ing the human self as a dramatic effect, a set of "me's"—all the men and
women are *merely* players. For Goffman, parts are changed from situation to situation, from episode to episode, so that his reader must finally ask, with Peer
Gynt, whether the human self is simply layers and layers of roles without a
heart, like an onion, the layers of which may be peeled away until nothing
remains. This depiction of the self renders futile any attempt to "find one's
identity," and Goffman has been severely criticized for offering such an image
of humankind,[29] yet several contemporary subjective playwrights, as well as
novelists, can be seen as supportive of this view. Kurt Vonnegut uses terms of
his own invention that closely parallel sociological concepts. *Foma,* for instance,
are harmless untruths, intended to comfort simple souls—clichés, such as
"prosperity is just around the corner," which we can use without thinking.[30]
Goffman, it must be added, never takes the stance that the use of "foma" is
"harmless." He doesn't say. We must draw our own conclusions.

If the checker in the supermarket were *not* to say "Have a nice day," would
we be upset? If, further, she were to leave her side of the check-out stand to
engage us more directly, at the same time weeping wildly, would we not be

more upset? Such a violation of expectations would require of us an involvement in someone else's life and problems that we might prefer to evade. Evasion of serious issues is preferable to confrontations simply because it is easier.

Ionesco demonstrates the implication of the conformity by most people to expected roles in the "Bobby Watson" sequence of *The Bald Soprano*. It turns out that everybody involved in a series of coincidences is a commercial traveler named Bobby Watson. This interchangeability of people, each separate identity dissolved in a society of Bobby Watsons, is an indication of the insecurity and social pressures that allow people to be easily molded by social norms (just as does the interchangeability of some of the roles in *The Deputy*, by Rolf Hochhuth). The faceless, nameless, unrecognized mass-man may be easily induced to perform acts the identifiable individual might resist. Ionesco shows, too, what happens when people, particularly those in subservient positions, step "out of character." Everyone in *The Bald Soprano* is shocked when Mary, the maid, attempts to join the rest of the group in relating her story:

MR. MARTIN: I believe that our friends' maid is going crazy . . . she wants to tell us a story, too.

FIRE CHIEF: Who does she think she is?

. . . . . .

MR. MARTIN: What I think is that a maid, after all . . . is never anything but a maid.

. . . . . .

MRS. SMITH: Go, my little Mary, go quietly into the kitchen and read your poems before the mirror.[31]

Here, finely drawn, are examples of Goffman's notions of the treatment of servants as either children or as "nonpersons," the expectations that maids will behave as maids and as nothing else, that the performance of improprieties may lead to the labeling of one as "mad," and that subordinates usually have less power than do superordinates to define the situation.[32]

Generally, it is easier to conform to expectations than to violate them, to tell little white lies, to use foma, to present the self that fits the occasion. Presumably we can find someplace where we can show our "true" selves, or find someone with whom we can "be ourselves," yet, as Pirandello implies in *Six Characters in Search of an Author*, it may be that we cannot stop telling lies, even to ourselves, for we live on the surface of our being, not in the depths.[33] How can we know ourselves when we cannot know others—if all we ever present are "accounts," not only to satisfy others but also to convince ourselves that our actions are justified? [34] The producer in *Six Characters in Search of an Author* asks: "What's truth got to do with it? Acting's what we're here for." And, as Gaskell remarks, that is the point—we are all actors in life and Pirandello puts onto the stage both the persons that we feel ourselves to be and the actors we inevitably become when we live among others, on the surface. [35] The symbolic interactionists would say that we become what we see reflected in the eyes of others, as though in a looking glass, but if we present shallow "types" to others, surely that is all that can be reflected, all that we can become?

Some of my students, especially the well-meaning reformists who look to sociology hoping to find sensible, swift solutions to deeply rooted social problems, become disheartened by the creative approaches to the study of society and find the subjective drama and literature, with which they supplement the sociological literature on social interaction, grotesque and depressing, containing little suggestion of release from misery or any kind of attainable happiness.

The sociologist Glenn A. Goodwin, while appearing to accept the existentialist notion that man's existence in society cannot escape being absurd and that there are no definitive solutions to the contradictions in which we are steeped, suggests that there are possible responses to this awareness. [36] He argues that much of the rebellion we witnessed in the 1960s by students and blacks may be seen as "meaning-seeking" activity, goal-oriented in that it sought order and unity from the chaos of our society. The rebellious act, even though the individuals involved are aware that there can be no resolutions, is itself a source of meaning which "transcends" the absurd, provides reason for living and integrity for the individual. This, claims Goodwin, is very different from the concerned reform-seekers who see no basic absurdity of social life. Their outlook he describes as "confusion coupled with hopefulness." Besides the rebels and the reformers, Goodwin discusses two more groupings. First are those social scientists who are neither aware of the absurdity of their existence, nor willing to act on anything. Such scientists see as their only goal knowledge for its own sake; they fail to concern themselves with the consideration that knowledge is only temporary and, in any case, is seen differently by each who observes it. He sees such scientists as valueless in that they refuse to discuss the concept of meaning. In the final grouping Goodwin includes Beckett with Camus, Sartre, and Kafka as those who recognize the absurdity of social life but whose characters fail to transcend the absurdity. The work of these authors, he suggests, demonstrates the continuous fatiguing effort of merely surviving in the face of absurdity and hopelessness. In this group are the apathetic and the withdrawn.

Goodwin's thesis may not be wholly acceptable. One would need many more indications than he provides that rebels *do* feel their struggle to be hopeless, and, further, his idea of rebellion and its attendant vision of violence is distasteful to many—needless to say, conflict need not be violent. Nevertheless, the notion that a conscious *awareness* of the absurd may provide a *catalyst* to action is an important one. The playwrights we have been discussing, instead of being viewed as doomsayers, might perhaps be seen as conveying a very different message.

The plays of the subjective dramatists violate all previously held notions of what a play should be: A play should have a beginning, a middle, and an end; there should be a plot; there should be tensions or mysteries that should be resolved in the final scene of the final act; a play should tell a story, preferably a "spanking good yarn." But, as Merleau-Ponty observes, these plays may have a beginning but no end, as in Ionesco's works; they may have neither a beginning nor an end, as in Beckett's plays. Events occur which have no apparent antecedents and which are never explained, as in Pinter's writing. (The funny orders for meals that come down on the dumb waiter are examples of totally unexplained and unexplicable events.) "At the end of a Pinter play a member of the audience has 'understood' when he has given up expecting an explanation. . . ." [37]

These plays can be seen as violating expectations in much the same way as "garfinkeling" violates everyday taken-for-granteds and, in so doing, exposes the flimsiness of "solid" institutions.[38] Ruby Cohn has described *Endgame* as the presentation of the "death of the stock props of Western civilization—family cohesion, filial devotion, parental and connubial love, faith in God, empirical knowledge, and artistic creation." [39] For many in the audiences of such plays, the traditional ways of doing things, the habitual responses to familiar stimuli, become inappropriate. The viewing of the crumbling away of the rocklike edifice of our social world is alarming and frightening to us. We are offended, affronted, unsettled. We laugh nervously, we jeer, or we leave, as did the audience in response to the plays of the absurd and to the Noh when first performed in Paris.

Such receptions have been accorded other expressions of art that have dared to go against the grain of expectations. In the Western world we take for granted as *natural* the ordering of the musical scale that is familiar to us. Yet the arrangement of tones in this manner dates only from the time of Bach. It was he who originally so tuned instruments, working from the ideas of Andreas Werckmeister, who was the first to divide the octave into twelve equal notes, each key now being equally in tune. The attempt to change this arrangement is popularly greeted as a kind of sacrilege, an effort to change the laws of nature. We tend to forget that over much of the world music is heard and enjoyed differently from our Western way, and those in the West who would utilize sounds differently from the ways of the past three centuries are greeted with impatience. The long silence in the contemporary composer Gyorgy Ligeti's *Fragments,* the use of taped sounds of the industrial world of Edgard Varèse, another twentieth-century musician and composer, the innovations employed by John Cage—all intended to convey the mood of the contemporary world, that the order we take for granted may not be there—are ridiculed and reviled by many. To enjoy such music, one must be subjected to a raising of consciousness such as most of us are too lazy, too disinterested, or too cowardly to embark upon.

Consciousness-raising is a technique, Marxist informed, whose aim is to help people to see that there are other ways of viewing taken-for-granteds than our way. This device is used, for instance, in women's liberation groups to arouse the awareness of women that theirs is a common plight, which can be remedied. While Beckett and other dramatists of this school have been called apolitical, their drama may be seen as a consciousness-raising device—one that has been greeted and responded to in similar ways to the reactions of women who denigrate the women's movement, refusing to acknowledge the absurdity of their own situation. Once one faces the possibility that there are more ways of living, of perceiving, of becoming, than one's own way, there is no turning back. One must then make decisions, perhaps painful decisions. These plays may be saying that we can be more than we are, we can be more than animals, that "rehumanization is everyman's task." [40]

Words strain,
Crack and sometimes break, under the burden,
Under the tension, slip, slide, perish,
Decay with imprecision, will not stay in place,
Will not stay still.

—T. S. ELIOT

CHAPTER FOUR

Language and the Structure of Daily Life

LANGUAGE, both written and spoken, is one of our major means of communication, yet the meanings of words are not always the same. What does it mean when I say "I love you"? One might think that a simple enough question to answer. Back in the 1930s, people sang:

I love you,
Yes I do.
I love you.
It's a sin to tell a lie. . . .[1]

If I say so, the song suggests, it must be so. It must be so because it is a sin to tell a lie, and yet in refuting the possibility that I could be lying, that very possibility is raised. Do we always mean what we say? Of course not! A declaration of everlasting love may be genuinely meant and received as such; it may be merely a device to gain some immediate gratification. The word itself—*love*— can be found in the dictionary, but it is not always used as the dictionary defines it; sometimes words dramatically different from "love" can be used to convey what the dictionary defines as love—perhaps even words that are defined as conveying hatred or degradation rather than love and ennoblement. The dictionary is of only slight assistance when we experience the realities of everyday life, for, as T. S. Eliot has said, words decay with imprecision; they will not stay in place.[2]

We know that every language changes with time. Chaucerian English is almost as difficult for us to read as is a foreign language. Similarly, biblical language has been modernized so that twentieth-century congregations might "identify" more easily with the stories of the testaments. A churchman said recently that, nowadays, "redemption" and "conversion" seem to be used more often by banks than by churches.[3]

Word usage changes not only over time but also according to situation. "Situation" includes place, participants (the ages and social standings of the people present and so on), the occasion of the gathering, the time and the setting, among other characteristics. Each person who says or hears a word may experience something different. The man with heart disease, for instance, thinks of *hills* very differently from the fit person. A fit man has no notion of the anxiety felt by one who fears the stabbing pains in the chest that come with undue exertion. "The hills of San Francisco," then, may conjure up for one person a romantic image of pastel-shaded houses, miniature gardens, and fingers of fog stretching over the Golden Gate Bridge; for another person, however, the phrase may call forth murmurs of dismay.

Meaning, both phenomenologists and ethnomethodologists stress, is indexical; it varies situationally and must always be sought anew. Yet, by and large, we do seem to be able to understand each other sufficiently to fit our lines of action together. Different aspects of this "ordinariness" of daily lived experience are of interest to different kinds of creative sociologists. Ethnomethodology, Harold Garfinkel has said, is not interested in the social construction of reality, as are phenomenologists, but in the *structure* of lived orderliness of daily life.[4] For Garfinkel, structure and orderliness are synonymous; his concern is with the production of structure *as* detail. Phenomenologists are concerned with the content of meaning, and if meaning is complex on the individual, subjective level, how much more complex it becomes at the intersubjective, or interactional, level. For social life to display regularity and stability, all interactions must proceed according to rules dictated by the context of the interaction. Rules that apply at a funeral do not apply at the annual office party.

The interest in language evinced by ethnomethodologists and phenomenologists focuses upon analyzing interactions to determine the ways in which the rules of language-use structure both the meaning to those involved and the orderliness of the situation. For Garfinkel, what goes on in people's heads is of no interest to the ethnomethodologist. We cannot read minds, but we can observe action. Attention is directed toward that which is overt; we can observe only that which shows itself. Certain rules, *constitutive* rules, tell us what "game" is being played. To violate them is to bring disarray to the situation. *Preferential* rules, on the other hand, are the proprieties which, if violated, bring sanctions to the violator but do not affect the situation in its totality. Neither kind of rule is always clear; one must sometimes feel one's way carefully, "step on eggs," delicately probe the situation to discover the prevailing rules.

According to Peter Berger "the subjective reality of the world hangs on the thread of conversation." [5] Our world first becomes real to us through conversations with parents, teachers, and friends. As time goes on, the reality of our world is maintained by the same kinds of conversations with spouses, friends, and others of personal importance. If the conversation is disrupted by the death or disappearance of these significant others, our world collapses; it loses it subjective plausibility. This is not meant to indicate that the world is necessarily comfortable when one is in the company of significant others, only that the world is subjectively real. The conversational bonds of two men who, to an audience, appear to be sharing a hellish, claustrophobic existence, are beautifully illuminated in Samuel Beckett's play *Endgame*. After a particularly ugly exchange of words, Clov, the servant companion, asks Hamm, the fiercely selfish, blind cripple, "What is there to keep me here?" "The dialogue," answers Hamm. [6]

"The dialogue"—this line draws incredulous gasps from the audience, addressed as it is to one who seems to have been pointlessly, repeatedly verbally abused by the other; yet it makes clear the dependency of each of these two upon the other for the provision of meaning in the world, for the structure of life itself. Eventually Clov is moved to leave Hamm, but only when his self has become threatened by the dialogue which formerly sustained it. The function of conversation is to reinforce continually the reality people have built for themselves. Conversation is both a reflection of, and a part of, that reality; repetition itself serves to reinforce reality. Talk may even effectively replace the activity talked about. Some would-be writers, for instance, might be well advised not to "talk out" the plots of their stories or plays in too great detail, for in the telling, the excitement of the production may be dissipated. The work may never get written because the talking has already made it real. It is done.

Creative sociologists, then, are not looking for "truth" in the content of language but seek instead the ways in which a seeming orderliness in social life is structured by means of language. What people say, the way they say it, and the setting in which they say it provide important clues toward discovering how what is said by people is shaped by, and shapes, their social worlds. The social world is a practical accomplishment of those who act within it; language, both verbal and written, plays a major part in this accomplishment.

The ways language is used are analyzed in various ways by ethnomethodologists and others who conduct research from within similar theoretical frameworks. Not only is face-to-face "talk" studied, but telephone behavior and exchanges by letter are examined, as are the nonreciprocated written outpourings of diarists and intended suicides. Before turning to some of these studies, it might be helpful to look toward the ideas of some of the linguistic philosophers and anthropological linguists informing contemporary ethnomethodology and phenomenology.

The distinction between the "positivistic naturalists" and the "interpretive humanists" is found in philosophy and linguistics as well as in sociology, psychology, drama, and other fields. Frequently the work of individual thinkers can be seen to change direction during its course, the later work representing an overturning, or a denial, of much that came earlier. So it was with Ludwig Wittgenstein (1889–1951) who, in *Tractatus Logico-philosophicus,* written in 1919, maintained that only through the methods of the natural sciences can knowledge of reality be gained. In his later work, *Philosophical Investigations,* published in 1953, he held that reality, or meaning, is expressed in ordinary, everyday conversation, and the task of philosophy is therefore the analysis of ordinary language, a concept which has profoundly affected philosophy as well as creative sociology.

Wittgenstein claims that we convey meaning to ourselves and others through language—through talk. It is from Wittgenstein that the notion of the situationality of meaning stems. Meaning depends upon its situated *use.* Wittgenstein also introduces the concept of situational language *games.* Games are always being played; the rules may not be clear to us but we must try to discern them if we are to play together, if we are to be social creatures, if we are to exist with others. Language is the social activity par excellence.

Another language philosopher whose ideas have provided important insights for creative sociology is John L. Austin (1911–1960). His major thesis, as is Wittgenstein's, is that through analysis of ordinary language we gain knowledge of the realities of the world the language talks about. Austin coined the term "linguistic phenomenology" to replace such existing slogans as "ordinary language analysis" and "linguistic philosophy" or "analytic philosophy." By "phenomenology," he means descriptive analysis:

> When we examine what we should say when, what words we should use in what
> situations, we are looking . . . not *merely* at words (or meanings . . .) but also at
> the realities we use the words to talk about; we are using a sharpened awareness of
> words to sharpen our perception of . . . the phenomena.[7]

By examining what people say to each other we can discern the structure of
the situation and the ways in which the interactants share reality within that
situation. Austin addresses the problem of intersubjectivity, a problem which
still remains to be solved adequately by phenomenological thinkers. In the
chapter of *Philosophical Papers* entitled "Other Minds," he attempts to make
clear, as does Schutz, that in understanding others we do not "introspect," we
do not read minds. Instead, we bring to bear our stock of knowledge, our experience, our skills learned in other, similar situations, to perceive how others feel
by what they say and the way they say it. We take a great deal for granted; we
trust. Without such trust, social existence would not be possible. Our trust, of
course, may be misplaced. Things may not be what they seem; the man who
appears angry with us may, instead, be deeply grieved by some occurrence that
has little to do with us, but, as we cannot see into his mind, we are guided by
what we think he conveys by his actions:

> A great deal depends on how familiar we have been in our past experience with
> this type of person . . . in this type of situation. If we have no great familiarity,
> then we hesitate to say we know: indeed, we can't be expected to say. . . . On
> the other hand, if we *have* had the necessary experience, then we can, in favorable
> current circumstances, say we know: we certainly can recognize when some near
> relative of ours is angrier than we have ever seen him.[8]

Further, in order to know what another feels, we must have experienced the
feeling ourselves before we can declare with assurance that the other feels, say,
anger, or pity, or grief. The assumption is that others experience such emotions
in much the same way as we do and convey these feelings in ways that we share.
To know that we share our ways of feeling does not mean that we "introspect"
when we attempt to understand others, rather, that we recognize the ways in
which those feelings show themselves in actions, which include talk.

Austin's mention of "types of persons" and "types of situations" is reminiscent of Schutz's use of "typifications"—part of each individual's stock of knowledge. For Austin, as for Schutz and all the creative sociologists, everyday life is
lived among others. Since the experienced reality of life shows itself in what is
said, Austin holds that the study of language is important to our understanding
of the form and structure of social situations.

Ethnomethodologists use the term "doing" to mean that in the telling about some occurrence or activity the reality of that occurrence or activity becomes established, both for the speaker and for the hearer(s). Telling is doing. This usage, and the ideas behind it, have much in common with the statements made in a series of lectures delivered by Austin at Harvard University in 1955 and published in 1962 as *How To Do Things With Words*. Austin divides utterances, spoken phrases or sentences, into *constatives* and *performatives*. Constatives are descriptive statements which tell *about* something, whereas performatives do not merely report, or describe, or constate anything; in the uttering of a performative, the speaker *does* something. The telling is the doing. In saying, for instance, "I bet you a quarter that it will rain this afternoon," not only am I forecasting the weather, I am also making a bet, entering a contract. I am *doing* something.

In the course of the several lectures in the series, Austin elaborates upon the notion of performative utterances, charting out the categories of utterances that might be included as performatives. As well as the more obvious first-person, declarative statements, such as "I do . . . ," "I promise . . . ," "I name this ship," are *verdictives, exercitives, commissives, behabitives,* and *expositives. Verdictives* are typified by the giving of a verdict by a jury, an arbitrator, or an umpire; *exercitives* are the exercising of powers, rights, and influences in such ways as appointing, voting, urging, advising, warning, and so on; *commissives* are utterances which commit the speaker in some way, by promising or otherwise undertaking; *behabitives* have to do with such attitudes or aspects of social behavior as apologizing, cursing, congratulating, challenging, and the rest; finally, *expositives* make clear how we are using words— "I reply," "I concede," "I assume." These types of performative utterances overlap somewhat, and Austin points out also that the uttering of performatives, although this may be the leading incident in performing an act, is not usually the sole necessity for the act to be perceived as performed. The words must be uttered in the appropriate setting and, usually, while performing other actions.

In regarding *all* utterances as doing something as well as telling something, ethnomethodologists take the ideas of Austin a step further. Even phrases or sentences that do not fit into any of Austin's performative categories are seen by ethnomethodologists as performing, because in the telling, describing, accounting, explaining, quoting, and every other way of verbalizing, the structures of situations are exposed, made real, and reinforced for speakers and hearers alike.

A contemporary linguist and philosopher whose work has influenced some creative sociologists is Noam Chomsky (1928–). Especially has Aaron Cicourel drawn from Chomsky's ideas, generally applying them not literally but analogously, and linking them to Schutzian formulations (such as "reciprocity of perspectives") to help in the understanding of how social order, or social interaction, is possible.[9] Chomsky's generative-transformational theory of grammar, simply put, is that underlying the ability of native speakers to manufacture, or "generate," an infinite number of grammatically correct sentences, most of which they have never used or heard before, is a "deep structure," a set of grammatical rules. From the deep structure, the competent native speaker can generate and understand grammatically correct utterances. This is achieved through the use of "transformational rules," which, presumably, are part of the deep structure. The sentences or utterances so generated are referred to as the "surface structure" forms.[10]

Cicourel uses the notions "deep structure" and "surface structure" in attempting to explain how human beings manage to discern the correct behavior in new situations, to choose the norms which apply, the rules which guide the game. These particular norms he compares to the surface structures of grammar. The properties making up the interpretive procedures are analogous to claims about linguistic universals—the deep structure—acquired early in life and fused with the acquisition of language. Cicourel then turns to Schutz's notion of a *common scheme of reference* that makes it possible for human beings to share their worlds. The concept of "reciprocity of perspectives"—the assumption that if two persons changed places with each other, each would, for all practical purposes, experience the scene in the same way—can be considered as one of the interpretive procedures included in the deep structure by which one is able to "generate" correct or suitable behaviors in both new and familiar situations. Reciprocity of perspectives instructs each participant to leave aside personal differences in assessing the situation so that each can commune with the other in ways that the situation demands. One draws from the deep structure only that which is pertinent to the present situation. This might also be seen as analogous to Zimmerman and Pollner's discussion of an "occasioned corpus," which is drawn from one's much broader individual corpus of knowledge.[11] In all interactions we converse in "pruned" or "deleted" phrases, selecting from much more elaborated versions, and we expect others to "fill in." Each must construct the other's deep structure if social interaction is to proceed intelligibly.[12]

Other interpretive procedures include the ability to categorize items as belonging in a larger set, including the deferring of judgment about an item until additional information is forthcoming. This has elsewhere been termed "using the documentary method of interpretation," first noted by Karl Mannheim.[13] It consists of treating an item as a "documentary of," as "pointing to," a presupposed underlying pattern. It may not be clear what is seen, or what it means, while it is being seen. It may be necessary to wait for additional information before attempting to fit an item into a pattern, to find an explanation.

A third interpretive property is that of a network of typifications:

> As I confront my fellow man, I bring into each concrete situation a set of preconstituted knowledge which includes a network of typifications of human individuals in general, of typical human motivations, goals, and action patterns. It also includes knowledge of expressive and interpretive schemes, of objective sign systems and, in particular, of the vernacular language. . . .[14]

Just as Chomsky, then, posits deep and surface structures of grammar, so Cicourel and other creative sociologists suggest a deep structure of cultural knowledge from which each individual draws, permuting and changing elements, so that he or she may act within accepted ranges of normative, or surface, rules as each situation requires.

The contribution of anthropology to the study of language in creative sociology has been mainly that of ethnographic semanticists and cognitive anthropologists whose studies have departed from traditional ethnographies. Their work is sometimes called "the new ethnography" and "ethnoscience." These ethnographers of communication are interested, as are ethnomethodologists, in the interpretive procedures by which members of groups or cultures make sense of each other's speech and thereby orient themselves, or create order, in their social worlds. The ethnographer attempts to find the rules of culturally appropriate behavior, to discover what in the social situation evokes and supports certain actions and inhibits others. This task is performed mainly, though not entirely, by reference to the way people talk about what they do.

Among the anthropologists most cited by ethnomethodologists are Charles O. Frake and Harold C. Conklin. The links between the ethnographic semanticists, the linguistic philosophers, and creative sociology are revealed in this statement by Frake: "Since the knowledge that enables one to behave appropriately is acquired from other people, it must be communicable in some symbolic system which can travel between one mind and another as code signals in a physical channel. . . ."[15] In much of his work, Frake seeks to reveal the knowledge that is communicated by talking, and both Frake and Conklin have discovered in their research that the meaning of words is invariably affected by the context of the situation. The prevailing cultural constraints must be sought in each situation. As Conklin puts it, "An adequate ethnographic description of the culture of a particular society presupposes a detailed analysis of the communication system and of the culturally defined situations in which all relevant distinctions in that system occur." [16]

Frake's work has shown that to get a drink in Subanun, it is not enough to know how to construct a grammatical utterance in the Subanun language, translatable from English, which merely asks for a drink. One needs more than a grammar and a lexicon, says Frake, one needs an "ethnography of speaking": a guide to what kinds of things to say, to whom, in what way, and in what kinds of situations. The drinking of *gasi,* a rice-yeast fermented beverage, proceeds in ways very different from the ways the British drink beer in a pub or Americans drink beer in a bar. [17] Similarly, the concept of litigation is perceived and conducted very differently across cultures, litigation itself not being recognized as such from the setting but only from the content and structure of the talk. The Subanun conduct litigation during festive drinking occasions, frequently arranging legal language forms into verse and then singing the verses to the tunes of drinking songs. To participate in litigation means something different in Yakan, where there are no distinctive settings in which litigation takes place, no distinctive paraphernalia associated with litigation, no distinctive dress. Among the Yakan, litigation is outside the domain of festivities or ceremonies; litigation is never performed as part of another scene. [18]

The work done by ethnographic semanticists is aimed, as is ethnomethodology, at discovering the ways members of a community themselves categorize their own behavior, how they themselves construe their world, rather than by imposing prior categories on what is observed. To achieve this end, procedures have been developed for asking questions which are sensible to the people in the group being studied. The researcher must find out how a person in a given society finds out from others in the group what they know, and use similar kinds of questioning in research. [19] It is then possible to define categories of objects as used by members of the culture.

A problem for ethnomethodologists is the assumption apparently made by ethnographic semanticists that language is stable enough within each culture for meanings of words to be discovered and then fitted into sets of categories, or taxonomies, which make sense to those of the culture. This assumes that every member of a group treats meanings in like manner, yet, if meanings are elusive, slippery, indexical, changing from situation to situation, there are limits to how adequately an ethnography of a culture can describe that culture, even if compiled from the members' own viewpoints. Ethnomethodologists, inspired by the work of "the new ethnography" attempt to extend that work, developing alternative methods of study that still maintain the basic tenets of the ethnographic semanticists but which take into account the indexicality of meaning within groups or cultures. This involves focusing on ways members of groups actually use titles, names, categories, and criteria in a large variety of ongoing situations.[20] While maintaining that *meanings* are situational, however, ethnomethodologists hold that modes of interpretation are trans-situational.[21] The discovery of these trans-situational modes, or universal procedures, is the task of ethnomethodology.

In recent years a variety of studies by creative sociologists investigating "talk, the fundamental material of human relations" have become available both in published form and in unpublished manuscripts that are circulated among interested persons.[22] These studies, each in its own way, demonstrate that what is said, how it is said, and the setting in which it is said all create, shape, and maintain the social world for both speaker and listener.

In his study of telephones and telephone users, Donald W. Ball examines voice-to-voice, rather than face-to-face, conversations to find and to make explicit the rules that guide this kind of "disembodied" talk.[23] Ball is less interested in the content of the talk than in its form or structure, and, while his is a working paper rather than the definitive work, it provides thought-provoking hypotheses. Some 400 million telephone conversations are carried on in the United States each day, yet we rarely consider the underlying routine grounds on which our telephone behavior rests; we take them completely for granted.

The very act of answering the telephone, suggests Ball, involves not merely the substance of speech but also a "performative utterance," in Austin's terms. As well as greeting someone, one also announces oneself as willing to converse and is then expected to play one's part in keeping the conversation going. To refuse to maintain the flow of talk is to leave oneself open to unflattering definitions by the caller. The threat to definition of self ensures that we do what is expected and so reinforces that expectation. The first expectation is that we will answer a ringing telephone, even though we are not sure who the caller might be. We usually answer the telephone even if it means getting out of a hot bath or interrupting love making. Ball points to Menotti's little opera *The Telephone,* in which the hero's attempts to propose marriage are constantly thwarted by the ringing of the telephone, which, of course, his beloved always answers. As one unwritten rule appears to be that the caller terminates as well as initiates the call, the one called is trapped until released by the caller. The very presence of these conventions means that they are potentially subject to manipulative exploitation. One may splash from shower to telephone only to discover that the caller is selling siding for the house or magazine subscriptions. To be rude to such a caller leaves one feeling boorish and uncouth, needing to justify or excuse the behavior, if only to oneself.

As Ball notes, the initiation and termination of conversations are governed by conventions, or rules. These conventions have been topics for close study by Emanuel A. Schegloff and by Harvey Sacks as part of their interest in formally analyzing "sequencing" in general.[24] Schegloff begins his discussion of conversational openings by pointing to the readily observed fact that in two-person conversations, the conversational sequence is abababab, where a and b are the parties involved.[25] It is a basic rule in conversation that people take turns. What, though, he asks, are the rules governing who speaks first? In telephone conversations, as we have already seen, the answerer speaks first. Put in Schegloff's more formal terms, *"the distribution rule for first utterances* is: the answerer speaks first," although what is said varies considerably. Violations of this distribution rule are conceivable but are apparently rare. Schegloff found only one deviation in approximately 500 telephone conversations. This deviant case, instead of being dismissed as an anomaly, invited further examination leading to the discovery that this distribution rule of first utterances is a derivation of more general rules applied in other conversational exchanges than those conducted by telephone.

While the ringing of a telephone bell can be seen as a summons calling for an answer, such attention-getting devices are not confined to telephones. Other ways to get attention include calling someone's name, or saying "pardon me," or tapping someone on the shoulder, or raising one's hand at a meeting or in a classroom. Sacks has remarked that children often use the form "D'ya know what?" in order to gain an adult's attention.[26] Some of the utterances are used in other ways but are usually distinguished as attention gainers by a rising inflection of the voice, as though questioning.

According to Schegloff, the properties of summons and answer, or SA, sequences include their *nonterminability*—they are preliminaries or prefaces to further activity—and their *nonrepeatability*—once a summons has been answered, the summoner may not begin another SA sequence. Further, once a summons is acknowledged, the one summoned is obliged to listen to the statements that follow. Another important property of SA sequences is that of *conditional relevance*—given one item of conversation, we know that a second item may be expected, and if it does not arise, its absence is felt. For instance, if I call someone's name, I expect him to answer. Simply put, A *is conditionally relevant on the occurrence of S.* If A is not forthcoming, I have adequate grounds for calling the name again. Further, not only is an answer expected but it is expected quickly, that is, within a constraint of *immediate juxtaposition.* If an answer is not forthcoming, even after the name is called again, and perhaps again, I will stop summoning. Schegloff terms this qualification of conditional relevance a *terminating rule;* repetitions of S will not exceed, perhaps, three to five. The terminating rule applies to the limited repetitions of S and can also be said to apply when an answer is given.

The importance of this kind of painstaking research lies in its discovery of the coordinated character of social interaction and the expectations associated with this coordination. Based upon the property of conditional relevance, for instance, interactants are able to make a variety of inferences. If, say, one calls someone on the telephone and there is no reply, the caller will assume that no one is home rather than that they decided not to answer. Similarly, if a husband, on returning home, calls his wife's name and she does not reply, he will assume that she is out. The experience of finding that she is, after all, at home will surely lead to an annoyed "Why didn't you answer when I called?" To refuse to answer a summons is a violation of the property of conditional relevance and requires explanation.

The troublesome "deviant" in Schegloff's data, the one case in 500 telephone calls in which the caller spoke first and so appeared to violate the distribution rule for first utterances, can now be interpreted as a variant in the formulations governing conversational openings. Under the rule of conditional relevance, an answer is conditioned by the occurrence of a summons. If A is not forthcoming, it is officially absent and warrants a repetition of S. The caller, following a one-second pause after the receiver was lifted then said "Hello," to which the one called responded. The structure of the datum, Schegloff explains, is thus seen as S, no answer, S, A.

A summons is clearly a powerful way of generating conversation with another. It requires that it be answered. Let us turn now to the rules governing conversational closings, for conversations, as anyone can observe, do not simply end; they are brought to a close. In "Opening up closings," Schegloff and Sacks develop a technical basis for the closing of a conversation. Their inquiry is addressed to the orderly manner in which achievements of this kind, closing a conversation, are routinely conducted—how, for instance, the final speaker indicates that this is the final remark of the conversation and not intended to generate the other's response. A solution is the exchange of "good-byes," or the use of a *terminal exchange.*

The terminal exchange is one of the broader group of *adjacency pair sequences,* which includes the summons-answer sequence already discussed, as well as the question-answer sequence and others. A basic rule of adjacency pair operation is that when the first pair part is given by one speaker, the other speaker should provide a second pair part that matches the first pair part. This sequencing, or turn-taking, is an important aspect of the production of both orderly language and orderly social interaction. Both greetings and endings employ adjacency pair sequences. Just as S calls for A, so one "good-bye" calls for an immediate "good-bye" or "see you" response, which, if not forthcoming, is perceived as a violation or a misunderstanding requiring an explanation.

While the second part of an adjacency pair sequence is an immediate response to the first part of the pair, this still leaves the placement of the first pair part to be explained. Schegloff and Sacks develop the notion of *closing sections* and their proper initiation. A possible *pre-closing,* for instance, might take the form of "We-ell . . . ," "O.K. . . . ," "So-ooo . . . ," and so on, with downward intonation contours—an utterance without coherence; such an utterance does not introduce a new topic for conversation but still makes it possible for the other to begin a new topic. *Possible* pre-closings are not guaranteed to bring conversations toward an end, although they provide a kind of warrant for undertaking to close a conversation. Telephone conversationalists have special techniques for initiating closing sections which, again, may or may not serve to halt conversation. For instance, the caller might say, "Well, I'll let you go. I don't want to tie up your phone," or "I know you're busy, I'll let you get on with your jobs," or the one called may say "This call must be costing you a fortune!" Similar warrants for closing are used in face-to-face interactions: "Well, I'll let you get back to your studying." Another kind of pre-closing that interrupts the topic of conversation is the "I gotta go" statement. Examples might be "I gotta go—stuff's boiling all over the stove!" or ". . . the baby's fallen down."

The notion of the terminal exchange, then, is insufficient in formulating the ways conversations are ended; properly initiated closing sections much be established before a terminal exchange can be made, these closing sections themselves comprising a variety of possible components.

Sequencing, or turn-taking, includes more than the openings and closings of conversations. Recently published work of Sacks, Schegloff, and Jefferson attends to the broader question of general turn-taking in conversation, although taking turns is a characteristic of many activities in daily life, including the playing of games, the regulation of traffic, the serving of customers in stores and eating places, debating, and so on. In their work, the attempt is made to characterize the organization of turn-taking for conversation in its simplest systematic form.[27] As is usual with these researchers, the data used are audio recordings of naturally occurring conversations and not recordings of interviews or otherwise directed or contrived conversations. The organization of turn-taking in its own right is the topic of investigation, rather than the content or the context of the talk, the aim being to discover context-free, or universal, or invariant characteristics of turn-taking—some formal apparatus which is itself context-free and yet can be accommodated to specific contents.

The system, or model, of turn-taking presented by Sacks, Schegloff, and Jefferson comprises two components and a set of rules. The first component is the *turn-constructional component,* that is, the type of unit with which a speaker sets out to construct a turn. A unit type may be a sentence, a phrase, a clause, or a single word. The completion of the unit indicates the end of the turn and the transfer of speakership. The second component is the *turn-allocation component* by which either the next speaker is allocated by the current speaker or the next turn is allocated by self-selection. For instance, in serving food onto plates, the server may ask "Do you want some, Jim?" thereby allocating Jim as the next speaker. Alternatively, a more general question such as "Has anyone here seen my copy of Plato's *Republic?*" would lead to self-allocated turns. These two components are accompanied by a basic set of rules that govern turn construction and provide for the allocation of a next-turn party. The system is then brought to bear on the audio-recorded data to test its compatibility and to discover the ways in which turn-taking violations are repaired within the terms of the turn-taking system.

The rigorous empirical analysis of conversation to discover the organization of language structures as phenomena in their own right is only one of the ways speech is examined by creative sociologists. A great deal of conversational and language analysis is aimed at demonstrating more directly the ways certain forms of speech serve to establish and maintain the structure of the situation or to create and reinforce the "image" of persons in the situation.

In his study of the social organization of dying, for instance, David Sudnow provides some clues to the way in which the announcement by the physician of the death of a close relative, tragic though it is, is located as a manageable event by the survivors through their engaging in "talk." [28] In "doing" talk, in acting in accord with the rules which, as we have seen, govern polite interchange—following turn-taking sequences, waiting for the other to stop before beginning oneself, sharing the talk among the participants, leaving the engagement by use of conventional modes of leave-taking—persons find themselves engaged in a recognizable form of regular, everyday social conduct. To abide by the conventions of speech is to demonstrate the control over oneself that prevails in the ordinary conduct of daily affairs:

> In constructing "talk," matters which otherwise might produce severe immobility, upsettedness, consternation, and fear, could be overlaid by ordinary conventions of interaction and thereby have their sense incorporated within and constrained by the requirements of ordinary social discourse. . . .
>
> The institutionalization of "talk," i.e., "sociable" talk or "conversation," here serves to provide a standardized way for bringing the participants into alignment and moving the encounter about from its position of initial disturbance to the point where a consideration of other matters might properly occur, e.g., signing an autopsy permit, arranging for the disposition of the body, obtaining personal belongings, etc. [29]

Where Sudnow's examples shows the function of talk in rendering situations of trauma manageable, Joan P. Emerson's study of gynecological examinations demonstrates how the use of particular terminology helps to sustain the definition of the situation when that definition is precarious. [30] In the gynecological examination, the site of the task is the woman's genitals. Because this part of the body is usually accessible only in a sexual context, the situation connotes sexuality and even though most people realize that sexual responses are inappropriate, participants are unclear about the degree of modesty required. Most other kinds of medical examinations are more readily acceptable as impersonal performances on the physician's part than is the gynecological examination.

For doctors and nurses in the setting, the scene is routine—they take part in dozens of gynecological examinations each day—while for each patient, the occasion is relatively rare. The staff, doctors and nurses, guide the patient through the precarious scene, their behavior reinforcing the definition of the situation as "a medical situation" in which no one is embarrassed and no one is thinking in sexual terms. The stance is thoroughly matter-of-fact. Were the reality not clearly defined as medical, the actions and talk would be construed as shocking and degrading violations of privacy. Yet, says Emerson, the definition of the situation as *only* medical is not sufficient in this scene where counterthemes must also be played. The body must be treated as more than a technical object. In deference to general community meanings, the patient is a person and the pelvic area is regarded as special. A balance between medical meanings and general community meanings must be sustained.

The balance is created anew at every moment. Emerson describes how the appropriate definitions, the themes and counterthemes, are embodied in routine procedures, proper demeanor, and *talk*. Scientific-sounding terms are employed to depersonalize and desexualize the encounter. The definite article replaces the possessive pronoun when body parts are discussed so that, for instance, the doctor refers to "the vagina" rather than "your vagina." Instructions to the patient are couched in terms such that sexual imagery is bypassed. "The vulgar connotation of 'spread your legs' is generally metamorphosed into the innocuous 'let your legs fall apart.' " [31] While staff use technical terms for body parts when talking among themselves, patients tend to avoid such explicit terminology, saying, for instance, "I feel uncomfortable down there," and doctors and nurses frequently use similar euphemisms when talking to a patient. This common avoidance of explicit terminology in staff-patient contacts, suggests Emerson, is an indication that despite all the precautions to assure that the medical definition prevails, many patients remain embarrassed by the occasion. Euphemisms are used to avoid provoking this embarrassment, just as jokes are designed to ease the patient into retaining a feeling of dignity which is difficult to sustain under the circumstances. Joking can be seen as a demonstration that the parties involved are able to remain detached:

> Dr. Ryan announces that he will do a rectal examination and the (elderly) patient protests, "oh, honey, don't bother." Dr. Ryan assures her jokingly that it's "no bother, really." The indirect message . . . is that one should take gynecological procedures casually. [32]

Through the writing of both Sudnow and Emerson, the reader becomes aware of the ways in which conversation sustains a definition of a situation as a normal, or everyday, routine occurrence, even though it may encompass an event which is either tragic or potentially embarrassing. Other writers have shown how some events become *real* events only in the telling. Does a tree in the forest fall even if no one sees it fall? That is an old philosophical question. Both Sam Burns and John H. Newman address themselves to a similar problem and indicate that unless events or ideas are talked about, they remain unknown and, hence, unreal.[33]

John Newman describes how a drug program, whose task was long-term treatment and rehabilitation of drug users in rural southwestern Montana, simply could not be "found" by those whose task it was to evaluate the effectiveness of "outreach" in that rural area. Even the staff, which numbered some forty persons, expressed doubt that any "real" program existed. The evaluation team saw the need to make the program visible to both the program staff and to the community. Newman explains how the staff members were encouraged to talk about their work with each other and with the evaluators, to give detailed accounts of the place in which they worked, so that a sense of location could be experienced. As they rendered clear accounts of their tasks and the location in which they were conducted, the program became a reality to all of them. Previously, the tasks of program workers were only vaguely defined and, hence, could be only vaguely articulated. When pressed to articulate clearly, to give accounts of where their work occurred to specify the relationship between their activity and the setting, the program came into focus for both outsiders and insiders.

Newman's study makes clear the *reflexivity* of talk, the way in which talking both clarifies and then reinforces "reality," and in Burns's paper, too, the underlying theme is the phenomenological character of the world as "presented" in talk. Burns examines the "ordinary accounting practices" in community development field work, by means of which the world becomes available and "real" both for those who render the accounts and for those who hear them. Burns describes the methods he uses to make sense of what field workers say, and to bring to the surface their common-sense understandings of the community, their jobs, their learning, and their social needs and concerns. People living in the world of everyday life employ their own common-sense theories of the world and the way in which it operates. The task is to uncover these theories and, hence, to see how reality is produced for the common-sense "theoretician." In asking questions of field workers that cause them to reflect upon, and bring to light, their theorizing work, the workers are helped to hear for themselves, and so have made real, their guiding assumptions. Questions of field workers are of the "tell me about, tell me more about, can you go back to what you said, could you describe what went on this morning, shall we go over that again" type, questions intended to discover the everyday typifications used by the field workers as they perform their field work tasks.

Ethnomethodologists insist that their work is not directed at attempting to establish some "real state of affairs" against which members' accounts can be compared for accuracy, and several provocative models have been proposed that draw attention to the uses of linguistic devices for maintaining a *sense* of reality or a *sense* of self in precarious or threatening situations. Among these are the formulations of *accounts* by Marvin B. Scott and Stanford M. Lyman, and of *disclaimers* by John P. Hewitt and Randall Stokes.[34] Both accounts and disclaimers can be seen as *aligning actions,* to use Hewitt and Stokes's term, which serve to bring problematic conduct in line with cultural constraints.

Scott and Lyman's use of the term "accounts" is somewhat different from its usual usage among creative sociologists, where it means any kind of "telling." Scott and Lyman combine terms provided by Austin and by Gresham Sykes and David Matza to derive a formulation of accounts as statements made by a social actor to explain unanticipated or untoward behavior, either his own or that of others.[35] Accounts are of two general types: *excuses* and *justifications.* An excuse is made when one admits that the behavior was reprehensible but attempts to relieve the personal responsibility by claiming some unforeseen or unfortunate circumstance as the reason. Among several kinds of excuses for untoward behavior that a person might offer are: that it was caused by an accident; that "I wasn't in complete control of myself"; that "I wasn't fully informed of the facts"; or that "someone else was to blame."

A justification is given when one accepts full responsibility but denies that the behavior was improper. The "techniques of neutralization" of Sykes and Matza are shown to be of wider use than in their original presentation, *denial of injury, denial of victim, condemnation of condemners,* and *appeal to loyalties,* each being seen as a way of justifying what may appear to others as wrongdoing. Denial of injury denies that anyone was hurt or damaged by the act; denial of victim expresses that the victim deserved the injury; condemnation of condemners suggests that others have behaved much worse; and appeal to loyalties asserts that the action served the interests of others important to the actor. Other responses to a request for an account may be those of avoidance. One such response is *mystification,* with which the actor admits his action but claims that there are reasons for his behavior even though he cannot, or must not, say what they are. Such matters are secret and cannot be divulged. Another evasive response is *referral,* with which the individual suggests that he is not the one to consult, that someone else may be better able to explain his actions.

Although "accounts" for Scott and Lyman are usually spoken statements made in immediate response to spoken stimuli, other forms of language than talking are deserving of sociological analysis within this framework. In my own work, I have examined letters for the accounts of challenged behavior given by their writers.[36] Writing, of course, permits a more careful arrangement of words than does face-to-face speech. Sentences can be polished, a fine phrase may be worked and reworked until the precise nuance is attained, flaws in logic may be seen and corrected. Accounts given in letters should, therefore, possess more of art than do accounts called for on the spur of the moment.

The correspondence examined followed the completion of a study of the treatment by the press of the women's liberation movement in the late 1960s in both Britain and Los Angeles. The study data comprised the results of content analysis of twelve British national newspapers and the two major newspapers in Los Angeles. The findings of the study have been documented elsewhere.[37] Analysis was thorough, every line, cartoon, photograph, letter, and advertisement on every page of every issue being carefully studied. The periods of analysis of newspapers were July 1968 through June 1969 for Los Angeles, and from seven to fifteen months prior to August 1970 for Britain, depending upon the availability of newspapers on microfilm. The differing time spans for analysis of newspapers were chosen because development of the movement in the two settings was not parallel.

Newspaper coverage was sparse, despite the fact that the movement existed and was growing in both settings, as I learned first by visiting Britain in 1970 and seeking the movement out, and second by a reconstruction of the women's liberation movement as it had existed in Los Angeles County in the summer of 1969. The reconstruction was accomplished by interviews, correspondence, and examination of movement literature and such records as existed. Only one newspaper, the London *Sunday Times,* covered the movement extensively during the period under study, accounting for more than 40 percent of the total "units" of measured coverage in the twelve British newspapers studied—one assurance by the press that a movement did, indeed, exist. The women's movement later received press coverage ad nauseam, but that was in the second stage in its history of media coverage.

The task became one of explaining the virtual blackout of information by the press of the movement during its early days. Why *was* so little attention paid to the emerging movement—a movement which was soon to become an important agent for social change? In an attempt to gain some understanding of the problem, I wrote to each of the newspaper editors, except that of the *Sunday*

Times, relating that the results of my study showed little or no coverage of the movement in its early days by his newspaper, and asking for some insights into the choice of items accepted or rejected for publication. This letter, which implied that some newspapers had covered the movement more extensively than the editor's own, appeared to act as a stimulus challenge that resulted in several "accounts" of behavior.

The replies by the editors of the British newspapers are broken down into the categories of accounts formulated by Scott and Lyman.

JUSTIFICATIONS

Daily Express, Oct. 12, 1971: "Perhaps the antics of some of the ladies, such as burning their undergarments has turned the movement in the public mind in Britain into something less than a serious attempt to campaign for a recognition of women's rights."[*Denial of victim:* They deserved what they got.]

The Sun, Dec. 3, 1971: "It is, of course, quite impossible to define precisely the criteria by which items are chosen for inclusion in our newspaper. News value judgements are seven-tenths of the editorial task, and are usually at least four-tenths instinctive rather than intellectual. But very briefly, I would say that it is our purpose primarily to entertain, because unless a newspaper entertains it cannot hold readers. We do, however, feel a mission to inform and influence as well as to entertain. Perhaps the success of The Sun (circulation has grown from 600,000 to 2,600,000 in the two years we have been running it) is founded on harmonisation of these two motives."[*Appeal to loyalties:* Justification for all actions is on the grounds of the mission of the paper to entertain, inform, and influence opinion, in that order. Primarily, however, the task is to sell papers.]

The Times, Oct. 14, 1971: "As a paper we have tried to treat the subject [of the Women's Liberation Movement] seriously when we have written about it." [This *denial of injury* is hard to sustain. When coding newspaper items for analysis, each unit of coverage was categorized as belonging in one of three directional groups: favorable, unfavorable, or neutral toward the movement. Neutral implied fair reporting of statements made by persons about the movement, even though such statements may have been favorable or unfavorable toward the movement. The favorable or unfavorable categories were used when the reporter injected opinions of either slant which were not direct reporting. An example of unfavorable coverage of the movement is part of the *Times*'s report of the Miss World Contest in November 1968. The Women's Liberation Workshops had jointly picketed the contest. The *Times* report included the following:

Outside the Albert Hall, a group of straggle haired feminists stamped around, noses pink with the cold protesting the exploitation of womanhood. They wore flesh pink banners stencilled with Miss-Fortune, Miss-Laid, and other such slogans.

"Equal pay, equal rights, equal jobs, now," they chanted but then when has beauty ever been equal? It was a dark night but could their protests have been jealousy?]

The Sunday Telegraph, Oct. 15, 1971: "I have read your comments with care and interest, and am obliged to say that I am not wholly in agreement with them. Our coverage of the feminist movement or any other comparable organisation is governed strictly by its relevance to the news, and above all, by its topicality." [*Denial of victim:* The feminists got the coverage they deserved.]

The Observer, Oct. 14, 1971: "More probably, I think, the reason [for lack of coverage] was the rather crazy picture of Women's Lib. that came to us from the United States in the early stages. I'm not sure if that was the fault of the British papers—or the movement itself—but it tended to be described here in terms of its wilder-man-hating, bra-burning-eccentricities." [*Denial of victim.*]

Morning Star, Oct. 14, 1971: "A second factor as far as we were concerned was that we had ourselves been campaigning for a very long period on many of the issues which the women's liberation movement has now taken up, including the questions of equal pay, nursery schools, abortion and birth-control facilities, etc. Because of this the actual issues involved in the movement were not new ones to us." [*Appeal to loyalties:* We were serving others.]

"I should think that during the past year the coverage we have given, proportionate to our total space would compare very favorably with that given by any other newspaper." [*Condemnation of condemners:* Others are worse.]

"I think it is also true to say that our approach to the movement and the issues it is dealing with is more serious and sympathetic than most other newspapers." [*Condemnation of condemners:* Of the small amount of coverage by the *Morning Star* during the time period studied, most was categorized as "favorable" towards the movement. It is interesting to compare this paper's reporting of a similar event to that reported by *The Times* (above). This item appeared on Sept. 10, 1969, and refers to the United States:

> It was only a year ago that the Women's Liberation Movement moved into action against beauty contests and all the extravagant superfluities they represent, . . . storming Atlantic City, chief hangout for the Contest Criminals. The WLM proposed, first a bra-burning (presumably to emphasize the ridiculousness of the values adhered to in most competitions); second, the crowning of a live sheep— the most beautiful sheep around, naturally.]

EXCUSES

The Observer, Oct. 14, 1971: "I enclose cuttings of a major series we ran in the Observer on Women's Lib. in January 1971. It wasn't until that time that the social significance of the movement really struck us. It may be that before then we had simply been slow to react or had too few women at decision-making level on the newspaper. . . .

"It wasn't until the end of 1970 that we began to see it differently [from its wilder-man-hating, bra-burning-eccentricity]." ["We weren't fully informed. We perhaps didn't have the right kind of leadership."]

EVASIONS

Daily Express, Oct. 12, 1971: "The Daily Express chooses news stories purely on their reader interest value. The Women's Lib caught the public interest for a time, and I know that during this year we have printed 30–35 stories, some quarter to half-page features—many of them with pictures. These our News Editor apparently considered were sufficient for a movement which is declining in general interest." [Discussion of time period in question is evaded.]

The Guardian, Oct. 8, 1971: "I find the results of your research into the Guardian's coverage of the Women's Liberation Movement hard to believe. Some people would say that we have a reputation for going on about it endlessly. Perhaps we were slow to pick it up in the first place though I doubt even this." [Denial renders an account unnecessary.]

"As to the criteria we apply, as a daily newspaper we are primarily concerned with the news of the day and as a strongly political paper we give the bulk of our attention to what we sometimes call 'government in the widest sense.' " [Evasion.]

The Daily Sketch, Oct. 14, 1971: "Thank you for your letter of October 4. Unfortunately, the Daily Sketch ceased publication last May and the editorial executives are now scattered. . . . [The need for an account is thus evaded.] However, my recollection is that Women's Lib received adequate coverage according to its news value." [The evasion is compounded by a justification: they got what they deserved.]

The Sun, Dec. 3, 1971: "I am not able to say very much about the earlier part of the period you have under examination, because the Sun changed ownership and editorial policy in late November 1969 and I have no contact now with anyone who might be able to advise you about editorial decision-taking before that date." [The need for an account is evaded.]

The Times, Oct. 14, 1971: "The Editor thanks you for your letter and has noted your comments on the coverage we have given to the Women's Liberation movement." [Evasion.]

The Sunday Telegraph, Oct. 15, 1971: "It is perhaps unfortunate that your research did not cover a slightly longer period, for if so you would doubtless have seen that we devoted a substantial article to the Women's Liberation Movement in Britain earlier this year." [Evasion of discussion of dates under study.]

The Daily Telegraph, Oct. 12, 1971: "I am sorry to have to tell you that we would in no circumstances reveal to any third party the reasons why we do or do not accept matter for publication. I am sorry to be so unhelpful, but I am certain that you will understand that there is a serious matter of principle involved." [Avoidance by *mystification.*]

As the *Sunday Times* had given extensive coverage to the women's liberation movement during the period under examination, the letter to the editor asked for insights regarding why this might be, when other newspapers had chosen to cover it minimally. The complete reply is reproduced below:

> Thank you for your letter. It may sound rather conceited on our part, but the Sunday Times' Editorial staff takes a pride in being ahead of the others in discerning the trend of public opinion and bringing changes to the attention of its readers. We have the space, especially in our 72 page issues, to go into developments in more detail than most of our competitors. Our staff is large and active and among them are some who might appear to be extreme in their views, but this gives us the opportunity to discover what out-of-the-way groups are thinking or planning. Where other editors might be reluctant to mention behavior which their readers might deplore, we let the light in wherever possible—at the expense of some readers, it is true, who regret such outspokenness, but gathering others at the same time who are interested in what the other half (or quarter) of the world is doing. . . . [The *Sunday Times*'s coverage of the movement, while it accounted for over 40 percent of the total coverage in the twelve British papers analyzed, was categorized as "unfavorable" for more than a third of the units.]

Of the editors of the two large newspapers in Los Angeles, only that of the *Los Angeles Times* replied, in spite of numerous follow-up letters to the editor of the *Herald Examiner.*

The first response from the *Times* is presented below:

> As the editor of the VIEW section, I beg to differ with your opinion of our women's liberation reporting. The late Maggie Savoy wrote often and well and at length on the subject. I think that some strong representatives of the move-

ment—including Aileen Hernandez and Pauline Buck—would back my statement. [Denial renders an account unnecessary]

To a second letter, carefully insisting that while the *Times* had indeed been
generous in its coverage *since* the period under study, it had given sparse coverage during the earlier period, the following reply was received:

> I knew I'd hear from you again—for I realize that, as much as the Times did in
> late '69 and '70 on women's lib, we certainly didn't spearhead the movement. To
> be honest, I don't know of any movement—labor union reform, civil rights,
> etc.—that newspapers led. Because newspapers generally reflect what the public
> (the mass) is thinking and doing, and the public is always late, albeit right in the
> long run, Viet Nam being the latest and best example.
>
> In other words, we're not perfect, and we are reporters first before we are ad-
> vocates and/or activists. Okay? [This is an excuse, an admission, in the form of
> "the blame lies elsewhere—because newspapers always reflect public opinion."]

As can be seen, the editors offered very few excuses in their letters, for excuses involve admission of the behavior for which an account is called, but several kinds of justifications and evasions were extended, some artful, few totally
lacking in subtlety. Analysis of these letters as accounts is useful in pointing up
some of the ways in which people, in this case editors, attempt to reason with
their critics, to placate, to save face, to maintain credence within acceptable
limits of good business and tact.

Whereas *accounts* are retrospective, offered to justify or excuse some behavior
which has already occurred, *disclaimers* are prospective, verbal devices given prior
to behavior which may possibly be seen as undesirable and which are designed
to ward off negative responses provoked by such behavior. Hewitt and Stokes's
model provides five kinds of disclaimers: *hedging, credentialing, sin licenses, cognitive disclaimers,* and *appeals for suspension of judgment,* all of which are familiar in
everyday conversation.

Hedging includes such remarks as "I'm no expert, of course, but . . ." and
"I haven't really thought this out very well, but. . . ." It implies minimal
commitment to the forthcoming statement; the statement is to be perceived as
offered only tentatively, with no claim to expertise needing to be defended.
People who *are* experts use slightly different hedging disclaimers, saying, for instance, "This is not really my specialty, but . . ." or "I'm not sure I understand your question as you phrase it, but . . ." or "I have a very poor memory
for dates. . . ." The message of this kind of disclaimer is that no great emphasis should be put on the accuracy, or otherwise, of what is about to be said.

Credentialing is used when the speaker knows that what he is about to say will discredit him, but he nevertheless feels committed to saying it. Examples of credentialing are "I'm not prejudiced, but . . ." and "Don't get me wrong, some of my best friends are Jews, but. . . ." The use of credentialing indicates that even though the speaker knows that the statement he is about to make has negative connotations, it must be said, for it will serve some good purpose. This kind of disclaimer serves as a protective device; it allows the speaker to "credential" himself as unbiased or unprejudiced, even though his statement may make him appear otherwise.

Sin licenses are used when a person is committed to making a statement which he knows will provoke a negative response and fears being perceived as a "rule breaker" or "irresponsible person." Sin licenses inform the listeners in advance that what is about to be said violates expectations but that there are occasions when breaking the rules is justified. One claims license to sin with such statements as "I know this is against the rules, but . . ." and "I realize you might think this is the wrong thing to do, but. . . ."

Cognitive disclaimers anticipate the doubt that a statement might raise and attempt to reassure the listeners that the speaker is in full possession of his wits and that there is no loss of cognitive capacity. Examples are, "I know this sounds crazy but I think I saw . . ." and "This may sound strange to you, but. . . ."

Finally, appeals for suspension of judgment ask that the listener wait until the statement is completed so that the full meaning can be discerned. "Hear me out before you explode . . ." is one example of an appeal for suspension of judgment or for a delayed reaction.

People use disclaimers to secure the success of their identity claims. If a disclaimer is used successfully, if it is accepted without challenge, the user's identity is sustained in the situation, at least for the time being. Aligning actions, such as accounts and disclaimers, serve to bring behavior that might be construed as of doubtful propriety into line with social and cultural expectations. In so doing, they both clarify and reinforce those expectations.

The ways the "expected" power relationships between the sexes are confirmed and reinforced in language use are shown in studies by Pamela Fishman and by Candace West and Don Zimmerman.[38] If, as Fishman says, "our understanding and views of ourselves and the world are produced in interaction," then the analysis of interaction—especially symbolic interaction, or speech—between men and women should help to make manifest the power position of each vis-à-vis the other. Fishman examined the conversational interactions of couples in their own homes to see how attempts at beginning, sustaining, and stopping talk were made. If A initiates a conversation but B does not respond, or bypasses the utterance made by A, then the attempt on A's part to initiate an interaction is a failure. Both parties must participate if the conversation is to continue, although participation is not enough for the interaction to have meaning or to be considered interesting for the participants. Fishman, then, examined two kinds of work involved in the interaction: the beginning, maintaining, and ending the talk, as well as the maintenance of the features necessary for interaction to be seen as having meaning. She asked how the work of interaction gets done and who does what type of work, among three couples, all the members of which consider themselves "sympathetic" to the women's movement or declared themselves feminists. Tape recorders were installed in the living rooms of the couples to record naturally occurring conversations. All six reported that they quickly forgot the recorders were present, and the naturalness of the recordings appears to confirm this.

As the investigator struggled to make sense of the fifty-two hours of tape recordings, she began to notice talk which seemed never to develop into conversation and which, after further study, turned out to represent a series of unsuccessful attempts by the women to get conversation going. The women tried more often, and succeeded less often, at interaction than the men, whereas the men tried less often and seldom failed at initiating and sustaining conversation. This success of the men's remarks was due to the interactional work of the women in response to men's remarks, while the men did not "support" the women's opening remarks in the same way. Fishman suggests that women work harder than men in interaction because they are less assured of success. Men's control over the choice of topic to be pursued was demonstrated in a variety of situations, a man frequently totally ignoring the woman's remarks if those remarks concerned herself rather than being about him.

Close analysis of the transcripts revealed several interactional strategies for ensuring, encouraging, and subverting conversation. Questions are the first part of question-answer paired sequences, and just as a summons calls for an answer, so a question from A should generate an answer from B. Failure to respond to a question violates expectations, for which breach of rules an explanation might be demanded. Fishman found that women asked questions of men between two and three times as often as men asked questions of them, indicating use of a tactical device which is difficult to ignore. Further, women used the question in "D'ya know what" form twice as often as did men—a tactic which has previously been noted as frequently used by children to gain the attention of adults. Men and women also used "minimal responses" such as "mmm" or "oh" or "yeah" in different ways. When used by men, they were said in ways not meant to encourage further discussion while women used them to demonstrate continuing interest in both the topic and in their partners.

In order to sustain conversation, then, women had to say something to catch and hold the interest of men, whereas men's statements rarely failed to be supported by the women, even though the statements themselves were inherently no more interesting than those made by women. It appears, from this admittedly small sample of interactions between couples, that topics of conversations are directed to what interests the man. When he displays interest, the woman follows through; the reverse is not true. While women do most of the interactional work, they are not the ones who control the conversation or who benefit from it the most.

West and Zimmerman go a step further than does Fishman in their discussion of the conversational "place" of women, comparing the positions of women and children and suggesting that women's power in conversation is restricted in similar ways to that of children. In their study, these two researchers compared interruptions in cross-sex conversations with similar data on adult-child verbal interaction and found striking similarities between the pattern of interruptions in both sets of data.

Interruptions, following Sacks, Schegloff, and Jefferson's model, may be viewed as violations of a speaker's right to a turn.[39] In five adult-child transcripts, adults interrupted eleven times, while only two interruptions were those of children. Similarly, in the cross-sex conversation excerpts, forty-six interruptions were by males and only two were made by females. West and Zimmerman suggest that these observed asymmetries reflect culturally legitimated differences in power, manifested by the violation of turn-taking rules, and attempt to move to a more specific account of this presumed power relationship.

Violations of turn-taking rules, say West and Zimmerman, are not culturally approved, whether it be women or children who are interrupted, and must be seen to be *warranted* if the one who interrupts is not to be perceived as domineering, boorish, or authoritarian. "Your pants are on fire!" would, for instance, be seen as a warranted interruption. As the adult-child conversations all took place in physicians' offices and were, more specifically, parent-child interchanges, parents' interruptions were warrantable if they were aimed at controlling children's behavior in an unfamiliar or nonroutinely rule-governed setting. In other words, the parent-child, or adult-child, relationship is essentially asymmetrical by our cultural standards; parents are justified in controlling children's behavior.

The analysis of male-female conversation showed that men found it warrantable to interrupt women when what women said appeared to the men to be incorrect. Twenty-five percent of the male interruptions directly corrected or sanctioned the female and, evidently, with more success at obtaining acquiescence than that obtained by parents from children under similar circumstances. Men's interruptions, the researchers suggest, are used as a *display* of dominance over the female, just as parents' interruptions communicate parental control. Further, the use of interruptions is in fact a control device as, once interrupted, the flow of conversation changes. Such displays of dominance in conversation on the part of males and submission on the part of females constantly reinforces the cultural expectations of male-female relationships, for, as West and Zimmerman point out, whereas children do not brook interruption without argument, often having to be told, at length, to "shut up," women seldom struggle when interrupted, usually responding with silence. By the time they are grown up, women, the investigators suggest, unlike many children, have learned their place.

With the exception of Emerson's analysis of gynecological examinations, most of the studies of speech and language discussed so far have dealt with face-to-face interactions of a few, usually two, people at a time, in relatively informal situations. One of the criticisms frequently leveled against creative sociology is that it cannot make the leap from small group situations to examine larger structures of organization. The response to this criticism by, for instance, Herbert Blumer and Norman Denzin is to suggest that, on the contrary, the creative or interactionist approaches offer powerful strategy for organizational analysis.[40] Large organizations, says Denzin, can be broken down into interactional units, each offering special ways of thinking and acting; they can be studied as separate units held together by a very few salient symbols, such as university X or hospital Y. Further, Blumer adds, whole mass societies can be analyzed using the symbolic interactionist framework. The interactionist approach can subsume all other approaches in its ability to analyze conflict, exchange, and other kinds of interchanges, whether these take place in small groups or in larger units. Human beings develop and construct action as they interpret the situation and it matters little whether the interaction is formal or informal in context.

Aaron Cicourel's work and that of Cicourel and Kitsuse, has been in large, bureaucratic organizations, such as school systems and juvenile justice systems.[41] Their analyses of interaction in such settings have demonstrated that the processes by which individuals make decisions, account for those decisions, and so structure their reality, are similar, regardless of the formality of settings in which those processes take place.

The decisions made in large bureaucracies frequently have direct effects upon the future prospects, both immediate and long term, of those about whom the decisions are made. We assume that choices are made rationally and on the basis of proper criteria when our children's progress files are being compiled in school, or when youngsters are called before law enforcement personnel. Cicourel and Kitsuse demonstrate that we assume too much, that decisions are not made entirely on the basis of organizational rules and procedures but rest, instead, on typifications included in the stocks of knowledge that decision makers bring with them to the situation and use to interpret what they see and hear. The actual practices by which records of school children and juvenile offenders are compiled are the result of "common sense" theories combined with organizational methods for "making sense" of a child's progress or behavior. Once the judgment is made and written as a record, this account of the reality of the child's achievements or actions accompanies him or her into the foreseeable future.

In *The Social Organization of Juvenile Justice,* Cicourel asks how police and probation officials "make the system work." How do they cope with the many problems associated with classifying juveniles? How do the day-to-day activities of the police, probation officers, and others associated with the court or detention facilities produce information that becomes part of the official file on the juvenile? These questions cannot be answered without understanding the everyday categories of law enforcement officials' stocks of knowledge—the "strange," "unusual," "wrong," and the "routine," "normal," "harmless," and "right"—and the ways officials use these categories to improvise the formal legal and clinical categories provided by official law enforcement guidelines.[42]

Cicourel takes information provided in the everyday language of reports and contacts between policemen, juveniles, probation officers, and parents, and tries to determine how this information is used as the basis for decisions by officials both of "what happened" and the next course of action. One of his examples, for instance, is of an interview between a juvenile with no previous record of misdemeanor and a police officer. The youngster was tidily dressed, answered questions respectfully, and demonstrated remorse—all indications of propriety. In this case, the officer offered to "forget it this time," provided restitution was made and the juvenile "promised" to "stay out of trouble." Cicourel constantly emphasizes the background expectancies of this kind which enter into police questioning and decision making. When a youngster's record showed that he had lied on previous occasions, the questioners assumed that the boy would lie on every occasion and appeared, by hints, direct accusations, and other techniques, to seek not merely "information," but, rather, evidence of the boy's "perpetual lying."

Cicourel's data richly demonstrate the interplay of "appearances," whether these be manifested verbally or nonverbally, and cultural expectations. He compares a transcription of a recorded interview between a fifteen-year-old girl and a probation officer with the probation officer's brief, informal notes based on that interview. The transcript shows how a previous definition of the youngster as "appealing and attractive" and as one who "wants very much to be liked and relates in a friendly manner to all around her" had led to a clinical interpretation of her stealing and other misdemeanors rather than to a criminal interpretation. Having previously established the juvenile as "sick," the probation officer worked to sustain this definition despite activities by the girl that appeared to contradict this label. The probation officer supplied a basis for clarifying or redefining "what happened"—in this case, a fight—into standard categories of rational conduct which could not be construed as violations of the conditions of probation. The juvenile's behavior was constantly reinterpreted, the probation officer repeatedly gaining affirmation from her that the remarks were, indeed, "correct," while simultaneously defining for the youngster what *was* correct behavior under the circumstances.

The brief note made by the probation officer reconstituted the "facts" of the case so that the juvenile's offenses were reported as "minor" incidents. The note includes reference to an earlier discussion with the girls' teacher, who had described the girl's attitude as "good." In using elements of past incidents, existing definitions of the girl were reinforced and the incidents under discussion on the occasion of the interview were neutralized. It could easily be argued, suggests Cicourel, that the probation officer's interview with the juvenile was structured entirely by the school official's remarks that the girl's "attitude was good," enabling the probation officer to enter the interview with the tacit assumption that nothing serious was involved and that the girl's "trouble" was not to be viewed as a critical violation of probation. "Having a good attitude" also meant agreeing with the probation officer, not talking back, and so coming to "see" things as they "should be seen." [43]

Cicourel's evidence indicates that decisions are made in the juvenile justice system not on the basis of "what happened" but based on an *account* of what happened, that account being compiled by a selection of contingencies which the decision maker uses for deciding that a particular behavior falls under a particular rule. The task of the researcher is to discover the criteria by which members accomplish the practical reasoning that leads to one definition or another, the ways in which youngsters are viewed as "delinquent" or "sick" or as "having a good attitude" or as being "punks" or "bitches."

Within high school systems, Cicourel and Kitsuse have found, decisions are made on similar ad hoc grounds as those in the juvenile justice system. [44] They note that not all high school students with good academic records and high I.Q. scores go to college and propose that the differentiation of students is a consequence of the administrative organization and decisions of personnel in the high school. Their task in their exploratory study was to investigate the processes by which students come to be defined and classified as college-bound or noncollege-bound and, if college-bound, headed for the "best" colleges rather than the less-than-best colleges. Their first research task "was to explore the 'vocabulary and syntax' of the language used by the school personnel to identify the variety of student types recognized as significant in the day-to-day activities of the high school"; their second task was to examine the consequences of those processes upon any given student's career within the high school. [45]

Much of the vocabulary used by counselors in compiling student evaluations is drawn from psychology and the language of "mental health." A student whose work shows a lack of congruence between ability and achievement may be characterized as "lacking in motivation" or as being in competition with his brother ("sibling rivalry") or, if he insists that he does not need counseling, as "reacting against dependency needs." Persistent learning problems might lead to a definition such as "emotionally disturbed," or "anxious," or "insecure." These kinds of characterizations often remain in a student's file, conveying an image other than that of "well-adjusted person." The increasing stress in our society upon good social and mental adjustment, the authors suggest, indicates the counselor's position of authority and power as a validating agent for the student's future opportunities.

From the time a student enters the high school as a freshman, his or her academic course is directed by the perceptions, decisions, and actions of school personnel. The evidence indicates that scores on scholastic aptitude tests and records of past achievement are not the only bases on which students find themselves assigned to college preparation courses. Other criteria, such as teachers' comments concerning the student, parents' expressions of concern regarding the prospects of realizing their plans for sending their children to college, or information about a student's "delinquent activities" may enter into a counselor's evaluations. As the student proceeds through the high school, his or her record is being compiled of information on test scores—only an imperfect indication of intelligence or ability—as well as history of family or personal problems, social adjustment problems, and the like, the interpretations of many of the entries being based on a combination of clinical and common-sense conceptions.

This is not intended as an indictment of the high school system in general. The data were gathered from only one high school, with additional information from outside counselors. The exploratory study, though, was an examination of a school whose methods of evaluation were highly bureaucratized, an increasing trend in school systems across the nation, and demonstrates that diffuse "subjective" criteria are considered, together with the seemingly "objective" methods of evaluation. The opportunity for elite status in the United States is based as much on "sponsorship" as on "contest." [46] It is widely believed that our educational system offers contest mobility, based on effort and ability. Sponsored mobility, on the other hand, is attained by the judgment of others that the aspirant has the qualities they wish to see in fellow members. While a candidate's effort and ability are among the criteria for sponsorship, they are not sufficient in themselves.

The several studies discussed here represent only a small part of the increasing body of work by creative sociologists which demonstrates the variety of ways in which language, both written and spoken, plays a major part in the practical accomplishment of structuring the reality and orderliness of society by those and for those who act within it. The meanings that persons, things, and actions convey are not determined once and for all time, but are sought, created, confirmed and reconfirmed in each social situation. It is largely through language that this task of creation is accomplished.

'You are old, Father William,' the young man said,
  'And your hair has become very white;
And yet you incessantly stand on your head—
  Do you think, at your age, it is right?'

—Lewis Carroll

CHAPTER FIVE

The Social Meaning
of Aging

WHAT IS *old?* What is *young*—or *middle aged?* Easy! To be old is to be over sixty years of age, middle age is from forty-five to sixty years, young people are those under thirty. Hmm! What about the period from thirty to forty-five years? We-e-l-l. . . . shall we call that *adulthood?* Or *youthful maturity?*

All these divisions are, of course, arbitrary. We label segments of life's flow of years and the labels themselves acquire a reality which, in turn, makes "real" the division of time. Yet we all know people who are "old" at twenty, or "young" at seventy, according to our own typifications of "old" and "young." To be old is, perhaps, to be dull and inflexible, or to be interested in the serious rather than the frivolous, whereas young people conversely are bright, fun-oriented, lively, and flexible. Each of us seems to view age differently, depending upon his or her own age and experience.

This difference of vision was illustrated especially clearly for me recently when I was listening with a group of people to an anthropologist. He was telling us about a witch who had cast a spell on his house in the interior of Brazil. The house had been broken into by burglars several times, each time a few small items being stolen. The witch, a woman renowned in the village for her magical powers, was called in to sprinkle herbs, chant incantations, and perform whatever was necessary to protect the house from further burglaries. Evidently the powers of the witch were such that nothing more was ever stolen. "How old was the witch?" was one question from the group. "Umm—about forty-five, I'd say," the anthropologist answered. "Oh!" exclaimed the questioner, a white-haired woman of, perhaps, sixty years, "a *young* witch!"

To some, forty-five is young for a woman or, at any rate, for a witch; to others it is unthinkably old. In my research, I often ask college students what they think they might be doing with their lives when they are forty, or fifty, or sixty, or seventy years old. Usually, one or two people, between seventeen and twenty years—always female—will answer "I hope I'll be dead before I am forty." To some, only the early years are valuable, and yet this often changes with one's own collection of years.

The fluidity of the meaning of age is often overlooked because a biological or physiological model underlies much research into social aging. There is no doubt that human beings undergo marked physical changes with the passage of years. Bodies usually "age" in sequence, one stage following another fairly predictably. Primary and secondary sexual changes occur within a range of years that we term puberty. The child-bearing years for women are limited by body processes, although the range of years during which men may procreate is less predictable. For both men and women, physical sexual activity can continue until death, although this may not be the general experience. The study of social gerontology, often called "life-cycle" study, usually parallels study of the stages of physiological aging. Human beings are seen to move, or develop, from one stage to the next: birth, infancy, childhood, youth, adulthood and middle age, old age, and death. Age ranges are chosen for these stages, each of which is categorized in a number of ways. Certain activities "belong" in some categories but not in others. One ages "optimally" or "poorly" according to each theorist's definition of "proper" aging.

A major theory current in the study of aging suggests that people gradually "disengage" from society as they grow into old age, reducing their involvement as the number of roles they perform becomes fewer.[1] This disengagement is considered good, both for the individual and for the society, and those who remain integrated within society, or who develop new interests as the earlier roles diminish, are seen as "unsuccessful disengagers." In another theory optimal aging involves continued integration into the broader society. Old people, this theory suggests, are happier and healthier if they maintain the high level of activity they enjoyed in earlier years. Neither of these theories appears to consider old age from the view of the old person. Some creative people never "retire;" they are happy to continue writing, studying, painting, playing music, composing, or performing publicly as actors or artists until they die. Other people are pleased to leave the world of work at the age of mandatory retirement, while still others loathe being cut off from their most salient identity-defining roles.

With advances in medical knowledge and technological skills, more people live to be old than at any time in history. That most people grow to "middle age" in good health is taken for granted, yet as recently as the turn of the century, even the "empty nest" or "post-parental period" was unknown as a problem. The median age of a woman when her last child married was about fifty-five years. She was probably a widow, her husband having died when she was about fifty-three. Her own life expectancy was similar to her husband's; she would probably live for another year or two after launching the last of her children.[2]

Both middle age and now old age are relatively new phenomena. How might a phenomenologist or an interactionist study "age?" These approaches emphasize that human beings experience their social reality through a filter of culturally provided symbols. Symbols, or images, of aging would have to be described as they are presented and received, as they are experienced and manipulated by both givers and receivers in everyday life. Such a study would not begin by imposing a theory upon the phenomenon of aging but instead would explore the ways in which all aspects of age are talked about, depicted in the media of mass communication, lived, endured and enjoyed, used, negotiated, and changed from day to day. The study would begin without presuppositions about these images, leaving aside any stereotypic notions held by the investigator. One would start on a program of discovery by asking, "What *are* the images of aging presented to the public on a regular day-to-day basis?" Other questions would include: "Does a uniform picture of each age group emerge from the popular culture, or do the images conflict? If they conflict, which seems to predominate?" Further questions follow from these, for if persistent stereotypes, or clichés, of particular age groups are found in popular culture, one can ask about the ways these images are received—taken for granted or resisted—and the effects of these perceptions upon people in several age groups. How closely do images of aging held by individuals and groups in the society correspond to those presented in the media? Do people accept the popular culture's definitions of age? How do people plan to spend their added years? Do they relish the prospect of old age? Why, or why not? Ultimately, perceptions of aging should be compared with the images of aging in the popular culture.

The precedents for this kind of study include recent literature on sex roles, for instance, which indicates that social expectations, manifested in the family, the educational system, the world of work and leisure, children's books, and so on, constrict and constrain both males and females in their aspirations and their achievements.³ Women employed in professions traditionally reserved for men still face the difficult task of having to "behave like women" while "thinking like men." Success in masculine-typed professions frequently invokes the label "unfeminine" from both men and women. The avoidance of such a label involves the juggling of several different roles. The successful professional must be a superwoman: good wife, good mother, good cook, good housekeeper, good worker, good-tempered, and good looking! While she may resist the generalized other's definition of woman's place, she may in part accept it or feel she must at least maintain an appearance of accepting it.

Women traditionally are said to deduct a few years from their chronological age as they leave what has been defined as youth. Jack Benny, the great comedian, remained thirty-nine years old until his death at around eighty. His audience laughed at him, as they were meant to, and they understood the joke. Men, though, have not been required to remain youthful in a childlike way, as have women.⁴ This may change. At present, advertisements for hairpieces for men stress the lost earning power of men who look old, but increasingly the emphasis is on remaining young-looking and sexually attractive. A recent magazine advertisement, showing a muscular young man, broad of chest and white of teeth, is headed: "Lie about your age . . . (We'll help you look young enough to get away with it!)."⁵ The body of the advertisement tells of the products which will "soften the little lines and wrinkles that otherwise too soon become deep lines and heavy wrinkles": super shape skin conditioner, skin toner, firming mask, enriched night cream, and under-eye concentrate (a dynamic, penetrating, highly refined combination of super-rich oils and emollients; used nightly before retiring, this soft-acting cream will keep your eyes looking young and wrinkle-free). Until recently, such advertising was directed only toward women.

While considerable research into sex-role and ethnic stereotypes has been conducted, far less information has been gathered about the images and expectations of people of particular chronological ages. "Racism" and "sexism" are familiar terms; "agism" is relatively new. All these terms imply that judgments are made about a person simply on the basis of his or her skin color or sex or age, regardless of other, more pertinent criteria. Stereotypical notions of blacks or women or old people or children place *all* blacks or women or old people or children into their respective pigeon holes. No matter what the circumstances, a member of any of these groups is endowed with characteristics that supposedly are typical of these groups. So, a man of sixty-two, who may be in excellent

health both mentally and physically, is removed from his employment along
with all men of sixty-two, because some of them may indeed be of declining
vigor after forty years on the job. Arbitrary decisions of this kind, made on the
basis of stereotypes, are termed "agist" by those who resist such wholesale
labeling.

Among the groups who are attempting to negotiate, or renegotiate, definitions, or images, of age, are the Gray Panthers. This coalition of both old and
young people aims to bring to public awareness the fact that an extra twenty or
thirty or even forty years of healthy life are of little value if there is nothing to
do during those years but play bingo, work jig-saw puzzles, and talk about the
past with others of one's own age. Of what use, they ask, are the extra years if
one is too poor to buy fuel for the winter or food for the table? Of what use are
the extra years if one is shunted aside as worthless and unproductive? Why
prolong life to its fullest extent if the time gained has to be "passed" and cannot
be used? Why prolong the years if it means age-segregated living, with old people cut off from the mainstream of life? Why invent the euphemism "senior cit-
izen" when only the name is changed and not the station? What is the nature of
a society which values human beings only for what they do and not for what
they are, which scraps people like out-dated machinery, which averts its eyes
from the substandard conditions in "convalescent" homes, which encourages the
spending of thousands of dollars on the ostentatious display of a funeral for a
"loved one," who may have spent twenty years in a "nursing" home, largely un-
visited and unwanted, waiting for death?

These are the kind of questions being asked by the Gray Panthers, whose attempts to bring radical changes in the society begin with tactics designed to
change definitions—stereotypes—of age. The Gray Panthers do more than ask
questions; they are prodders and probers and they demonstrate their concerns by
picketing and by performing colorful guerrilla theater, among other actions.
They experiment with age-integrated housing in which college students live
with much older people, and with transgenerational schooling in which people
of all ages participate and learn together. The Gray Panthers are not merely a
service organization for the elderly, they are angry people whose rage at the in-
dignities and inhumanities suffered by persons because of their age (or any other
irrelevant criteria) propels them to action. They are prepared to claw and spit
and gnaw, in keeping with their name, if that helps to bring changes in mandatory retirement rules that waste talent and skill; changes in "care" services,

including medical practices, that profit from human misery; changes in existing images of people that rest on arbitrarily chosen age ranges.

Phenomenologists might ask what kinds of people become Gray Panthers. What is it that moves some old people to work for others in the society, while others ask only for help for themselves? Have old Gray Panthers always been political activists? How do they perceive themselves? How do they manage to resist stereotypes which they see as prevalent in the culture and as guiding social policy? My own data, so far, indicate that each of the men and women in leadership positions in the Gray Panthers comes from either a deeply committed religious background or a family which stressed service to the community, or both, but that these factors were not enough in themselves to promote political activism. The impetus for activism seemed to be generated through some event or turning point that had a radicalizing effect. Maggie Kuhn, the national convener of the Gray Panthers, had always been deeply concerned with social issues but was somewhat constrained in her activities because of her employment by the United Presbyterian Church. When she was told that she would have to retire at the prescribed age, she experienced first shock, she said, then *rage*—an overwhelming rage that she was to be put out to pasture while she was still capable and active. Maggie Kuhn, together with a few others who were also facing mandatory retirement, founded an organization to combat the cultural notion that old people were unproductive and therefore useless. The group was determined to realize the responsible use of their enforced "freedom."

Other leaders and workers in the movement were radicalized in other ways. For one person, the influence towards radicalism arose from the events of the Great Depression; for another, it was being told that she was too old for a full-time job as a social worker at the age of thirty-five, even though she had worked in the field satisfactorily for a number of years. For still another, a man who had been a church missionary for most of his adult life, it was the example of Gandhi in India that originally inspired him toward political activism in behalf of those in the society who are defined as inferior to or in some way less desirable than others in the society.

Are the Gray Panthers justified in their anger against the prevailing cultural stereotypes of old age? Although there has been detailed examination of the way the sexes, particularly women, are depicted in the popular media, much remains to be researched in the area of aging. A preliminary study by Craig Aronoff, based on 2,741 characters in prime-time network television drama sampled between 1969 and 1971, indicated that the elderly comprise less than 5 percent of the characters, about half their share of the total population.[6] The average female character is almost ten years younger than the average male. In television drama, females age earlier and faster than males. Chances of male villainy increase with age, but while most males in prime-time drama fail because they are evil, females fail just because they age. Aronoff's data indicate that aging in prime-time television drama is associated with increasing evil, failure, and unhappiness. "In a world of generally positive portrayals and happy endings, only 40 percent of older males and even fewer (older) female characters are seen as successful, happy, and good." [7]

While careful research remains to be conducted, a casual sampling of the most frequently viewed television programs reveals generally negative images of middle-aged and old people, with some notable exceptions. The popular Jefferson family has as one of its members a grandmother who, although "well preserved," well coifed, and well dressed, is presented as an interfering busybody. Two stereotypes are perpetuated for the price of one: the possessive mother-in-law and the demanding old woman. Rhoda's mother, too, is presented as interfering and pushy, here emphasizing the stereotype of the "Jewish mother" as well as of the woman whose nest is empty and whose interests remain centered on her children's activities. (She also probes into the lives of those who threaten the well-being of her offspring, once advising the former wife of her son-in-law, as she appraised her face and body, that she had better catch another man "while the goods are still in good condition," a particularly ugly reminder that only youthfulness is desirable in a woman.) Even Maude, that model of proud, strident, self-assured middle-aged womanhood, breaks down and seeks help from a psychiatrist as she approaches her fiftieth birthday. Her husband, Walter, had been similarly overcome by depression as he reached his midcentury mark. Archie Bunker, of "All in the Family," is continually reminded of his advancing years by the pressures of his work; he must keep insisting that he is as strong and as capable as the younger fellows on the job. In one program, Edith Bunker was depicted as experiencing stereotypic menopausal symptoms, her erratic behavior both sad and funny to watch.

Although one cannot deny that the body does change at menopause, the "symptoms" may be caused as much by cultural expectations as by physical changes.[8] My mother, for instance, experienced no adverse sensations during menopause because, as she put it, "I didn't know I was supposed to." Her own mother had undergone a hysterectomy before menopause and had not, therefore, exhibited any menopausal symptoms. It was only later, when my mother read about symptoms of menopause that she realized that she *had* experienced minor "hot flashes" but had paid them no heed as she did not know that they signified anything important. She had viewed them as merely normal discomforts. This seems to illustrate that reality is what one believes or, put more elegantly by William Shakespeare, "There is nothing either good or bad, but thinking makes it so." Experiences and actions appear to proceed on the basis of a person's interpretation of reality. Another example, for instance, is that placebos, when given as "medicine" or as drugs and believed to be such, have the effect of drugs; the human brain triggers profound chemical changes in the body. It is not clearly understood why this is so.[9] What does seem clear is W. I. Thomas's dictum that if something is perceived as real, it is real in its consequences. Unlike most depictions of the elderly on television, the grandmother and grandfather of "The Waltons" are old people whose contributions to the family are vital and valued, whose advice is frequently sought and often followed. Everyone knows, though, that the Waltons are from "the olden days" and that extended farm families of their kind are rarely found now. The appeal of the Waltons resides in nostalgia, evoking a yearning for times gone by, which, although hard, had their rewards in love, companionship, and mutual respect. Similarly, kindly old "Doc" Bogert is recognized as one of a vanished breed, whose like is no more to be found in New York City, if anywhere else in the United States.

If older people are often shown as tiresome nuisances on some television programs, in television advertisements they are most often seen, when they are seen at all, as recommending ways of putting back the clock or of coping with the "inevitable" discomforts of aging. Both men and women look "better" if they use hair coloring, and although the spoken message is upbeat—"You're not getting older, you're getting better"—the underlying message is that you are getting better if you look younger. Advertisements directed at old people are largely for denture adhesives, laxatives, over-the-counter sleeping medicine, and pain relievers. Old people in advertisements for saving banks warn those not yet of retirement age to save now rather than risk ending up as destitute as the character portrayed. That these old people allegedly "play" themselves makes their sad plight even more poignant.

In a recent exploratory study of daytime television advertisements I discovered that old people were shown in slightly over 3 percent of the 458 advertisements examined, although 10 percent of the population of the United States are sixty-five or older. Six commercial television channels were carefully monitored for five weeks in July and August, 1975, with monitoring spaced so that morning, afternoon, and early evening advertisements were represented. Twenty hours of television programming were taped for analysis, revealing only fifteen advertisements in which old people were either addressed directly or appeared among other age groups. In the daytime, the images of aging presented on the television screen, although rare, are not entirely negative or depressing. Two of the fifteen commercials showed the Kentucky Colonel, who is clearly an old man but who is also a lively and active man. An advertisement for ketchup, also recorded twice during the twenty hours under study, showed a grandmotherly type and a small girl of between seven and ten years enjoying a meal together. Both characters were wearing identical large-lensed, metal-rimmed spectacles. This kind of charm is unusual and, hence, is worthy of mention, as is a similarly charming view of an old woman given in a margarine advertisement. Father, mother, and children in turn extol the virtues of the margarine and, finally, an old woman with a quavering voice adds, "Toast tastes better!"—and she winks, saucily, at the viewers.

One of the fifteen advertisements was for a center that claims to help people to stop smoking. The testimonial was given by a man who announced himself to be almost eighty and told how he had smoked for over sixty-five years; his voice was going bad, his energy was low. The advertiser helped him to stop smoking, and now he feels great! The remaining advertisements were for denture adhesives, savings and loan associations, and heating rubs for the pain of arthritis. Only rarely were old people shown among groups of people of varied ages.

During the daytime, few advertisements are addressed directly to middle-aged people, although the middle-aged are shown among varied age groups. Those in my sample who did advertise products for middle-aged persons emphasized the retention of youthful appearance and sexual appeal. They included advertisements for creams to minimize dry skin lines—"Discover the secret. Look as young as you can"—and an exerciser body-shaper that "Helps you look *years* shapelier." Eye drops were recommended by a woman who announced, "I'm over forty, so my eyes are over forty, and eyes over forty produce only half the youthful moisture they used to . . . become irritated, red, that's why I use X because X has a methyl cellulose formula that replaces youthful moisture . . . I am over forty, but my eyes tell you something else." As she made her final statement, she removed a pin from the back of her head so that her hair was loosened and bounced around her face. She smiled seductively. An advertisement directed at men offered hair transplants that would so transform appearance that "that lovely young lady won't call you 'sir' any more." Middle-aged people as well as old persons frequently appear in advertisements for denture adhesives and cleansers. Those for cleansers play on the fear of giving offense to others. In one such advertisement, the "mother of the bride" expressed her happiness in the assurance that her mouth was "odor free."

Much more study is needed to discover the full range of depictions of people of various age groups in television advertisements and programs. This medium is particularly important in that it is available to most people in the United States, some programs being received in more than 50 million homes simultaneously. The direct effects of television are not yet fully known or understood but the millions of dollars invested annually by advertisers would seem to indicate that the effects are thought to be considerable—at least by those with something to sell. The aim of a phenomenological study would be to discern whether viewers' perceptions of various age groups are affected by television images and how this might, in turn, affect their expectations of themselves and of others.

Other media which might be examined for the images of aging they convey are, among many, popular novels and songs. Once more, although considerable attention has been directed toward these media in discerning the images of the sexes they convey,[10] little work has been concerned with images of age or aging. Because so few reports of rigorous studies in these areas exist, any discussion about depictions of age in novels and songs must necessarily be tentative and thought-provoking, rather than definitive.

A careful study of popular novels might begin with a sample of those that have been listed among the top ten best sellers across the nation and/or are available through book clubs, and that include reference to old age or middle age. Among the popular books of recent years is Doris Lessing's *Summer Before the Dark*, which tells the story of a woman of forty-five whose children are attaining independence and whose husband has wide interests he would prefer to pursue without her. Told largely through the words of the heroine, Kate Brown, the narrative leads the reader through the experiences of a single summer of crises and discovery, during which Kate passes from youthful maturity to the realization and acceptance of old age.

At the beginning of the book, Kate is described as a "pretty, healthy, serviceable woman." She dresses in ways her husband and children approve; she behaves in ways "proper" for her age and station in life. With her entire family away for the summer, she rents her house and takes a job, well paying and interesting, at which she excels, using both her considerable talents as a translator and the skills acquired and polished as wife and mother. Her employer regards her highly, is deferential and considerate of her wishes. She can afford to buy lovely and expensive new clothes. To this point, Kate's life seems like the ideal to which women whose children have grown are encouraged to aspire.

Kate, though, is not satisfied. The roles she is asked to play differ little from the familiar ones she has known for more than twenty years: nurse, nanny, mother—"a parrot with the ability to be sympathetic about minor and unimportant obsessions." She longs to be free.

The struggle for freedom leads her through a disastrous affair with a man much younger than she, who is taken ill while they are traveling in Spain. While waiting for her lover to recover, she contemplates the recent past, the constraints of family expectations and realizes that her love affair has become another mother/child, nurse/patient relationship, with Kate once more serving another, confined, longing for freedom—for what, she does not know. Returning to London, she becomes ill herself. In a hotel room in Bloomsbury, the size of the smallest bedroom in her home, the weeks of her illness pass, the gray pushes up into her now lank, tarnished red hair. She loses weight, her skin becoming "creased and shabby." She longs for her husband and family, all far away. When she finally summons enough energy, she climbs on a bus and travels the several miles to her home, to find that her neighbor and friend of years does not recognize her. At first hurt by the lack of acknowledgment, she then becomes elated that she was not known; as though she's been set free. Upon reflection she is relieved to discover that friendship is shallow and easily disproved. Suddenly, it no longer matters to her that she was not seen—those who *are* seen, who turn heads, begin to appear to her as parodies, as animals. At the theater one evening, she looks around her:

> But what a remarkable thing it was, this room full of people, animals rather, all looking in one direction, at other dressed-up animals lifted up to perform on the stage, animals covered with cloth and bits of fur, ornamented with stones, their faces and claws painted with colour . . . and their hair . . . their hair was the worst: mats and caps and manes and wigs of hair, crimped and curled and flattened and lengthened and shortened, hair dyed all colours and scented and greased and lacquered. It was a room full of animals, dogs and cats and wolves and foxes, that had got on their hind legs and put ribbons on themselves and brushed their fur.[11]

Kate's own hair was now a dry, brassy, crinkly mass, her face an old woman's. In a flash of revelation, she realizes that she has spent weeks, months, even years of her life in front of mirrors, to see how others would judge her. She had even limited her facial expressions to a small "acceptable" range. That no one sees her now, that no heads turn when she walks past a group of men, is both liberating and achingly confusing. The indifference of others, her seeming invisibility, makes her realize that it was the notice of other people that had held her upright all her life. Yet, a well-fitting dress, a little attention to her hair, is sufficient to attract men's notice. She realizes that the difference between drawing attention and failing to draw attention rests on small care taking, on wearing masks, on fitting oneself to a pattern.

Seething with rebellion and determined to use the time left to her—until October when her family will return—to be free, Kate moves again, to a less expensive place, where she befriends Maureen, a girl of her own daughter's age who knows her only as she has now become—"a thin monkey of a woman." But the call to return to her family comes sooner than expected. As the result of an illness, Kate's son will be home three weeks early. Suddenly she is caught up in the familiar pattern of telephoning, arranging, organizing—until an outburst by Maureen stops her in her tracks. Maureen turns on her for what she sees her becoming—just like her own mother: nurse, servant, helper, housekeeper—what Maureen, herself, must become if she marries conventionally. Kate changes her mind, sends wires, cancels plans. The family must manage without her for a while; she still has unfinished business. She must indulge her fantasies.

Out in the street she passes a group of laborers. They do not notice her; she is angered. She walks away, takes off her jacket to show her fitted dress, ties back her hair dramatically with a scarf, then strolls again in front of the workmen. This time, she receives a storm of whistles, calls, invitations. She makes her small transformation once more. Once more she walks by unnoticed. Her anger grows to consuming proportions. She realizes that this is what she has been doing for years and years and years—acting as sex object. She again delays going home; she needs more time. She must gather strength, for when she returns she will walk into her home with her hair undressed, tied back, rough and streaky, with a wide band of gray at each side of the parting.

Lessing's book presents middle age as a time of terrible struggle, of agonizing reappraisal of the past, of recognition that, after the torment of stripping away pretenses, one must face "the dark." The dark. The imagery of hair, the silken strands which snare the opposite sex, appears again and again through the story. The choice for Kate, the only moral choice Lessing gives her, is to abandon the artifices of youthfulness, to let her hair be gray, to face herself, to be old. In examining the past Kate realizes that the pressures of social expectations have constrained her, have allowed her to be less than she could have been. Youth—lovely, smooth-limbed, rosy-skinned youth—has been wasted. And the future is dark.

The middle-aged man in Joseph Heller's *Something Happened* is also shown as suffering through a period of appraisal, of looking backward, and looking forward, and of realizing that he is trapped. For 565 pages, Bob Slocum agonizes over what he has become, the games he has had to play in order to move his family to better and better suburbs. His view of others is cynical, malicious, distrustful, but his own ambition has cooled. After years of studious manipulation to reach his present goal, he has become bored:

> I am bored with my work very often now. Everything routine that comes in I pass along to somebody else. This makes my boredom worse. It's a real problem to decide whether it's more boring to do something boring than to pass along everything boring that comes in to somebody else and then have nothing to do at all.[12]

Only crisis on the job excites him, but it frightens him, too. Although there are peaks of challenges and elation, his work life is largely monotonous, yet he is making no plans to leave: "I have the feeling now that there is no place left for me to go."

At home, Bob Slocum's wife is "unhappy, bored, and lonely." She is beginning to drink during the day. "We have had better times together, my wife and I, than we are having now: but I do not think we will have them again." His fifteen-year-old daughter is testing her autonomy, challenging her parents with swear words, with disdainful expressions, with insults. Underneath the bravado, she is lonely and frightened. His nine-year-old son is timid, anxious to please, easily worried. Slocum is deeply fond of this child, although he sometimes hurts him, upsets him, unwittingly. Meal times frequently become occasions for bickering, for raised voices, and, sometimes, for raised hands. One more child completes the family, a younger son, born brain-damaged ("I wish I were rid of him now, although I don't dare to come right out and say so.").

Looking back on his life, Slocum asks, "What happened to us? Something did. I was a boy once, and she was a girl, and we were both new. Now we are man and woman, and nothing feels new any longer; everything feels old. . . ."

The book is an outpouring of regret for the past, for hurts inflicted on others that can never be undone: a flood of guilt, of pain, of yearning for another chance: "I know at last what I want to be when I grow up. When I grow up I want to be a little boy."

The future holds bleak promise. His beloved son is already growing up, growing away from him; a stream of foreboding floods his consciousness:

> I don't want him to go. My memory's failing, my bladder is weak, my arches are falling, my tonsils and adenoids are gone, and my jawbone is rotting, and now my little boy wants to cast me away and leave me behind for reasons he won't give me. What else will I have? My job. When I am fifty-five, I will have nothing more to look forward to than Arthur Baron's job and reaching sixty-five. When I am sixty-five, I will have nothing more to look forward to than reaching seventy-five, or dying before then. And when I am seventy-five, I will have nothing more to look forward to than dying before eighty-five, or geriatric care in a nursing home. I will have to take enemas . . . I will be incontinent. I don't want to live longer than eighty-five, and I don't want to die sooner than a hundred and eighty-six.[13]

In the very last pages of the story, Slocum suffocates his cherished nine-year-old boy, believing him to be dying after a road accident and desperate to relieve him quickly of his pain. No one knows but Slocum. This is one more burden he must carry with him into the future.

Both Lessing and Heller, fine, sensitive writers whose works are widely read, depict middle age as a crisis point, as a time of reckoning, of coming to terms with the past, as a transition. This transition, this crossing over from one stage of life to another, leads into a darker, grimmer place than the one left long behind. Old age holds little hope. Only youth held promise. And that is gone.

What, then, of novels dealing with those well past middle age? Do they offer a similarly depressing view of the life of the elderly? Kingsley Amis, of *Lucky Jim* fame, has written *Ending Up,* the story of several old people sharing a house together some seven miles from the nearest town (Newmarket, in England), and three miles from the nearest village. *Ending Up* is a farce, a painfully savage portrait of life among septuagenarians. The characters are grotesque, ghastly in their afflictions, their fractiousness, their bitterness, their malicious practical jokes. While Amis may be saying that people who are dull, or garrulous, or wise, or stupid when young will be more dull, garrulous, wise, or stupid when old, the story he tells is moving, and frightening, at the same time as it is funny. The closing scene is reminiscent of Shakespeare at his bloodiest, dead bodies in bizarre positions strewn across the set.

The grandchildren, on their rare visits, fret with boredom. Neglected, cut off from the flow of life, there is little left for these old people to do but to torment each other into the grave. Amis's characters are creatures of petty human failings who are in no way compensated by their years. No special wisdom, no extra virtues, are theirs. Only their weaknesses are strengthened.

A different picture of old age is that painted by Saul Bellow in *Mr. Sammler's Planet*. Artur Sammler, a tall, white-haired man with only one functioning eye, is in his seventies. Born in Poland, he fell early in love with England, where he worked more than twenty years as London correspondent for Warsaw papers and journals. His working life has been among writers, historians, economists, and intellectuals, but he has endured the horrors of war and of the death camps. He has learned to see but to appear not to have seen, to keep quiet, to monitor his expression. He has known much, but he has lasted:

> He didn't in fact appear to know his age or at what part of life he stood. You could see that in his way of walking. On the streets he was tense, quick, erratically light and reckless, the elderly hair stirring on the back of his head. Crossing, he lifted the rolled umbrella high and pointed to show cars, buses, speeding trucks, and cabs bearing down on him the way he intended to go. They might run him over but he could not help his style of striding blind.[14]

This tall, spare man lopes through New York seeing pickpockets and pimps at work, observing the deterioration of the city, the smashed telephones, the filthy urinals, the squalor. Always observing, even with only one good eye, he notices the passing fashions in clothing, in theater and art, in entertainment. He listens more than he talks, his mind constantly alert, registering, digesting, analyzing. He sees much that is in decline, a lowering of standards, a raising of demands. University students who come to help save his sight by reading to him appear ill-educated, needing lengthy explanations of the works they stumble through. He wearies of them, preferring to read for himself, if only a few sentences at a time.

At a large university meeting, which he has agreed to address under the impression that it was to be a small seminar, he is insulted by members of the audience. Rather than being personally offended by the event, he is not sorry to have met the facts—the reality, the howling of present-day youth—however regrettable the facts. He feels himself severed from the rest of mankind, not by his age as much as by the realization that, intellectually and spiritually, he is out of place, out of step, out of time. To the young he is an old bore:

> The worst of it, from the point of view of the young people themselves, was that they acted without dignity. They had no view of the nobility of being intellectuals and judges of the social order. What a pity! old Sammler thought. A human being, valuing himself for the right reasons, has and restores order, authority.[15]

Throughout, in spite of all the affronts that he faces, Sammler retains his sense of dignity; he values himself. He remains sane in the face of insanity, recognizing it but not being drawn into it. His anger, slow to stir, is not directed at those who have hurt or offended him, it is aroused by brutality shown to others.

The words Sammler whispers mentally at the death of a friend are fitting for Sammler himself:

> He was aware that he must meet, and he did meet—through all the confusion and degrading clowning of this life through which we are speeding—he did meet the terms of his contract. The terms which in his inmost heart, each man knows. As I know mine. As all know. For that is the truth of it—that we all know, God, that we know, that we know, we know, we know.[16]

Popular novels reach perhaps several hundreds of thousands of readers and may provide "cues" for the actions of many actors in society—but popular music reaches many millions of listeners, most of them young. A search for the images conveyed in recent best-selling albums reveals, with few exceptions, regret and sadness at growing old, loneliness and despair, and, sometimes, helplessness. Some of the most popular recording artists of recent years have used the theme of aging: the Beatles and, later, the individual Beatle Paul McCartney; Elton John; Simon and Garfunkel and, later, Art Garfunkel; Neil Diamond; and Harry Nilssen.

"Morningside," sung by Neil Diamond, tells of an old man who dies alone and unmourned, leaving behind a table which he had built with his own hands. Inside the table he had carved the words "For my children," but no children come to claim it:

Morningside, an old man died,
And no one cried,
He surely died alone.
For not a child

Would claim the gift he had,
The words he carved became his epitaph:
For my children.[17]

Art Garfunkel also sings of an old man's dying, lonely, unwanted, given little comfort:

You want to stay, I know you do,
But it ain't no use to try,
'Cos I'll be here, and I'm just like you,
Goodbye, old man, goodbye.

Won't be no God to comfort you,
You taught me not to believe that lie,
You don't need anybody, nobody needs you,
Don't cry old man, don't cry,
Everybody dies.[18]

Both Elton John and Harry Nilsson use the symbolism of soldiers grown old in a time when there are no wars to fight. A man grows useless when he can no longer ply his trade or use his tools:

I'm an old forgotten campaign hero,
Left without a cause,
Because they took away my war.
I'm an old forgotten railroad,
Looking at the empty old train,
And my rusty ammunition,
Has been left out in the rain. . . .[19]

and

You'll always see me staring at the walls and at the lights,
Funny, I remember, Oh, it's years ago I'd say,
I'd stand at the bar with my friends who've passed away,
And drink three times the beer that I can drink today.
Yes, I know how it feels to grow old.

. . .What do they know what it's like
To have a graveyard as a friend?
'Cos that's where they are, boy, all of them.
Don't seem likely I'll get friends like that again.[20]

Looking toward the future, old age holds little promise. Elton John sings:

Who'll walk me to the church
When I'm sixty years of age?
When the ragged dog they gave me
Has been ten years in the grave . . .

. . . You know the war you fought in,
Wasn't too much fun.
And the future you're giving me
Holds nothing for a gun,
I've no wish to be living,
Sixty years on.[21]

The lyrics of those songs that look into the future indicate that there is little left to do but sit on park benches, like bookends, thinking about the past, dreading the future:

. . . The old men,
Lost in their overcoats,
Waiting for the sunset. . . .

Can you imagine us
Years from today
Sharing a park bench quietly?
How terribly strange
To be seventy.

Old friends,
Memory brushes the same years.
Silently sharing the same fear. . . .[22]

Even more grim is the vision of helpless old age painted by Paul McCartney:

Treat her gently,
Treat her kind
She doesn't even know her own mind.

Treat her simply
Take it slow
Make it easy
Let her know
You'll never find another way.

Here we sit
Two lonely old people
Eking our lives away.

Bit by bit
Two lonely old people
Keeping the time of day. . . .[23]

One of the few cheerful and lively popular songs about growing older is the
Beatles' "When I'm Sixty-Four." The tune is jaunty, unlike the plaintive melo-
dies of most other songs about aging, the message is hopeful, even though it
conveys some doubt about how lovable one might be during one's later years. I
may have lost my hair, and my youthful good looks, is the message, but there
will be lots of things we can do together. We'll have fun—and in any case,
you'll be older, too!

. . . I could be handy, mending a fuse,
When your lights have gone.
You can knit a sweater by the fireside,
Sunday morning, go for a ride.
Doing the garden, digging the weeds,
Who could ask for more?
Will you still need me, will you still feed me,
When I'm sixty-four? [24]

By and large, though, the images of aging in the examples of popular culture
given here appear to be negative, even frightening. What is less clear is the way
in which these images affect those who receive them. Ultimately, a complete
study of age should attempt to seek the linkages between the images projected
and the images perceived. Are people influenced by media presentations? If so,
is the influence direct or indirect? Is it filtered through a screen of personal experience?

Considerable research has been conducted over the years into the perceptions
that people of all ages, including old people themselves, have toward the elderly,[25] although little has been done to determine how closely cultural ideas
match, affect, or shape actual beliefs and behavior. Perhaps the crucial groups
in study of this kind are those not yet old, for their perceptions may color their
expectations and plans for their own future, as well as their behavior towards
those already old. Ideally, then, responses should be sought from a wide sample
of ages and types of people from all parts of the country, different methods
being used as suitable. Analysis of essays by children and young people, titled,
perhaps, "What it is like to be old," might be revealing of expectations of old

age. The experiences of these people should be taken into account: Do they have grandparents or great-grandparents living with them, or living nearby?

A phenomenologically oriented investigator would tend to avoid questionnaires and set interviews, preferring to use open-ended questions of the "Tell me about . . . , How do you feel about . . . ?, What do you think about . . . ?, What do you like about . . . ?" variety, so that preestablished categories would not limit the responses. Some researchers have used preset questions to which respondents must answer "agree" or "disagree." Examples of such questions are: "Old people are annoying," or "Old people make friends easily," but answers to questions of this kind are difficult both to give and to interpret. How does a person answer if he or she knows some old people who are annoying and some who are not, or if he or she thinks *all* people are annoying, regardless of their age?

A phenomenological study of aging, then, would impose no prior theories, hypotheses, or expectations upon the topic. It would explore as freely and as fully as possible, using interviews, observations, discussions, participation techniques, content analysis of essays, letters, diaries, songs, books, television programs, advertisements, magazine stories and articles, in an effort to discover what age means to people of many ages and types, and how cultural images affect, and are affected by, these meanings.

PART THREE
Reflections

All living things are critics.

—Kenneth Burke

CHAPTER SIX

Creative Sociology: Detractors and Defenders

CRITICISMS of the creative approaches to the study of society have risen from moral, methodological, theoretical, and political grounds. Some commentators, for instance, see all the creative sociologies as inherently and unavoidably conservative politically, while others, paradoxically, view them as implicitly and potentially revolutionary in political intent. Further, the image of the human being presented in the dramaturgical view of the interaction process as constantly plotting and manipulating to win support for the self he or she presents has been deplored, as has the game framework used by creative sociologists for its cynical presentation of humankind as learning to play the game of life in order to reap the most rewards. Other critics find that the concepts of self, role, role-taking, role-playing, and so on are vague and difficult to measure empirically, and the accusation is also made that the creative approaches are micro-sociological only and cannot be used to study the large-scale, or macro-sociological, organization of society. A still further criticism is that the language used by enthnomethodologists, in particular, renders incomprehensible the ideas being put forth both to the generalist in the field and to students.

Mention of the jargon, the prolix style, the tortuous sentences of the eth-nomethodologists rarely fails to invoke laughter at any gathering of two or more sociologists. Ethnomethodologists themselves have long grown weary of the easy jibes and the easily won amusement at their expense. Where it once was the work of Talcott Parsons that served as the exemplar of the heavy sociologese that muddies meaning and deters even the most conscientious of students, the writing of ethnomethodologists now plays this role. The accusation is justified. Much of what ethnomethodologists write cannot be understood without several readings, underlinings, and abstracting and précis work. I advise my students to attempt to draw out the major ideas and rephrase them. In fact, I occasionally rely upon them to do this, not only for themselves and for others in the class, but also for me. The style is without style; it is disarming though not charming; editing is often minimal, if attempted at all. One of my students once threw up her hands in despair and declared, "They write like oxen!"

The question, then, is *why* do ethnomethodologists write the way they do? It surely is not because they do not know how to use more conventional, readily understood language. Some clues are given in Alan Blum's introductory remarks to *Theorizing:*

> The following work contains a variety of analyses which appear eccentric and is organized through a language that appears unorthodox. The analyses were not designed to be eccentric nor is the usage designed to be unorthodox. I found it the most truthful way of speaking, a mode of speaking which my commitment requires.
>
> I could attempt to teach you to read the following work but such an effort would deny my argument. Therefore I will not characterize the book or present you with a position from which to read it for that would create a beginning for you which you ought to recover for yourself in your own reading. I will not then anticipate objections which you might raise (and which I have inventoried myself in assembling this work over the resistance generated by innumerable concrete exchanges) by attempting to convincingly disarm these objections, and instead, I shall trust you to achieve the reading which I require (which is less of a concrete 'position' than a level of involvement). My writing is intended, then, to invite you to reconstitute yourself through the very inter-action of the reading as one engaged in the 'problem' of the possibility of reading itself as exemplified in the relationship between speech and its ground.[1]

If I understand him correctly, Blum is suggesting that, as ethnomethodology questions the very grounds upon which common-sense language and meaning rests, some other language than the taken-for-granted usages must be employed if we are not to be lulled by the ordinariness of expected language forms into missing the very points ethnomethodology makes. Our ordinary language must be bracketed so that an awareness of *how* one understands what one reads is attained and maintained. To translate the language ethnomethodologists use into more familiar language is to undermine the ethnomethodological enterprise. Without a commitment to the discovery of the grounds of everyday meaning, one cannot do ethnomethodology. By this token, the task I have set myself in this book to demystify ethnomethodology, or make it understandable in ordinary language, is futile, for it removes the readers to the domain of everyday life instead of allowing them to remain in, and to work from, the domain of meaning of the ethnomethodological approach.

Part of this defensive argument by those criticized is that whereas physicists and chemists, among others, use technical language without criticism by laymen, sociologists, as scientists, are not permitted to use a language that is suited to their particular purposes. The theoretical framework of ethnomethodology calls for a special terminology if the scientist is to stand aside from the world being described. Objectivity demands definitions that are different from those of the "reality" under study.

However plausible these arguments may be, the fact remains that many students and members of the profession alike find the writings of some ethnomethodologists difficult to read and to understand. If a new language is to be learned, someone must teach it. At present, many outside the charmed circle of those trained as ethnomethodologists dismiss ethnomethodology as worthless out of exasperation. They remain unconvinced that the labor of deciphering the writings will deliver anything other than the puniest of ideas.

Attacks on the image of humanity projected by Erving Goffman, Stanford Lyman and Marvin Scott, and other creative sociologists range from mild to devastating and, in turn, lead to a debate about the political implications of such a view of the nature of men and women.

Perhaps the most severe criticism of Goffman's "man" comes from George Psathas, who maintains that although Goffman's view of humanity is one-sided, unreal, and incomplete, it is, nevertheless, dangerous because of the great popularity of Goffman's work.[2] Goffman's man is always on stage, always playing a part, always guiding and controlling his behavior to create the impression that the situation demands. In playing his part he must, nonetheless, appear honest, appear to *be* the character presented. He uses what he knows about manipulation of others' views of him to control his portrayal. Others in the situation, of course, use similar techniques in playing their parts and in judging the honesty of others' performances. Society is presented by Goffman as a series of interactions in which definitions of reality are precarious, sustained only by mutual cooperation. Each strives for credible performances; the self is an appearance. Further, says Psathas, each self is alone. In *Asylums,* Goffman gives an account of how the individual is manipulated and degraded, mortified and tyrannized. Yet, says Psathas, in his adaptation to the situation, Goffman's man uses the rules to advance his own cause. He does not attempt to overturn or reform the institution that oppresses him. He does not challenge the system, he "works" it. This man, suggests Psathas, lacks emotion and passion. He lacks a soul. The danger of this image of man, Psathas claims, lies in the cynicism with which he has been created. This man reflects Goffman's blindness to love, caring, and intimacy. No room is left for the possibility of sincerity, honesty, openness, and trust. How can we ever know that another is not merely presenting one of his "selves," acting a part? Goffman's man is immoral, degraded, and without self-worth or dignity. He trusts no one and so is, finally, alone.

Irving Zeitlin, too, sees an explicit and fundamental cynicism pervading Goffman's work. Goffman, he suggests, wants to "transform us all into agents who expose and discredit others, fearing all the while that we ourselves shall soon be discovered and exposed." [3] Similarly, Robert Friedrichs writes of Goffman's man as having no identity other than those attributes that arise out of intimate interaction with the contingencies of staging performances. Goffman's man, according to these critics, is a hollow shell, lacking any self besides that which is "presented" and "performed." [4]

Just as Goffman presents an image of man as stage-managing his every action, Lyman and Scott provide, in their *Sociology of the Absurd,* a picture of the human being as a calculating creature who uses what he knows about interaction, and about game-playing, to reach his goals most effectively. [5] Machiavelli is the model for this man, who can make others believe in illusions that are mere calculated performances; who can achieve his ends through an appearance of respectability, through the assumption of masks, through being continuously aware of the requirements of behavior in public places. This Machiavellian model, it has been suggested, denies the possibility that human beings are capable of something other than merely "acting," "performing," or "playing." Lyman and Scott counter this criticism by insisting that it is not the game framework that presupposes a particular human morality; it merely indicates that skill in games has payoffs. Not all players are equally good at games or at acting and one may admire the skilled player—or deplore him.

Although the existentialism of Jean-Paul Sartre springs from phenomenological roots, as does the interactionist approach of Goffman and of Lyman and Scott, Sartre sees man as moral only if he denies the expectations of others when they violate his expectations for himself; only by choosing freedom above conformity can man live authentically. These creative sociologies, in presenting an image of the human being as using a repressive system to further his own ends, rather than joining with others to rebel against a society which demands inauthenticity, have been accused of being essentially conservative politically. Other creative sociologies, too, are included in the accusation because of their underlying assumptions and their methods of study. Defenders deny an inherent conservative bias, claiming, in fact, the political radicalism of the creative sociologies. The debate concerns ethnomethodology, dramaturgy, the sociology of the absurd, symbolic interactionism, and phenomenology.

Ethnomethodologists have found, in studying the manner in which people construct reality, that people behave as if reality is real and concrete, but what they actually convey in their accounts is elusive, changeable, varying from situation to situation. Ethnomethodologists use quasi experiments to demonstrate that the social world is not really solid at all even though, most of the time, most of us "trust" our environment and the people around us. We accept definitions about reality without challenge; we take them for granted. This ethnomethodological viewpoint, suggest Randall Collins and Michael Makowsky, is potentially *revolutionary* in its implications.[6] We do not have to accept our roles in a docile way. If social structures appear solid, it is only because people *believe* that they are solid and unchangeable. If people refuse to take for granted what others around them take for granted, if people dare *risk* the possible social disapproval of those who believe unquestioningly, then they can puncture the myth, they can reshape "reality" by redefining it. The revolutionary potential in ethnomethodology is in its demonstrations that reality is negotiable, and, while we are all aware that those with economic or military power are more able to make their definitions of reality stick, disbelief in organizations can occur; existing power structures can be challenged: "Human social order is ultimately a symbolic reality that exists only as long as it is believed in and changes as people struggle to shift those beliefs to their own advantage." [7]

As do others, Collins and Makowsky see Goffman as more conservative than the ethnomethodologists; they term Goffman a functionalist "who is ready to see things as necessary simply because they exist":

> Goffman sees ceremonies as functionally necessary to maintain social order. He explores the underside of life, but he is not really sympathetic to the underdog. . . . Goffman's analysis of the rules of politeness and social ceremony is carried on without irony. In his view individuals who do not live up to the rules of polite interaction are justly punished by embarrassment, self-consciousness, or ostracism, for such rules are functionally necessary for the social reality to be kept alive. . . .[8]

Collins and Makowsky, then, view the ethnomethodologists as potentially revolutionary, even though, they say, ethnomethodologists do not spell out the implications of their approach and simply confine themselves to analyzing the rules that seem to govern people's everyday behavior. They see Goffman as conservative, as a functionalist, adding that he does not follow through to show either how people struggle to impose their own definitions of reality on others, or the liberating effects that this could have when people begin to realize just how this operates.

A similar criticism is leveled by Robert S. Broadhead against the sociology of the absurd of Lyman and Scott.[9] Broadhead suggests that, in their extreme reaction to the oversocialized conception of man implied by functionalism,[10] Lyman and Scott present an *undersocialized* conception of man and, in so doing, make of the sociology of the absurd a duplicate of functionalism. Broadhead sees two assumptions underlying the absurd: first, the social world is continually created and recreated by man and denies the existence of any social world that influences or channels the behavior of people;[11] and, second, far from society being based on consensus, cooperation, loyalty and competition, human beings are in a constant state of conflict with other humans. Each is out to maximize his own interests, conflict is the fundamental nature of social interaction and, therefore, every social situation is problematic for those involved.

Both functionalism, with its oversocialized view of man, and the absurd, with its undersocialized view of man, says Broadhead, "boast of tackling and dealing with the Hobbesian question: How is social order possible?" Both, he suggests, avoid dealing with the problem.

According to Broadhead, Lyman and Scott claim that the sociologists of the new wave seek to place *man* at the center of study, but they fail in this because, like the functionalists, they see man as both the victim and the function of forces greater than he. In functionalism, man's behavior is seen to be the function of the reified social system, while in the absurd man's behavior is seen as the function of "absurdity." So, the absurd becomes a type of functionalism, not like Parsonian functionalism, where human behavior is the function of socially shared norms or rules, but just the opposite; human behavior is seen to be the function of the *lack* of socially shared rules or norms—a function of meaninglessness. Broadhead concludes that the "absurd's reaction to functionalism becomes so extreme that it makes a full circle and, like a reflection in a mirror, becomes both its antithesis and its duplicate."[12]

Another, and one of the most recent, of the accusations of conservatism of the creative sociologists is by Scott McNall and James Johnson, who maintain that these kinds of theories, with their similar structure, purpose, and intellectual roots are, in their *implications,* detrimental to the development of sociology as a critical perspective for viewing society; they lead to a conservative stance that inhibits a concern for fundamental social change.[13] McNall and Johnson set out in some detail the similarities between phenomenology, symbolic interaction, and ethnomethodology and the methods used by each to study social interaction. The implicit assumption, they say, is that it is the actual *methods* by which people make the world accountable to themselves and to others that orders people's actions and determines the nature of the social order. This disregards the fact, they maintain, that most people can manipulate only trivial events that do not relate in any way to basic life chances. It ignores the fact of the values, or power, or status, or economic base as ordering actions and determining the nature of the social order. It offers a one-sided interpretation that denies the reality of the social structure. It is one thing, they say, to argue that everything is relative, and quite another thing to ignore the fact that some people's definitions of reality carry more weight than others' and may even impose upon others. These approaches, say McNall and Johnson, assume that Everyman is in a position equal to everyone else.

The statement made by Lyman and Scott about the *intention* of the sociology of the absurd is criticized by McNall and Johnson. Lyman and Scott write that social engineering or social change is not the primary objective of the sociology of the absurd. This is meant to demonstrate that the perspectives they defend are merely designed to help people to understand themselves, but, say McNall and Johnson, in fact, their methods, techniques, and assumptions about the nature of man deny the worth of institutional analysis aimed at social change. This is why their theories are essentially and inherently conservative—they are neither concerned with the possibility of social change nor are they opposed to it. They bypass social reality because they start with individual consciousness.

Further, the argument for free will quickly leads to an ideological justification for the way things are. If man creates his own world, then he must be responsible for his own actions. This is seen by McNall and Johnson as antirevolutionary. They cite Szymanski, who writes, "A revolutionary analysis . . . understands behavior to be the result of the social system—a social system which must be transformed by revolutionary action."[14] The assumptions of the creative sociologists can lead away from change, say McNall and Johnson. Human beings are simply not in a position to exercise the control over their lives that these approaches assume. They say, too, that there have been no studies from these perspectives dealing with economic development, imperialism, or war, because they are not concepts that fit into the system. There has been relatively no concern with the nature of power or its distribution in society with, they concede, the possible exception of Goffman's work on asylums in which he deals with the power of the institution to determine the reality that will be accepted. Finally, McNall and Johnson suggest that the view of society and man as presented by ethnomethodologists, symbolic interactionists, and phenomenologists leads to a conservative, astructural, ahistorical, situational perspective—one that causes one to concentrate on the deviant and the abnormal and to ignore the social conditions that give rise to abnormalities. Everyman is not in control of his own destiny and to suggest that he will be liberated by being given a glance at the strings by which he is controlled is to offer him a false liberation.

Against this severe criticism is an earlier paper by T. R. Young, which sees creative sociology as potentially *revolutionary*. [15] He suggests that if we adopt a *radical perspective* when we view the writings of Goffman and Garfinkel, they can be read as a "producing mine of radical insights."

Beginning with Goffman, Young agrees with the critics that Goffman is ambiguous regarding a political stance. [16] His approach is without a "metaphysics of hierarchy"—that is, Goffman does not support the point of view of any group of people over any other point of view; the view of patients is as important as that of doctors, the view of criminals is as important as that of policemen. Yet, by not sustaining the point of view of the official hierarchy Goffman appears to be "against those advantaged by it." The ambiguity in Goffman's work *can* be resolved by politically radical sociologists: first, by simply interpreting Goffman as being against the stratification system; second, by using Goffman as a point of departure to settle the question "Should the stratification system in these arena be dismantled or some other policy preferred?"; and, third, by searching in Goffman's work for specific instances where he condemns stratification mechanisms in implicit terms. Young says that this is the way he has used Goffman's work in his own classes and so has "politicized Goffman more than he might wish."

Young feels it is valid to accuse Goffman of focusing on the immediate and the episodic, and in so doing ignoring the permanent and hostile features of society. Goffman's model of man is one who accepts and "works" a dehumanized system of society instead of rebelling against it or rising above it. Goffman really teaches the art of gamesmanship—how to get by—which can be seen as conservative. Yet, surely what Goffman is doing, says Young, is providing insights about the social conditions that make such gamesmanship necessary. Goffman's work can be used to stimulate *awareness* of the managing and packaging that goes on in schools and colleges, the manner in which face is sustained, and the costs of maintaining the face of "inauthenticity."

The dramaturgical view of society—that social reality requires a script, actors, body idioms, ethos, involvement norms, clearance norms, relevance rules, conventions of boundary closure, disengagement norms, and the rest—has political payoffs, claims Young, for we understand that the script for reality may be changed and that new and more humane forms of reality may take the stage, given adequate political means for choosing between scripts. Let us assume, he suggests, that those who read Goffman have a sociological perspective and can see that the conning behavior which Goffman stresses is symptomatic of a poorly organized social world and that these "symptoms are acts of silent rhetoric by which a person communicates the anguish, hostility, alienation, and rage that the social situation elicits from him." Young rejects any interpretation of the political meaning of Goffman's work as hostile to "the radical romance." He is vital to it, says Young. "Goffman should be read as a radical sociologist and he will open radical vistas that are impossible to come by when reading him as apolitical." [17]

In his discussion of ethnomethodology and Garfinkel's contribution to sociology, Young sees this as essentially radical politically, with methods of study and demonstration that make very clear the underlying characteristics of the society. Ethnomethodologists poke and probe and provoke and puncture the social system in order to make its characteristics visible. These methods Young sees as the beginnings of the science of a conflict methodology. Ethnomethodology, he says, provides us with other ways of knowing than the methodology that provides the technical basis for a police state. He sees survey methods as a tool serving such a police state. Large-scale, funded research, he suggests, is based on tact, consensus, cooperation, persuasion, and establishment sponsorship. Such research serves the large-scale organizations of business, government, the military, finance, and education. Conflict methodology, on the other hand, exposes that which is withheld by such large-scale powerful organizations—information that would enhance the interests of the general public, were in divulged. In Young's view, Garfinkel and, to a lesser extent, Goffman embody the precepts of a conflict methodology and must be appreciated on those terms; they have advanced radical sociology.

Young is not alone in his view that Goffman's concepts, as well as those of others who work from within the symbolic interactionist framework, can be examined as contributing to the emancipatory consciousness necessary for revolutionary movements. "They offer us a strategy in locating the oppressive and discriminating 'other' in the social structure. Overcoming 'false' consciousness must be preceded by a self-awareness, understanding and evaluation of one's own situation." [18] Goffman himself is cautious in response to those who accuse him of a political conservatism:

> Of course, it can be argued that to focus on the nature of personal experiencing—with the implication this can have for giving equally serious consideration to all matters that might momentarily concern the individual—is itself a standpoint with marked political implications and that these are conservative ones. The analysis developed does not catch at the differences between the advantaged and disadvantaged classes and can be said to direct attention away from such matters. I think that this is true. I can only suggest that he who would combat false consciousness and awaken people to their true interests has much to do, because the sleep is very deep. And I do not intend to provide a lullaby but merely to sneak in and watch the way the people snore. [19]

In turning to the labeling theory which stems from, and contributes to, symbolic interactionism, Alex Thio sees it as politically conservative in that beneath it flows an undercurrent of class bias, by which he means tacit support of the power elite. [20] Students of deviance, he says, tend, although not exclusively, to focus on the deviance of the powerless class, neglecting the deviance of the powerful. They support the power elite in their concentration on the individual deviant or his immediate milieu and in their neglect of analysis of the established power structure in their society. While the labeling perspective emerged with the aim of taking the side of the powerless class, the actual consequence of its application is to imply subsurface support for the power elite, just as did earlier approaches to deviance such as those of the "social pathologists" and the "value-free" social scientists. The source of this focus lies in the definition of deviant behavior by labeling theorists: deviance is a consequence of labeling by superordinate parties. As it is mostly the powerless who are so labeled, research activities are deflected from study of deviance typically committed by the powerful. Indeed, Thio posits that labeling theory equates deviance with powerlessness and, further, that the emphasis on "secondary deviation"—when the one labeled deviant comes to perceive himself as such—deflects the research interest away from the reason the act had originally occurred. Thio's accusation rests on labeling theorists' failure to work with a clear view of the causal relations between power structures and deviance. Because labeling theory focuses on the *reactions to* behavior and the manner in which it becomes defined as deviant, observability becomes vital to the labeling theory enterprise. It is appreciably easier to observe the actions of the powerless than of the powerful and so to reinforce the class bias in sociology and in the broader society.

In a slightly later article, Thio supplements his earlier position accusing labeling theorists of class bias by adding phenomenological sociology to his discussion, insisting that this suffers from the same kind of bias.[21] In their reliance upon the subjective, the phenomena as seen from the point of view of the social actor, phenomenologists rely heavily on the method of participant observation, but this technique demands ease of observability. The powerful are unlikely to consent to observation of their deviant activities and so phenomenologists also focus their research on the deviance of the powerless only.

So far, we have joined the debate concerning those creative sociologists who make no claim that their work is either revolutionary or conservative in political intention; the critics have "read in" the "inherent, essential" conservatism, or the "potential, implicit" radicalism. Brief mention should be made of those working within a phenomenological framework who *do* claim to present a radical point of view, or who can be seen as having presented such a radical viewpoint.

C. Wright Mills, whose work and actions provided impetus for current radical sociology, has been described as believing "that the center of truthfulness lies in individual subjectivities rather than in the objective network of institutions." [22] In such writing as "Situated Actions and Vocabularies of Motive," Mills demonstrated the value of the phenomenological approach for understanding the linkage of individually expressed motive to systems of action.[23]

Several contemporary "idealistic" Marxists, criticized by their more "materialistic" fellows, have been influenced by Edmund Husserl, Maurice Merleau-Ponty, and Georg W. F. Hegel, among others, and term themselves phenomenologists.[24] Among these is John O'Neill, who suggests that "for anyone concerned with the nature of the construction of social reality, Marx will always remain a classical analyst of the deep structures of economic and social life." [25] Another might be Fred R. Dallmayr, whose discussions of Enzo Paci, Paul Picone, and John O'Neill indicates a feeling that a blending of Marxism with phenomenology and existentialism may "recapture the human dimension and purposive thrust of Marxism." [26]

In the main, though, most of the creative sociologists make no political statements and yet are interpreted as "potentially" and "inherently" revolutionary or, quite the opposite, as "serving the power elite." The more fundamental question, perhaps, than whether these approaches are conservative or revolutionary, concerns the use of sociological theory. Should sociological theory direct social change or should it direct sociological research? If the answer is the former, is it not, rather, revolutionary-activist theory which is being sought? Is not the important *sociological* question about a theory, "Does it generate new knowledge?" Useful theory, I would suggest, is, like the creative approaches, not determinable as either inherently revolutionary or conservative, although the manner in which it is *used* may lead to either of these conclusions. This is nicely demonstrated by Paul Schervish in his discussion of the manner in which labeling theory research has tended to focus on the underdog as a helpless victim of the labeling process by superordinates.[27] The existing bias, he suggests, is directly opposed to what we would expect from analysts who are committed to Mead's insistence that individuals are in constant reflective dialogue with reality rather than being simply determined by it. He goes on to demonstrate that research within the labeling theory framework can be directed to the study of the ways in which those labeled actively resist, or counter, the labeling process. Further, such studies need not be limited to individuals within small groups but may consider cases in which negotiation of labels occurs between groups. Examples abound of individuals and groups undercutting existing value orientations by aggressively seeking to win acceptance for their views of reality as expressed in the labels they attempt to legitimate. In San Francisco, for example, the aggressive approach of various groups ordinarily labeled "deviant" has made it possible for a cultural climate to develop that allows for a tolerance of, and an accommodation to, their style of life. Study of such groups is possible and has, indeed, been conducted. Schervish provides examples of research projects of this kind from within the labeling and symbolic interactionist frameworks and also suggests a number of macro-level cases of political resistance to labels for further study.

Useful theory may provide material for political activists or political conservatives, as has been shown by the materials cited above, especially by the manner in which Goffman and Garfinkel's work has been utilized by Young. Young admits, however, that in his use *he* has politicized Goffman, has added interpretations that are not explicit in Goffman's writings.

Karl Mannheim observed that the theories of scientific thought become amalgamated with political thought, with the resulting amalgamation demonstrating negative as well as positive effects. He reminded us that theories can be used by the dominant to maintain their dominance, or they can be used by the oppressed to gain release from their oppression. Both oppressed and oppressors, however, can *misuse* theory, applying only those aspects which serve them and casting a blind eye over those which would shake their belief or paralyze their desire to change things.[28] I would suggest, then, that the creative sociologies are neither conservative nor revolutionary politically but can, because they are useful theories that add to our stock of knowledge about human behavior, be used by either conservatives or revolutionaries to further their aims. We should remain alert to their possible misuse.[29]

The dramaturgical analogy, the likening of society to theater, also has its share of opponents and proponents—those who find that such an analogy provides useful insights into everyday life and those who see it as unrealistic and misleading.

Richard Dewey sees the "world as theater" approach as overplayed by social scientists and as contributing little to the understanding of human interaction.[30] The theatrical analogy, he says, entails the application of words and concepts designed for one set of restricted relationships to significantly different and more expansive sets of relationships. The theater is not the equivalent of society; the application of the dramaturgical model is therefore an instance of reductionism in conceptualizing societal phenomena. Such a model carries with it some of the same limitations that beset the organic analogies or models that were once fashionable in sociology. To the extent that the analogue differs from the sociocultural system being studied, the conclusions are apt to be unwarranted, with both conceptions and perceptions distorted. To be sure, Dewey indicates, some play-acting, some make-believe, takes place in the world of everyday life, but there are important differences between the theater and the larger society.

Goffman himself agrees that all the world is not a stage. Even the theater is not entirely a stage. One needs a place for cars to park and coats to be checked, and these had better be real places which had better carry real insurance against theft.[31] Still, he points out, even though all the world is not a stage, it is *like* a stage, and we can watch the actors strutting and fretting upon it.[32]

Another critic who finds major problems in the use of the theatrical analogy is George Psathas. In the theater, he writes, the actor has already interpreted the part he is to present, and he knows how he wants the audience to respond. The audience, in its turn, is awaiting the revelation of the character, anticipating and interpreting as the characterization unfolds. The actor is "on," says Psathas; he knows that he is performing and that the world of the theater is not the world of everyday life. He is fully aware that he has entered another domain of meaning and that the character he presents is not himself. The stage actor knows that, although he may bring himself into the part of Hamlet, he is not Hamlet—and after Hamlet dies on the stage, *he* arises to take his bow and to play the same part again:

> The character in the play is the "same" character, the performers vary. In everyday life, the performers are the same, the performances vary. Performing and being are not identical—and the analogy breaks down just as surely as the human performer would "break down" if he were to be "on" all the time. To be told that man is a performer, that the world of everyday life can be analogized to theater, is to misrepresent the reality of everyday life.[33]

Proponents, on the other hand, stand firm in their support for the dramaturgical view. R. S. Perinbanayagam, for instance, in direct contradiction to Goffman, says it is not that social reality is like drama, but that it is drama insofar as social reality is drawn out of the communication and symbolism by which socially constructed persons talk to each other, define situations, and interact.[34] The use of the drama of social life, he maintains, is not mere metaphor; it is the stuff and fiber of social relations. We constantly negotiate our ongoing definitions, responding to each other on the basis of our images of each other. Each creates, or attempts to create, desired images through dramatization. Dramatization, he says, is not manipulative or exploitative; it is a genuine act, or technique, of communication. The rituals of everyday life, he adds, are theater. Religious ritual is a way of establishing a personal relationship with impersonal forces; weddings and funerals are personal transformations, or rites of passage drawn from life and put on the stage. The drama on the stage is merely a microcosmic representation of the drama of life.

From the more deliberately political activist perspective of Jeanne Boland and T. R. Young, society, especially contemporary society, is also equated with staging.[35] Ours, they say, is a dramaturgical society, one in which the behavior and consciousness of people are shaped and managed by the technology of the theater, of the behavioral sciences, and of mass communications. Images of service, of quality, of the economy, of accountability constantly impinge upon our thinking; reality and make-believe converge, the midline between the two becoming progressively obscured. Our organizations demand that we adopt and discard temporary identities. Emphasis is placed upon image rather than substance. Politicians, both those striving for office and those who hold office, aim for "credibility." They are packaged and sold on their ability to fit a particular image, play a particular role. In the world of business, the art of public relations is developed and polished so that the images conveyed are plausible and favorable. Fund raisers for colleges and universities assure their financial supporters that their establishments fit an acceptable image of academic life.

Dramaturgical techniques, say Boland and Young, are taught to children; in the process of socialization by parents, teachers, and others, they learn to project "correct" impressions, they learn to play roles. In a mass society, advertising augments and replaces socialization for the construction of social reality. Needs and wants are generated by advertising techniques. In folk societies, Boland and Young write, when others see a person, they also see the social identities of that person, but in mass society a person needs dramatic cues in order to determine who he or she is supposed to be in any particular situation. Our roles bear little relation to our own self-structure. Clearly, these writers deplore the dramaturgical society they describe and see the dramaturgical mode of social analysis as presenting a useful way of examining a society in which human beings and organizations are not trying to do and to be, but to *seem* to be doing and being.

The dramaturgical mode of analysis, then, has its supporters and detractors, as do the research methods of all the creative sociologists. It is probably the research techniques of creative sociologists which have drawn the heaviest fire from attackers of these approaches.

One criticism is of the use of participation observation and the interpretations drawn from such observations. Such studies as those of Cicourel and of Cicourel and Kitsuse demonstrate that official data do not parallel either the frequency or types of delinquent acts, or the potential ability of high school students to cope academically at the college level.[36] Official data demonstrate, instead, the constructions of agency workers, and of teachers and counselors, which are based on background expectancies, taken-for-granted views, and stereotypes. The reports, though, become "reality" and shape the life prospects for those named in them. These studies inform us that official data are socially constructed phenomena and should not be accepted uncritically.

These ethnomethodological studies, however, are seen by Bob Gidlow as having costs that may outweigh their usefulness.[37] The methods used by Cicourel and Kitsuse, being little more than "glorified participant observation," are subject to the same criticism as participant observation and have similar limitations. Any major attempt at scientific rigor, writes Gidlow, is neglected; no rules of procedure are used to decide what should be counted as evidence beyond the investigator's own interpretations and subjective assessments. What are the criteria, he asks, by which the investigator selects or discards "relevant" information? What about the possibility of alternative interpretations? While the investigator may impute plausible background expectancies by interpretation, one cannot say if the report he makes is true or false.

Peter Winch and Joan Huber join the discussion by insisting that one does not know that one's interpretation is valid in any *verstehende* approach.[38] Huber addresses the question in her critique of the methods of study recommended by Herbert Blumer. Blumer calls for "observation" and "inspection," involving the use of "informants." What, asks Huber, if well-informed observers disagree? How do investigators choose one view over another? And what insures the objectivity or reliability of the investigators? The methods of symbolic interactionism are not replicable, they do not meet the criterion of practicability. Symbolic interactionists go into research without hypotheses; theory is to "emerge" from the observations. But, Huber asks, how can one be sure that the emergent theory is not shaped by the researchers' own interpretations, drawn from their own social givens?

Blumer's answer is that the symbolic interactionist investigator is no less able to test his assertions and hypotheses about the empirical world than is the researcher operating with "prior constructions of logically related propositions."[39] Validity can be tested. Disagreements between conflicting parties are not insoluble; they can be resolved by "talking it over." Researchers can always continue scrutiny until they are satisfied that their interpretations are correct. How, responds Huber, do researchers know when they have scrutinized enough?[40] Blumer does not say.

Further, what appears to arise from the context of interaction may be based in some other experiences of the actors. Jacqueline Johnson adds a criticism of symbolic interaction that is also based on the problems of participation observation as a research technique.[41] In the symbolic interactionist view, self alters its shape and form according to roles to be played, according to the expectations of others. But, implies Johnson, while role imagery may help explain certain behaviors, it is possible that some people possess a core set of self attributes as consistent cognitive representations of who they are which does not vary with the things they do. The ahistorical, temporal orientation of "the situation" may be seen as superficial. The phenomenological approach, Johnson suggests, is an alternative of greater potential richness; it takes us beyond a current situation and seeks the individual's reconstruction of his past in order to understand the experience and organization of self and roles. Participant observation alone cannot reveal the determinants of the actor's experience.

Perinbanayagam, on the other hand, finds phenomenology and ethnomethodology limiting, relative to the symbolic interactionist/dramaturgical approach.[42] Schutz, he says, fails to come to grips with the problem of interaction—that meanings and definitions are *negotiated* between participants and not merely constituted by self or ego. The subject's actions are not shaped and determined only by past events; a capacity for voluntarism remains in participation in the definition of the situation and the creation of meaning. Schutz's ideas need the added insights of Mead and, perhaps, of other thinkers if they are to be useful in explaining intersubjective understanding.

This exchange of fire seems to make clear the need for more techniques of research than one. Paul Attewell adds to the discussion that understanding of the life world of actors must involve the full range of determinants of actors' experience. All the things ethnometodologists bracket, he suggests—the intention of the actors, their biographies, their substantive memories of previous interactions—must be taken into account in any attempt to understand current interaction.[43]

Perhaps these critics fail to consider that in newly developing, or recently revived, or unconventional approaches, research techniques, like the theoretical underpinnings that generate them, are being developed through experimentation and innovation. Methods of *many* kinds are tried for the insights they might provide, and are refined or discarded as necessary. Few investigators within the frameworks of the creative sociologies limit their research techniques to the extent suggested by some critics. Further, while the research methods of the creative sociologists may be considered rudimentary and still to be perfected, the findings of some of these sociologists undermine the notion that the methods of more conventional social scientists are any more reliable or valid. Harold Garfinkel's revelations of the way "objective" coding is conducted implies that coding of questionnaires and other research data depends on individual decisions rather than upon scientific criteria. His study indicated that coders employed ad hoc practices for making sense of information contained in official records, despite the provision of a set of elaborate coding instructions.[44] Ethnomethodologists deny that findings of this kind are intended as a critique of standard research methods. They merely serve to make clear that scientists employ the same methods to "do" science as do persons in everyday activity;

scientists and lay persons alike use the "documentary method of interpretation." The reliability and validity of research instruments are notoriously difficult to insure in any approach to the study of society. Researchers of all points of view continuously seek to perfect their field methods.

Not only are the interpretive methods of the creative sociologists called into question, but their very concepts are found inadequate, vague, and difficult to observe empirically. How are "self," "role," "role-taking," and "role-making," for instance, to be defined and measured? Attempts to derive tools for measuring subjective meanings have not proved an unqualified success and, although efforts at refinement continue, concepts remain largely tentative and imaginative.[45] While Herbert Blumer feels that concepts should serve as tools to "sensitize" the researcher to what is observed, others are less contented with such casually drawn guidelines. Goffman's work, especially, has been attacked for its lack of development of concepts. His studies, it has been said, are impossible to replicate; he presents no methodological discussion, and no indication of how his classifications are derived.[46] The body of concepts he uses differs in each of his many works. Goffman's response is that he makes no claim that his examples are typical or systematically gathered. They are not presented as proofs or facts, he says, but as clarifying depictions, as typifications, "as frame fantasies which manage, through the hundred liberties taken by their tellers to celebrate our beliefs about the workings of the world. . . ."[47] Goffman willingly admits the shortcomings of his data in a way that, perhaps, makes it more difficult for other researchers working from the interactionist perspective to legitimate their conceptual and methodological frameworks. Few researchers have Goffman's eloquence or his elegance of style; most strive to meet current definitions of scientific rigor, including clear analytical concepts to guide work in the field.

The writing of Peter Berger and Thomas Luckmann has also been the target of a number of critical comments. Their book, *The Social Construction of Reality*, presents an attempt to derive a multifaceted theory through a synthesis of the phenomenology of Alfred Schutz, the social factism of Émile Durkheim, and the sociology of knowledge of Karl Marx. As with all syntheses, each of the components has become slightly modified.

According to Berger and Luckmann, human beings themselves produce society so that it becomes an objective reality for them. The ongoing creative processes by which this is achieved are externalization, objectification, and internalization.[48] We structure our existence through patterned institutions and interactions and we then *externalize* our subjective interpretations of society in speech and other symbols; our reality, including the reality of ourselves as individuals, so becomes *objectified*. Objects become "real" in the telling and, in turn, through *internalization* become part of our subjective reality, as well as of that of the generations that follow.

Internalization, Berger and Luckmann claim, accounts for the necessary stability of societies if they are to survive over time, but some phenomenologists, among other critics, regret the emphasis on social determinism manifested in the heavy stress upon internalization. Children are born into an existing society; they learn the nature of that society from their parents and teachers. They absorb the social reality as it is presented to them, apparently without acting upon the definitions provided. If we are taught what our parents know, suggests Richard Lichtman, we have no part in what we are socialized to believe or to understand.[49] Even though parents may have had some choices in the definition, the children have to have it explained to them and legitimated. Unclear in Berger and Luckmann's work are the ways in which societies may change, the ways in which individuals may free themselves from their internalized reality in order to bring into being new modes of thought and action; although the individual externalizes his or her thoughts into the society, the content of the input appears to be drawn from the society itself. Why, asks Lichtman, is society chosen as the defining unit, rather than the individuals who may deviate from the societal definition?

The autonomous aspect of the human self, the "I," has presented theorists with difficulties of conceptualization ever since its early formulation by George Herbert Mead. Mead himself was much less vague in his definition of the "me" than of the "I," and it is considerably easier to account for the aspect of self that internalizes the culture and, thereby, reinforces it, than it is to show how individuals work back on the distribution of knowledge so as to increase its potential for emancipation and change.[50] Jack Douglas has remarked that in the grafting of structural ideas onto situational analyses, Berger and Luckmann have largely denied the necessary freedom of individuals implicit in the whole idea of situated meaning and have reinstated the "objectified" absolutist tyranny of the structuralists.[51] Robert Friedrichs, however, himself a "synthesist," admires Berger and Luckmann's revision of Schutzian phenomenology in that it shakes "man free . . . of the fictions that he himself has constructed quite unselfconsciously into an 'everyday reality' that in fact serves to imprison him and manipulate him."[52] Those like Friedrichs, and many others, whose work stems from a tradition different from that of the creative sociologies, feel strongly the "one-sidedness" of these approaches and welcome attempts at synthesis. Although published in 1939, Robert S. Lynd's remarks parallel closely the views of present-day commentators:

> While the understanding of a culture trait or a complex of traits . . . must include full analysis and understanding of the trait or traits *as the culture is wont to view them*, analysis and the hypotheses that evoke analysis must not stop there; the hypothesis . . . must also wrench analysis clear of the popular pattern of acceptance and rejection and set the phenomenon under study in a wider context of relationship and meaning. . . . It is the failure . . . in current research to take the . . . step of seeing an institutional area in relation to other known things, a wider scheme, that is here questioned.[53]

The creative sociologies, with their emphasis on the importance of intersubjectivity, of the social interaction from which social reality is generated and created, are viewed by critics as offering only a partial description of society. The criticism is couched in more ways than one: There are those who say that the divisions in sociology are not merely between the "positivists" and the "humanists" but, rather, that the difference is one of scope. Helmut Wagner, for instance, suggests that the "fallacy of displaced scope" is committed whenever a theorist assumes that a framework based on microsociological considerations fits macrosociological considerations, and vice versa. Symbolic interactionists, he says, claim that, from their viewpoint, one can make the leap from small interactions to the larger society; society is an interactional network tied together by symbolic communication—but, Wagner intimates, the declaration is unsupported by demonstration.[54] Others suggest that the creative sociologies complement rather than replace the positivistic approach to research; they sensitize positivistic sociology to major aspects of social reality that might otherwise be neglected, but neither approach is complete in itself.[55] While admitting the usefulness of phenomenology as a starting point in explaining the meaning of action, Robert Bierstedt feels that if it leads only to the view that society emanates from intersubjective processes and obscures, or clouds, the reality of the exteriority of the society and the constraints society imposes upon human beings, then it leaves something wanting.[56] Yet, as soon as a synthesis is attempted between the situationalists and the positivists, the synthesis ends up in the framework of the positivists, just as does Berger and Luckmann's sociology of knowledge.[57]

Some creative sociologists deny that there is such a thing as a "microsociology" separate from a "macrosociology." Even though Erving Goffman and Harold Garfinkel have stated that they are microsociologists, or microecologists, Stanford Lyman sees this as a misreading of the nature and the significance of their own work, saying, at the seventieth annual meeting of the American Sociological Association, that it behooves others to rescue that work for what it really is! [58] The distinction between micro and macro sociology, Lyman suggests, is rooted in a paradigm that the "new" sociologies are supposed to have overturned—structural functionalism—and when subjected to careful, critical scrutiny, falls quickly apart. What, asks Lyman, is a macrosociological unit? How small does a sociological unit have to be before it becomes designated microsociological? Most people would agree that if the unit studied comprised two persons, it would be a microsociological unit. But consider, suggests Lyman, if it were a sociological analysis of the President of the United States and his encounter with the Premier of the Soviet Union. Would the study then be called micro- or macroanalysis?

Far more important than this quibbling over the size of the sociological unit and whether the gap between the small group and the larger society can be bridged, is the question of the nature of the sociologies of the "new wave." It is not that these creative sociologies deal with the small scale and the trivial while structural functionalists and others are concerned with the "big problems and the big issues." What ethnomethodologists and phenomenologists of all stripes are doing, says Lyman, is questioning the logic that underlies most of Western social science and Western philosophy. Lyman terms as "the Aristotelian thesis" the belief that everything is moving on, changing slowly, inexorably, and teleologically, to its appointed end, and that the task of science is to discover the direction, nature, and process of the change. The Aristotelian thesis, Lyman intimates, pervades the thinking of laymen as well as academicians and scientists, and the problem that everyone has to face is that, instead of things moving on and changing slowly, inexorably, and teleologically, a welter of *events* interferes with the process. What creative sociologists have been trying to do is to "get at the qualifications that human beings introduce to account for the recalcitrance of events in the face of the hypothesized process." [59] Whether the social unit studied is big or small, *accounts* are given to help maintain the belief that the social world is orderly, and moving slowly on its preordained path.

A synthesis, then, of the creative sociologies with the positivistic, or naturalistic, or structuralist, or social system sociologies, is seen by Lyman, and by most other sociologists working from within an interpretive framework, as neither useful nor, indeed, as possible. The impossibility of synthesis is also seen by Alan Dawe, who declares that two distinct sociologies exist side by side, each grounded in diametrically opposed concerns. The "social action" theorists stress autonomous man, able to realize full potential and to create a truly human social order when freed from external constraints, while the "social system" theorists stress that society is prior to its participants and that external constraints are of paramount necessity for social stability.[60] The values underlying these two sociologies are in conflict at every level.

In his autobiography, Bertrand Russell wrote that diversity is essential, in spite of the fact that it precludes universal acceptance of a single gospel. What we have seen in examining the criticisms and defenses of the creative sociologies is a considerable diversity of opinion, the differences often being based less on purely objective and "scientific" grounds than upon personal values and beliefs in the nature of human beings and society. Cynics abound, both within and without the creative sociologies, as do believers in the inherent goodness and kindness of humanity. Values cross the boundaries between sociological approaches, frequently making difficult the drawing of distinct lines between them.

Academic disciplines grow through diversity; lively debates keep scholars alert to new possibilities. Dialogue is necessary if knowledge is to be enriched— but dialogue is valuable only if each party to the exchange hears, and understands, what the other is saying.

One never steps in the same river twice.

        —HERACLITUS

CHAPTER SEVEN

The River Flows on

EACH OF OUR EXPERIENCES affects us in some way. Events may influence us dramatically, changing the direction of our thinking and our plans, but more often the influences are barely perceptible. We learn, we grow, we change, slowly but inexorably, from day to day. The creative sociologies view "truth" not as a fixed entity but as evolving, changing with the experiences of human beings as they live together and negotiate their reality. Meaning, therefore, is not easily replicable in the sense that the physical sciences demand replicability. The river is not the same for each person who steps into it. Yet some things *are* the same. To maintain the analogy, the water in the river keeps moving but it flows in a direction determined by the push and pull of nature. Even though the direction of the flow can be diverted, the river is not likely to flow away from the sea. Similarly, although human beings change day by day, they remember what they were, and where they have been, and what they have seen. Even though the memory becomes distorted with time and situation, the past is part of the present. To understand meaning, one must take the past into account. The objective present provides us with too little information to understand the full richness of the content of meaning.

The present, though, can provide us with enough information to discern recurring patterns of interaction: invariables. Ethnomethodologists are not concerned with past events, biographies, or histories as are phenomenologists, symbolic interactionists, and other creative sociologists. Their concern is with the *processes* by which meaning is attained in the situation. While existentialists and absurdists—the dramatists, especially—are inclined to show the ways in which words, clichés, *hide* meaning, ethnomethodologists turn toward the study of language use to show how a sense of meaning is attained. The contradiction is more apparent than real, for although ethnomethodologists study words to discover how people make sense of them, they recognize, as do other creative sociologists, that this is only a *seeming* sense but that the seeming sense provides guidelines for action, or, to use Harold Garfinkel's phrase, for all practical purposes.

While there are differences between, among, and within the creative sociologies, they all belong together in their resistance to using the methods of the natural sciences in studying social phenomena. Underlying them all is the assumption that human beings are different from the subject matter of other sciences in that they create, or construct, their social reality in interaction. They are joined in their opposition to sociological approaches that assume that human behavior is determined by social structure. Sociology is not the only discipline experiencing schisms of this kind. It is well known that the field of psychology is sharply divided between "humanists" and clinical or experimental psychologists,[1] but it is, perhaps, less commonly known that similar differences divide anthropologists and historians of science, as well as those in other disciplines, including some of the natural sciences. In the history of science, the debate is between the "internalists" and the "externalists." The question concerns whether the origin and growth of science depend upon factors external to the substance of science itself, such as social and economic influences, or whether scientific ideas have a life of their own, insulated from the general cultural, economic, and social state of a nation or a community of nations.[2]

Anthropology, like sociology, has been undergoing a period of innovation influenced by the cognitive anthropologists, the "new ethnographers." The debate over ethnoscience within the field has matched that within sociology regarding the usefulness and the paradigmatic novelty of ethnomethodology. Discussion now seems to be waning, one writer beginning his article with the question, "What ever happened to ethnoscience?"[3] As was noted earlier, ethnomethodologists have been considerably influenced by ethnoscientists but have recognized the limitations of their approach and have been careful to avoid its pitfalls.[4] The new ethnographers seemed unable to move beyond the analysis of simplified semantic domains in their assumption that each culture can be understood only by analyzing the meanings of words as defined by those of that culture. The search for cultural meanings becomes endless and, ultimately, of little value, according to the current approach of the "transformationalists," who, following Chomsky, seek a universal language design—invariant properties underlying all languages.[5] The search for "invariants" occupies ethnomethodologists, too, and leads them away from the concept of "meaning."

Content is of little interest, but the forms in which that content is conveyed assume crucial importance.

Does that mean that ethnomethodologists are not interested in the "social" and are, therefore, not sociologists? The computer is among their major aides—does this concession to the use of the tools of the "hard" sciences mean that they are "positivists" and are not interested in human beings as *human* beings? My own understanding is that, although they may appear to lack interest in the concept of meaning, in the long run their work is directed toward understanding social interaction and the structuring of social reality through language use. The findings of their painstaking "objective" analyses of naturally occurring conversations between and among groups of two or a few persons build bridges toward a clearer comprehension of the ways in which the larger society is created and sustained. The findings of the studies of male and female patterns of dominance and submission, for instance, are not confined to small groups but are applicable to the larger society where similar power relationships can be seen to prevail.[6] The division of labor involved in conversations between men and women reflects the division of labor in the world of work and, ultimately, mirrors the scope of opportunities open to women for high level decision-making positions. Close study of the family setting differs little from study of larger organizations and though we may treat relationships in the "micro" and "macro" social settings as of different quality and dimension, the distinction is an analytical one. It may be that these so-called microsociologies, or "contextual sociologies," will be able to explain social change on a national, or international, scale more plausibly than can structural theories. Examinations of newly developing or "modernizing" nations have demonstrated that few of these countries have proceeded according to predictions drawn from conventional theory. It may be more valuable to examine change in a developing area from the viewpoint of the members themselves rather than to attempt to preimpose a theory upon the situation.[7]

It has long been held that two kinds of sociology coexist within the discipline. Helmut Wagner has proposed that the differences between sociological approaches are a matter of the scope, of the scale, of the entity examined.[8] With the newer work of the ethnomethodologists, however, the unbridged gap Wagner posits between micro and macro sociological units becomes far less problematic. According to Alan Dawe, the two sociologies within the field are a sociology of social action and a sociology of social system.[9] These two approaches, he says, are grounded in dramatically opposed concerns with two central problems, those of *order* and *control,* the one viewing man as needing to be kept in line, constrained, the other seeing human beings as autonomous, able to create a truly human society only when freed from external constraints. Underlying each are sets of biases, of values, making impossible value-neutral research and interpretation. Each presents a doctrine, a social philosophy, as well as a system of concepts or of general propositions.

While I agree with Dawe that value-free science, whether that science be social or natural, is a myth, after perusing the hundreds of writings that provide the background information for this book, I am no longer convinced that the dichotomy is as clear-cut as either he, or I, have suggested. Such a dichotomy seems to imply that the field is divided into conservatives and liberals, or humanists and anti-humanists, or, even good guys and bad guys, along the same lines as "subjectivists" and "objectivists." It seems to me, now, that this division is too simple and that radicals, revolutionaries, liberals, and conservatives, are to be found within both camps. Radicals among the structuralists accuse the creative sociologies of conservatism; radicals among the creative sociologies level the same accusation against the structuralists.

The distinctions between the two sociologies are, perhaps, not entirely matters of scope or of political philosophy, but are, rather, differences of focus. The one sees society from the outside in, the other from the inside out. Both are valuable, but the choice of focus may depend less upon personal philosophy than upon indoctrination into certain ways of thinking early in one's academic career. Indoctrination is perhaps a strong word to use when referring to the academy that purportedly aims to provide opportunities for students to learn of many points of view and to choose freely among them. I draw upon Liam Hudson for the use of the term here,[10] for when I read his description of his training in psychology, I realized that my own educational experience in America was similar in some ways to his training in psychology in English universities. Hudson was offered only one approach to psychology, the experimental, and during his years in the university he learned nothing about other ways of viewing human behavior. He learned a way to think, and found it difficult, if not impossible, to consider other ways of thinking. The works of phenomenological psychologists and existentialists still remain difficult for him to read. He finds, simply, that they make little sense. Those who are students in psychology departments that are wholly clinical or experimental—and there are such departments, just as there are economics departments that teach only supply-and-demand economics and history departments that leave women out of history—

must similarly become biased in their thinking. One rejects "evidence" from other points of view, even before hearing it.

In my own case, my introduction to sociology was through phenomenological thinkers, who, in addition, were inspiring and lively lecturers. As mine was a tiny undergraduate department, I was relatively untouched by structural functionalism and other theoretical approaches. In graduate school, however, there were no creative sociologists, only, at that time, solidly "objective" quantitatively oriented theorists and researchers. Although I passed my qualifying examinations without difficulty, I recall that my reference to R. D. Laing and existentialism in answering one of the questions was rejected out of hand as being without value. Existential ideas had certainly not been promoted, or encouraged, during my graduate training. One of my fellow graduate students, who, as an undergraduate, had studied at Berkeley with Herbert Blumer, was so tormented by his fellows that he disappeared from the campus, never to be seen again; symbolic interaction was not to be taken seriously. I fared somewhat better than he for I kept hidden my undergraduate training in the phenomenological approaches. That undergraduate training had left me with much to learn in graduate school, having demanded courses neither in research methodology nor in statistics. I set about learning it and learned it well, gaining, thereby, a decent exposure to previously neglected aspects of sociology. But my intellectual commitment was to those ideas with which I had first been introduced to sociology, and I find myself increasingly drawn back to them.

In preparing this book so that others might be introduced to this way of sociological seeing, I've indicated that I lean toward the creative sociologies, but it is also clear that, in the writing, I have changed my own thinking in some ways. Learning continues, change continues. . . .

Notes

CHAPTER ONE: WHY "CREATIVE" SOCIOLOGY?

1. George A. Lundberg, "The Postulates of Science and Their Implications for Sociology," p. 47.

2. Max Weber, *The Theory of Social and Economic Organization,* p. 88.

3. Émile Durkheim, *The Rules of Sociological Method.*

4. Jean-Paul Sartre, *Existentialism and Human Emotions,* p. 23.

5. See Alan Dawe, "The Two Sociologies," for a discussion of the "problem of order" versus the "problem of control," and Maurice Natanson, ed., *Philosophy of the Social Sciences,* among others, for opposing views in the social sciences.

6. Paul Tillich, *Theology of Culture,* p. 46.

7. See Robert W. Friedrichs, *A Sociology of Sociology,* especially chapter 11.

8. The current debate among Marxist sociologists (see Horton, 1972, and Keller, 1974) seems to stem, at least in part, from this dichotomy. Simply put, it appears that Marx's statement that existence determines consciousness, but that consciousness also determines existence, has been torn into two parts, one part only being defended by each side.

9. For a useful introduction to the topic of *Verstehen* see Marcello Truzzi, ed., *Verstehen: Subjective Understanding in the Social Sciences.*

10. Some ethnomethodological research can be seen to be based on some other foundation than phenomenology. Whether such an ethnomethodology can be included as a "creative" sociology is a matter which will be discussed in chapter 2.

11. For a profound description of the various phenomenologies, see Maurice Roche, *Phenomenology, Language, and the Social Sciences,* which includes an unusually extensive and scholarly bibliography.

12. Roger Jehenson, "Social Construction of Reality and Social Distribution of Knowledge in Formal Organizations."

13. Joseph Kockelmans, ed., *Phenomenology,* especially the introduction.

14. See Herbert Spiegelberg's scholarly two-volume work, *The Phenomenological Movement: A Historical Introduction.*

15. Ibid., pp. 78–79.

16. Ibid., part five.

17. John Wild, *Existence and the World of Freedom,* pp. 72–73.

18. For discussion of "reduction," see the introduction by Helmut R. Wagner to Alfred Schutz, *On Phenomenology and Social Relations.*

19. See Alfred Schutz, "The Stranger: An Essay in Social Psychology."

20. Wild, *World of Freedom.*

21. See Richard Schmitt, "In Search of Phenomenology."

22. Edmund Husserl, *Ideas: Pure Phenomenology,* p. 189.

23. Weber, *Social and Economic Organization.*

24. Max Weber, *The Protestant Ethic and the Spirit of Capitalism.*

25. This short description of Schutz's life draws from George Walsh's introduction to Alfred Schutz, *The Phenomenology of the Social World,* and from Thomas Luckmann's preface to Alfred Schutz and Thomas Luckmann, *The Structures of the Life-World.*

26. Loosely translated as "the meaning (or meaningful) construction of the social world" or, as in the Walsh and Lehnert translation, *The Phenomenology of the Social World.*

27. Schutz, *Phenomenology of the Social World,* p. 90.

28. For further clarification of concepts in this section see Schutz, "The Stranger."

29. This section draws heavily from Alfred Schutz, "Concept and Theory Formation in the Social Sciences," and "Common-Sense and Scientific Interpretation of Human Action."

30. For detailed information about provinces of reality, see especially Alfred Schutz, "The Stratifications of the Life-World," chapter 2 in *The Structures of the Life-World.*

31. Some works of Søren Kierkegaard include *Concluding Unscientific Postscript* and *Either/or; A Fragment of Life.* See also John Wild, *World of Freedom,* pp. 19–20.

32. See chapter 1 of Stanford M. Lyman and Marvin B. Scott, *A Sociology of the Absurd.* Although these authors are basically existential-phenomenological in their approach, they select from all the creative sociologies presented in this chapter, especially the neo-symbolic interactionism of Erving Goffman. Their work illustrates, as does this chapter, the convergences between and among these sociologies. Discussion of divergences will be presented in the following chapter of this book.

33. See Georg Simmel, "The Adventure."

34. Lyman and Scott, *Sociology of the Absurd,* p. 27.

35. Peter L. Berger and Thomas Luckmann, *The Social Construction of Reality,* p. 104 and throughout.

36. Ibid., p. 130.

37. The sociology of knowledge of Berger and Luckmann, although clearly in the "creative" camp, also draws from the social factism of Émile Durkheim as well as from the sociology of knowledge of Marx. Chapter 2 of this volume will attend to the variations among the sociological approaches discussed in this chapter.

38. Among the writings of Marx that emphasize the creative aspect of human beings, see especially his "Theses on Feuerbach," the *Economic and Philosophical Manuscripts of 1844,* and throughout Karl Marx and Frederick Engels, *The German Ideology.*

39. To deal fully with the ways in which Marxist thought and phenomenological philosophy converge and diverge would require more discussion than is called for by the scope of these brief introductions. For a deeper investigation of the topic, see Phillip Bosserman, *Dialectical Sociology: An Analysis of the Sociology of George Gurvitch;* Fred R. Dallmayr, "Phenomenology and Marxism: A Salute to Enzo Paci"; Maurice Merleau-Ponty, *Sense and Non-Sense* and *The Primacy of Perception;* John O'Neill, *Perception, Expres-*

sion, and History: The Social Phenomenology of Maurice Merleau-Ponty; and Enzo Paci, *The Function of the Sciences and the Meaning of Man.*

40. Jerome G. Manis and Bernard N. Meltzer, eds., *Symbolic Interaction: A Reader in Social Psychology,* p. 1.

41. W. I. Thomas, *The Unadjusted Girl.*

42. W. I. Thomas, *The Child in America,* cited in Edmund H. Volkart, ed., *Social Behavior and Personality,* p. 81.

43. The four major collections of lectures and lecture notes were published as: *G. H. Mead, The Philosophy of the Present* (1932); *Mind, Self, and Society* (1934); *Movements of Thought in the Nineteenth Century* (1936); and *Philosophy of the Act* (1938). A collection of works published during his lifetime is to be found in *Mead: Selected Writings.*

44. William James, *Psychology,* p. 176.

45. Charles Horton Cooley, *Human Nature and the Social Order,* p. 121.

46. Mead, *Mind, Self and Society,* p. 47.

47. Herbert Blumer, *Symbolic Interactionism: Perspective and Method;* "Commentary and Debate: Sociological Implications of the Thought of George Herbert Mead"; "Society as Symbolic Interaction"; and "What is Wrong with Social Theory?"

48. Blumer, *Symbolic Interactionism,* p. 23.

49. Ibid., p. 39.

50. Not all symbolic interactionists are as opposed to the methodologies of the natural sciences as is Blumer. Manford Kuhn's "self theory" is a variant of the Meadian tradition that does attempt to operationalize and measure the concepts of symbolic interaction theory in ways other than the *verstehende* approach of Blumer. Kuhn is probably best known for the development of the Twenty Statements Test, which asks respondents to answer, in up to twenty statements, the question "Who am I?" The answer to the question, and others similar to it, represents a definition of the self of the respondent, a self that is considered to determine the person's actions. This approach stresses the *structure* of the self rather than its processual character. See Manford H. Kuhn and Thomas S. Mc-Partland, "An Empirical Investigation of Self-Attitude."

51. Cited in Manford H. Kuhn, "Major Trends in Symbolic Interaction Theory in the Past Twenty-Five Years."

52. Mirra Komarovsky, *Women in the Modern World: Their Education and Their Dilemmas.*

53. Monica B. Morris, " 'I Enjoy Being a Girl': The Persistence of Stereotypic Views of Sex Roles."

54. Robert Rosenthal and Lenore Jacobson, "Teachers' Expectancies: Determinants of Pupils' IQ Gains."

55. See, for instance, Sarane S. Boocock, *An Introduction to the Sociology of Education,* pp. 136–38.

56. Joseph A. Kahl, "Educational and Occupational Aspirations of 'Common Man' Boys."

57. William Peters, *A Class Divided.*

58. Helen B. Andelin, *Fascinating Womanhood,* p. 7.

59. Ibid., p. 164.

60. John W. Kinch, "A Formalized Theory of Self-Concept." The story may be apocryphal, says Kinch, but it makes the point nicely.

61. Howard S. Becker, *Outsiders*, pp. 9–13.

62. Erving Goffman, *Frame Analysis*, pp. 1 and 124.

63. Lyman and Scott, *Sociology of the Absurd*, chapter 1 and throughout.

64. For instance, Garfinkel's paper "Studies of the Routine Grounds of Everyday Activities," which appears as chapter 2 in his 1967 book, was published in *Social Problems* 11 (Winter 1964), 225–50; Aaron V. Cicourel and John I. Kitsuse's book, *The Educational Decision Makers*, which uses an ethnomethodological approach, was published in 1963.

65. Lyman and Scott, *Sociology of the Absurd*, chapter 1.

66. Harold Garfinkel, *Studies in Ethnomethodology*, p. 11.

67. Ibid.

68. Harold Pinter, *The Caretaker and the Dumb Waiter*, pp. 97–98.

69. For the concept "gloss," see Harold Garfinkel and Harvey Sacks, "On Formal Structures of Practical Action."

70. Garfinkel, *Studies in Ethnomethodology*, chapter 1.

71. An article which attempts this grouping is Paul Attewell, "Ethnomethodology Since Garfinkel." Attewell is not entirely sympathetic toward ethnomethodology but provides some useful categorizations. Differences within ethnomethodology are considered in chapter 2 of this volume.

72. See chapters 2 and 4 of this book.

73. Comments by Garfinkel at the American Sociological Association meetings in Montreal, August 1974.

74. Don Zimmerman, in a talk given at the University of Southern California, May 1971.

75. See Emanuel A. Schegloff and Harvey Sacks, "Opening Up Closings," and Harvey Sacks, Emanuel A. Schegloff, and Gail Jefferson, "A Simplest Systematics for the Organization of Turn-Taking for Conversation." Other studies include D. Lawrence Wieder, "Telling the Code," a study of a half-way house for narcotic-addict felons on parole, and David Sudnow, *Passing On: The Social Organization of Dying*, a study of death and dying in a hospital setting. See also Arlene Kaplan Daniels, "The Social Construction of Military Psychiatric Diagnoses," in Hans Peter Dreitzel, ed., *Recent Sociology No. 2* pp. 182–205; and Aaron V. Cicourel, *The Social Organization of Juvenile Justice*.

CHAPTER TWO: DISTINCTIONS AMONG, BETWEEN, AND WITHIN THE CREATIVE SOCIOLOGIES

1. James M. Edie, *Phenomenology in America*, p. 14.

2. Jack D. Douglas, "Understanding Everyday Life," in Jack D. Douglas (ed.), *Understanding Everyday Life*, p. 43.

3. John D. Wild, *Existence and the World of Freedom*, pp. 72–73.

4. Edward A. Tiryakian, "Existential Phenomenology and the Sociological Tradition"; Peter L. Berger, "On Existential Phenomenology and Sociology (II)."

5. See chapter 1.

6. See Jacqueline Johnson, "A Phenomenological Alternative to the Analysis of Sex Role Conflict," for an interesting application of the ideas presented in this section.

7. William Peters, *A Class Divided.*

8. Helmut R. Wagner, "Signs, Symbols, and Interaction Theory."

9. Nicholas C. Mullins, *Theories and Theory Groups in Contemporary Sociology,* chapter 8.

10. Don H. Zimmerman and Thomas P. Wilson, "Prospects for Experimental Studies of Meaning-Structures."

11. George Psathas, "Ethnomethodology as a Phenomenological Approach."

12. See Helmut R. Wagner, "Displacement of Scope: A Problem of the Relationship between Small-scale and Large-scale Sociological Theories," and Herbert Blumer, "Society as Symbolic Interaction."

13. See Don H. Zimmerman and D. Lawrence Wieder, "Ethnomethodology and the Problem of Order: Comment on Denzin."

14. See Aaron V. Cicourel and John I. Kitsuse, *The Educational Decision Makers;* Aaron V. Cicourel, *The Social Organization of Juvenile Justice;* and Jerry Jacobs, "A Phenomenological Study of Suicide Notes."

15. W. I. Thomas, *The Unadjusted Girl;* Herbert Blumer, *Symbolic Interactionism: Perspective and Method* and "Commentary and Debate: Sociological Implications of the Thought of George Herbert Mead."

16. Virginia L. Oleson and Elvi W. Whittaker, *The Silent Language: A Study in the Social Psychology of Professional Socialization.*

17. Melvin Pollner, "Sociological and Common-Sense Models of the Labelling Process."

18. Howard S. Becker, *Outsiders.*

19. See the debate between Norman K. Denzin, "Symbolic Interactionism and Ethnomethodology: A Proposed Synthesis," and Zimmerman and Wieder, "Ethnomethodology and the Problem of Order." Both may be found in Douglas, *Understanding Everyday Life.*

20. It should be noted that other important schools of social-psychology and social interaction exist and flourish within sociology: the field theory of Kurt Lewin and Leon Festinger, exchange theory of George C. Homans and John W. Thibaut and Harold H. Kelly, among others. The route to ethnomethodology, however, is traced through the Chicago tradition, rather than through these other approaches. For more extensive discussion of the history and developments of symbolic interaction, see Mullins, *Theories and Theory Groups,* chapter 4; Bernard N. Meltzer and John W. Petras, "The Chicago and Iowa Schools of Symbolic Interactionism," in Jerome G. Manis and Bernard N. Meltzer, eds., *Symbolic Interaction,* pp. 43–57; and Larry T. Reynolds et al., "The 'Self' in Symbolic Interaction Theory: An Examination of the Social Sources of Conceptual Diversity."

21. See Herbert Blumer, "What is Wrong with Social Theory?"

22. From Manford Kuhn, "Lectures on the Self," cited in Meltzer and Petras, "The Chicago and Iowa Schools," p. 49.

23. See Paul Attewell, "Ethnomethodology Since Garfinkel," p. 184.

24. Thomas, *The Unadjusted Girl,* p. 42.

25. Harvey Sacks, mimeographed lecture notes, May 22, 1968.

26. Harvey Sacks, Emanuel A. Schegloff, and Gail Jefferson, "A Simplest Systematics for the Organization of Turn-Taking for Conversation"; Matthew Speier, "Some Conversational Problems for Interactional Analysis."

27. Sacks, Schegloff, and Jefferson, "A Simplest Systematics."

28. Speier, "Some Conversational Problems," p. 398.

29. Aaron V. Cicourel, *Cognitive Sociology.* This book comprises a collection of five papers published in various journals and books between 1970 and 1972.

30. See Attewell, "Ethnomethodology since Garfinkel" for various ethnomethodologists' adjustments to the notion of invariance.

31. Don H. Zimmerman and Melvin Pollner, "The Everyday World as a Phenomenon."

32. Ibid., p. 95.

33. Peter McHugh, *Defining the Situation.*

34. Stephen Mennell, *Sociological Theory: Uses and Unities,* p. 50.

35. See Peter L. Berger and Thomas Luckmann, *The Social Construction of Reality,* p. 142, and chapter 1 of this book.

36. Peter L. Berger, *The Sacred Canopy,* chapter 4.

37. For a carefully reasoned view of this deficiency in Berger and Luckmann's theory, see William M. Lafferty, "Externalization and Dialectics: Taking the Brackets off Berger and Luckmann's Sociology of Knowledge." American Sociological Association, San Francisco, August 1975.

38. Stanford M. Lyman and Marvin B. Scott, *A Sociology of the Absurd,* pp. 4, 22, and 23.

39. See Robert W. Friedrichs, *A Sociology of Sociology;* Alvin W. Gouldner, *The Coming Crisis in Western Sociology;* Mullins, *Theory and Theory Groups;* George Ritzer, *Sociology: A Multiple Paradigm Science.*

40. Some of the final section of this chapter appeared in Monica B. Morris, " 'Creative Sociology': Conservative or Revolutionary?"

41. Randall Collins and Michael Makowsky, *The Discovery of Society.*

42. Stanislav Andreski, *Social Sciences as Sorcery.*

43. Tiryakian, "Existential Phenomenology," cited in Andreski.

44. John H. Goldthorpe, "Review Article: A Revolution in Sociology?"

45. Zimmerman and Pollner, "The Everyday World." See the section in this chapter on the differences between ethnomethodology and symbolic interaction for explanation of this "confounding."

46. Zimmerman and Pollner, "The Everyday World," cited in John H. Goldthorpe, "Review Article," p. 449.

47. It seems that Goldthorpe is confused by the indexicality/invariance paradox within ethnomethodology.

48. Zimmerman and Wieder, "Problem of Order," cited in Goldthorpe.

49. Doug Benson, "Critical Note: A Revolution in Sociology."

50. John H. Goldthorpe, "Correspondence: A Rejoinder to Benson."

51. Z. Bauman, "On the Philosophical Status of Ethnomethodology," p. 20.

52. Ibid., p. 21.

53. Mullins, *Theories and Theory Groups.*

54. Jeff Coulter, "Language and the Conceptualization of Meaning."

55. Attewell, "Ethnomethodology Since Garfinkel."

56. Psathas, "Ethnomethodology as a Phenomenological Approach."

CHAPTER THREE: "THE DRAMA IS IN US, AND WE ARE THE DRAMA"

1. Ronald Gaskell, in *Drama and Reality: The European Theatre since Ibsen,* presents *three* perspectives in the theater: naturalistic, subjective, and religious. This excellent book is recommended for a detailed elaboration of these categories.

2. Ernst Bloch, *Man on His Own,* pp. 7–18.

3. Erving Goffman, *Behavior in Public Places.*

4. Pirandello, *Six Characters in Search of an Author,* in *Naked Masks,* p. 224.

5. Jessie Bernard, *The Future of Marriage.*

6. Harold Pinter, "Writing for the Theatre."

7. Ibid.

8. Samuel Beckett, *Waiting for Godot,* p. 23.

9. I am indebted to Grace Holden, Ann Goldschmidt, and Steve Thompson, students in Social Interaction, a Pomona College course, for their profound sociological analyses of several dramas of the absurd. Some of their insights are scattered throughout this chapter.

10. Eugène Ionesco, *Notes and Counter Notes,* pp. 109–110.

11. Ibid., p. 227.

12. Beckett, *Waiting for Godot,* pp. 41–42.

13. Norman O. Brown, quoted in a lecture given at Pomona College by Robert N. Bellah.

14. William H. Form, "Auto Workers and Their Machines: A Study of Work, Factory, and Job Satisfaction in Four Countries."

15. See Ely Chinoy, *The Automobile Worker and the American Dream,* pp. 94–95.

16. Samuel Beckett, *Proust,* p. 8.

17. Beckett, *Waiting for Godot,* p. 27.

18. A considerable literature on "the empty nest" period is available. See, among others: Pauline Bart, "Depression in Middle-Aged Women: Some Sociocultural Factors"; Barbara R. Fried, *The Middle Age Crisis;* Bernice L. Neugarten, ed., *Middle Age and Aging.*

19. Leonard Cabell Pronko, *Theater East and West.*

20. Robert Kemp, *Le Monde,* June 27, 1957, cited in Pronko, *Theater,* p. 106.

21. Pronko, *Theater,* p. 108.

22. Martin Esslin, *The Theatre of the Absurd,* p. 29.

23. Beckett, *Proust,* cited in Esslin, p. 29.

24. "A Conversation (Pause)," from an interview with Harold Pinter by Mel Gusson. Reprinted from the *New York Times* in *Center Monthly* 6 (May 1972).

25. Pronko, *Theater,* p. 108.

26. Steven L. Morris, *"Night:* Commentary," unpublished paper.

27. Cited in Pronko, *Theater,* p. 68.

28. Maurice Merleau-Ponty, *Sense and Non-Sense,* translator's introduction.

29. Robert W. Friedrichs, *A Sociology of Sociology.*

30. Kurt Vonnegut, Jr., *Wampeters, Foma, and Granfalloons.*

31. Eugène Ionesco, *The Bald Soprano,* in *Four Plays,* pp. 34–36, passim.

32. Erving Goffman, *Behavior in Public Places.*

33. Paraphrased from Gaskell, *Drama and Reality,* p. 122.

34. See Stanford W. Lyman and Marvin B. Scott, "Accounts," in *A Sociology of the Absurd.*

35. Gaskell, *Drama and Reality,* p. 123.

36. Glenn A. Goodwin, "On Transcending the Absurd: An Inquiry in the Sociology of Meaning."

37. Merleau-Ponty, *Sense and Non-Sense,* translator's introduction.

38. See chapter 1 for an explanation of "garfinkeling."

39. Ruby Cohn, cited in Pronko, *Theater,* p. 108.

40. Lyman and Scott, *Sociology of the Absurd,* p. 1.

CHAPTER FOUR: LANGUAGE AND THE STRUCTURE OF DAILY LIFE

1. "It's a Sin to Tell a Lie." Lyrics by Billy Mayhew (Bregman, Voco, and Cohn, Inc., 1933).

2. T. S. Eliot, "Burnt Norton," *Four Quartets.*

3. *Los Angeles Times,* Saturday, August 16, 1975.

4. Remarks at the American Sociological Association Meetings, August 1975, San Francisco.

5. Peter Berger, *The Sacred Canopy,* pp. 16–17.

6. Samuel Beckett, *Endgame,* p. 58.

7. J. L. Austin, *Philosophical Papers,* p. 182.

8. Ibid., p. 104.

9. See Aaron V. Cicourel, "The Acquisition of Social Structure: Toward a Developmental Sociology of Language and Meaning," and "Interpretive Procedures and Normative Rules in the Negotiation of Status and Role," as well as chapters 1 and 2 in *Cognitive Sociology.*

10. For a clear introduction to Chomsky's theory, see John Lyons, *Noam Chomsky.*

11. Don E. Zimmerman and Melvin Pollner, "The Everyday World as Phenomenon."

12. Cicourel, "Interpretive Procedures."

13. Karl Mannheim, *Essays on the Sociology of Knowledge,* p. 47.

14. Alfred Schutz, *Collected Papers,* vol. 2, pp. 29–30.

15. Charles O. Frake, "Notes on Queries in Ethnography."

16. Harold C. Conklin, "Lexicographical Treatment of Folk Taxonomies."

17. Charles O. Frake, "How to Ask for a Drink in Subanun."

18. Charles O. Frake, "Struck by Speech: The Yakan Concept of Litigation."

19. Frake, "Notes on Queries."

20. D. Lawrence Wieder, "On Meaning by Rule."

21. Don H. Zimmerman and D. Lawrence Wieder, "Ethnomethodology and the Problem of Order: Comment on Denzin."

22. Quotation from Stanford M. Lyman and Marvin B. Scott, *A Sociology of the Absurd,* p. 111.

23. Donald W. Ball, "Toward a Sociology of Telephones and Telephoners."

24. Emanuel A. Schegloff, "Sequencing in Conversational Openings;" Emanuel A. Schegloff and Harvey Sacks, "Opening Up Closings."

25. Schegloff, "Sequencing."

26. Harvey Sacks, mimeographed lectures, University of California, 1966.

27. Harvey Sacks, Emanuel A. Schegloff, and Gail Jefferson, "A Simplest Systematics for the Organization of Turn-Taking for Conversation."

28. David Sudnow, *Passing On: The Social Organization of Dying,* pp. 148–152.

29. Ibid., p. 150.

30. Joan P. Emerson, "Behavior in Private Places: Sustaining Definitions of Reality in a Gynecological Examination."

31. Ibid., p. 82.

32. Ibid., p. 90.

33. Sam Burns, "Making the World Available: Ordinary Accounting Practices in Community Development Field Work"; and John H. Newman, "From Space to Place: Locating a Rural Drug Program."

34. See Marvin B. Scott and Stanford M. Lyman, "Accounts," in Lyman and Scott, *Sociology of the Absurd,* pp. 111–143; John P. Hewitt and Randall Stokes, "Disclaimers."

35. See Austin, *Philosophical Papers;* Gresham M. Sykes and David Matza, "Techniques of Neutralization."

36. Monica B. Morris, "Excuses, Justifications, and Evasions: How Newspaper Editors Account for Their Coverage of a Social Movement."

37. Monica B. Morris, "The Public Definition of a Social Movement: Women's Liberation," and "Newspapers and the New Feminists: Black-Out as Social Control."

38. Pamela M. Fishman, "Interaction: The Work Women Do"; Candace West and Don H. Zimmerman, "Women's Place in Conversation: Reflections on Adult-Child Interactions."

39. Sacks, Schegloff, and Jefferson, "A Simplest Systematics."

40. See Herbert Blumer, "Society as Symbolic Interaction"; Norman K. Denzin, "Symbolic Interactionism and Ethnomethodology: A Proposed Synthesis."

41. Aaron V. Cicourel, *The Social Organization of Juvenile Justice;* Aaron V. Cicourel and John I. Kitsuse, *The Educational Decision Makers.*

42. Cicourel, *Juvenile Justice,* pp. 112–113 and throughout chapter 4.

43. Ibid., pp. 163–164.

44. Cicourel and Kitsuse, *Educational Decision Makers.*

45. Ibid., p. 11.

46. See Ralph H. Turner, "Sponsored and Contest Mobility and the School System," for this discussion.

CHAPTER FIVE: THE SOCIAL MEANING OF AGING

1. Elaine Cumming and William Henry, *Growing Old*. The theory of disengagement has undergone considerable modification and refinement since its formulation in 1961.

2. Bernice L. Neugarten and Joan W. Moore, "The Changing Age Status System."

3. See, for instance, Lenore J. Weitzman, et al., "Sex-Role Socialization in Picture Books for Preschool Children"; Diana Scully and Pauline Bart, "A Funny Thing Happened on the Way to the Orifice."

4. See Susan Sontag, "The Double Standard in Aging," *Saturday Review/Society*, October 1972.

5. Advertisement by Baxter of California, *The New York Times Magazine*, September 28, 1975, p. 57.

6. Craig Aronoff, "Old Age in Prime Time."

7. Ibid., p. 87.

8. See Karen E. Paige, "Women Learn to Sing the Menstrual Blues," for the effects of social expectations upon the symptoms of menstruation.

9. *Saturday Review/World*, July 13, 1974. These comments were included in a commencement talk at the College of Medicine of the University of Oklahoma.

10. See, among others, Kate Millett, *Sexual Politics*.

11. Doris Lessing, *The Summer Before the Dark*, p. 175.

12. Joseph Heller, *Something Happened*, p. 14.

13. Ibid., p. 557.

14. Saul Bellow, *Mr. Sammler's Planet*, p. 10.

15. Ibid., p. 49.

16. Ibid., p. 316.

17. "Morningside," lyrics by Neil Diamond.

18. "Old Man," lyrics by Randy Newman.

19. "Old Forgotten Soldier," lyrics by Harry Nilsson.

20. "Talking Old Soldiers," lyrics by Bernie Taupin and Elton John.

21. "Sixty Years On," lyrics by Bernie Taupin and Elton John.

22. "Old Friends," lyrics by Paul Simon.

23. "Treat Her Gently—Lonely Old People," lyrics by Paul McCartney.

24. "When I'm Sixty-Four," lyrics by John Lennon and Paul McCartney.

25. See Donald G. McTavish, "Perceptions of Old People: A Review of Research Methodologies and Findings."

CHAPTER SIX: CREATIVE SOCIOLOGY: DETRACTORS AND DEFENDERS

1. Alan F. Blum, *Theorizing*, p. xi.

2. George Psathas, "Goffman's Image of Man."

3. Irving Zeitlin, *Rethinking Sociology*, p. 214.

4. Robert W. Friedrichs, *A Sociology of Sociology*, pp. 252–253.

5. Stanford M. Lyman and Marvin B. Scott, *A Sociology of the Absurd.*

6. Randall Collins and Michael Makowsky, *The Discovery of Society.*

7. Ibid., p. 212.

8. Ibid.

9. Robert S. Broadhead, "Notes on the Sociology of the Absurd: An Undersocialized Conception of Man."

10. See Dennis Wrong, "The Oversocialized Conception of Man in Modern Society."

11. This can be seen as a misunderstanding of Lyman and Scott and, indeed, of all the creative sociologists, in that it omits the basic underlying assumption of these approaches—that the social world is constantly created and recreated by humans *in interaction with others.* This omission makes it possible to misunderstand Lyman and Scott as denying that others influence or channel behavior. What does the "social world" comprise but "others?"

12. Broadhead, "Notes," p. 43.

13. Scott G. McNall and James C. M. Johnson, "The New Conservatives: Ethnomethodologists, Phenomenologists, and Symbolic Interactionists."

14. Al Szymanski, "Marxism or Liberalism: A Response to Pozzuto."

15. T. R. Young, "The Politics of Sociology: Gouldner, Goffman, and Garfinkel."

16. See Alvin W. Gouldner, *The Coming Crisis in Western Sociology.*

17. Young, "Politics of Sociology," p. 278.

18. R. S. Perinbanayagam and Rosanne Martorella, "The Radical Critique of Social Theory: The Case of Symbolic Interactionism."

19. Erving Goffman, *Frame Analysis,* p. 13.

20. Alex Thio, "Class Bias in the Sociology of Deviance."

21. Alex Thio, "The Phenomenological Perspective of Deviance: Another Case of Class Bias."

22. Ernest Becker, *Angel in Armor,* p. 178.

23. C. Wright Mills, "Situated Actions and Vocabularies of Motive."

24. For this debate see, among others, John Horton, "Combatting Empiricism: Toward a Practical Understanding of Marxist Methodology," and Robert L. Keller, "Marxism and Methodology: Toward a Dialectically Empirical Sociology."

25. John O'Neill, *Sociology as a Skin Trade,* p. xiii.

26. Fred R. Dallmayr, "Phenomenology and Marxism: A Salute to Enzo Paci."

27. Paul G. Schervish, "The Labeling Perspective: Its Bias and Potential in the Study of Political Deviance."

28. Karl Mannheim, *Ideology and Utopia,* pp. 37–38.

29. Some of the material in this section appeared as part of my article "Creative Sociology: Conservative or Revolutionary."

30. Richard Dewey, "The Theatrical Analogy Reconsidered."

31. Goffman, *Frame Analysis,* p. 1.

32. Ibid., p. 124.

33. Psathas, "Goffman's Image of Man," p. 4.

34. R. S. Perinbanayagam, "The Definition of the Situation: An Analysis of the Ethnomethodological and Dramaturgical View."

35. Jeanne Boland and T. R. Young, "The Dramaturgical Society."

36. Aaron V. Cicourel, *The Social Organization of Juvenile Justice;* Aaron V. Cicourel and John I. Kitsuse, *The Educational Decision Makers.* See chapter 4 of this book for discussion of these studies.

37. Bob Gidlow, "Ethnomethodology—A New Name For Old Practices."

38. Peter Winch, *The Idea of a Social Science;* Joan Huber, "Symbolic Interaction as a Pragmatic Perspective: The Bias of Emergent Theory."

39. Herbert Blumer, "A Note on Symbolic Interaction."

40. Joan Huber, "Reply to Blumer: But Who Will Scrutinize the Scrutinizers?"

41. Jacqueline Johnson, "A Phenomenological Alternative to the Analysis of Sex Role Conflict."

42. Perinbanayagam, "Definition of the Situation."

43. Paul Attewell, "Ethnomethodology Since Garfinkel."

44. Harold Garfinkel, *Studies in Ethnomethodology,* pp. 18–24.

45. See Sheldon Stryker, "Conditions of Accurate Role-Taking: A Test of Mead's Theory," pp. 41–62; and Darwin L. Thomas, David D. Franks, and James M. Calonico, "Role Taking and Power in Social Psychology."

46. George Psathas, "Goffman and the Analysis of Face-to-Face Interaction."

47. Goffman, *Frame Analysis,* p. 15.

48. See chapter 1 of this book for a somewhat more detailed explanation of these processes.

49. Richard Lichtman, "Symbolic Interactionism and Symbolic Reality: Some Marxist Queries."

50. William M. Lafferty, "Externalization and Dialectics: Taking the Brackets off Berger and Luckmann's Sociology of Knowledge."

51. Jack D. Douglas, *Understanding Everyday Life.*

52. Robert W. Friedrichs, *A Sociology of Sociology,* p. 309.

53. Robert S. Lynd, *Knowledge for What?* pp. 121–22.

54. Helmut R. Wagner, "Displacement of Scope: A Problem of the Relationship between Small-Scale and Large-Scale Sociological Theories."

55. See Jeff Coulter, "Deconceptualized Meaning: Current Approaches to *Verstehende* Investigations," and Edward A. Tiryakian, "Existential Phenomenology and the Sociological Tradition."

56. Robert Bierstedt, *Power and Progress,* pp. 87–92.

57. Alan Dawe, "The Two Sociologies."

58. Stanford M. Lyman's statements on "The State of Sociological Theory," presented at the annual meeting of the American Sociological Association, August 1975, San Francisco.

59. Ibid.

60. Dawe, "The Two Sociologies."

CHAPTER SEVEN: THE RIVER FLOWS ON

1. See Liam Hudson, *The Cult of the Fact,* for a discussion of this division in psychology.

2. George Basalla, ed., *The Rise of Modern Science: External or Internal Factors?*

3. Roger M. Keesing, "Paradigms Lost: The New Ethnography and the New Linguistics."

4. See chapter 4 of this volume.

5. See Brent Berlin and Paul Kay, *Basic Color Terms: Their Universality and Evolution,* for a rejection of the traditional doctrine that the language of each culture predisposes its members to see the world, including colors, in different ways from people of other cultures.

6. See chapter 4 of this volume.

7. See W. Randall Ireson, "Socio-economic Components of Agricultural Decision-Making: The Adoption of Multiple Cropping in Northern Thailand."

8. Helmut R. Wagner, "Displacement of Scope: A Problem of the Relationship Between Small-Scale and Large-Scale Sociological Theories."

9. Alan Dawe, "The Two Sociologies."

10. Hudson, *Cult of the Fact.*

Bibliography

Amis, Kingsley. *Ending Up*. New York: Harcourt, Brace, Jovanovich, 1974.

Andelin, Helen B. *Fascinating Womanhood*. Santa Barbara: Pacific Press, 1965.

Andreski, Stanislav. *Social Sciences as Sorcery*. New York: St. Martin's Press, 1972.

Aronoff, Craig. "Old Age in Prime Time." *Journal of Communication* 24 (Autumn 1974): 86–87.

Attewell, Paul. "Ethnomethodology Since Garfinkel." *Theory and Society* 1 (1974): 179–210.

Austin, J. L. *How to Do Things with Words*. New York: Oxford University Press, 1962.

———— *Philosophical Papers*. Oxford: Oxford University Press, 1970.

Ball, Donald W. "Toward a Sociology of Telephones and Telephoners." In *Sociology and Everyday Life*, edited by Marcello Truzzi, pp. 59–74. Englewood Cliffs, N.J.: Prentice-Hall, 1968.

Bar-Hillel, Yehoshua. "Indexical Expressions." *Mind* 63 (1954): 359–79.

Barrett, William. *Irrational Man*. New York: Doubleday, 1958.

Bart, Pauline. "Depression in Middle-Aged Women: Some Sociocultural Factors." Ph.D. dissertation, University of California, Los Angeles, 1967.

Basalla, George, ed. *The Rise of Modern Science: External or Internal Factors?* Lexington, Mass.: D. C. Heath, 1968.

Bauman, Z. "On the Philosophical Status of Ethnomethodology." *The Sociological Review* 21 (February 1973): 5–23.

Becker, Ernest. *Angel in Armor*. New York: Braziller, 1969.

Becker, Howard S. *Outsiders*. New York: Free Press, 1963.

Beckett, Samuel. *Waiting for Godot*. New York: Grove Press, Evergreen, 1954.

———— *Endgame*. New York: Grove Press, Evergreen, 1958.

———— *Proust*. New York: Grove Press, Evergreen, 1958.

Bellow, Saul. *Mr. Sammler's Planet*. New York: Viking Press, 1970.

Bendix, Reinhard. *Max Weber: An Intellectual Portrait*. New York: Anchor, 1960.

Benson, Doug. "Critical Note: A Revolution in Sociology." *Sociology* 8 (January 1974): 125–29.

Berger, Peter L. "On Existential Phenomenology and Sociology (II)." *American Sociological Review* 31 (1966): 259–60.

———— *The Sacred Canopy*. New York: Doubleday, 1967.

Berger, Peter L. Brigitte Berger, and Hansfried Kellner. *The Homeless Mind*. New York: Random House, Vintage Books, 1974.

Berger, Peter L., and Thomas Luckmann. *The Social Construction of Reality.* New York: Doubleday, 1967.

Berlin, Brent, and Paul Kay. *Basic Color Terms: Their Universality and Evolution.* Berkeley: University of California Press, 1969.

Bernard, Jessie. *The Future of Marriage.* New York: Bantam, 1972.

Bernstein, Basil. *Class, Codes and Control.* Theoretical Studies towards a Sociology of Language, vol. 1. London: Routledge and Kegan Paul, 1971.

Bierstedt, Robert. *Power and Progress.* New York: McGraw-Hill, 1974.

Bittner, Egon. "Objectivity and Realism in Sociology." In *Phenomenological Sociology: Issues and Applications,* edited by George Psathas, pp. 109–125. New York: John Wiley, 1973.

Blackham, H. J., ed. *Reality, Man and Existence: Essential Works of Existentialism.* New York: Bantam, 1971.

Blasi, Anthony J. "Symbolic Interaction as Theory." *Sociology and Social Research* 4 (July 1972): 453–65.

Bloch, Ernst. *Man on His Own.* New York: Herder and Herder, 1970.

Blum, Alan F. "The Corpus of Knowledge as a Normative Order." In *Theoretical Sociology: Perspectives and Developments,* edited by John C. McKinney and Edward A. Tiryakian. New York: Appleton-Century-Crofts, 1970.

———— *Theorizing.* London: Heineman Educational Books Ltd., 1974.

Blumer, Herbert. "What is Wrong with Social Theory?" *American Sociological Review* 19 (February 1954): 3–10.

———— "Society as Symbolic Interaction." In *Human Behavior and Social Processes,* edited by Arnold M. Rose, pp. 179–92. Boston: Houghton Mifflin, 1962.

———— "Commentary and Debate: Sociological Implications of the Thought of George Herbert Mead." *American Journal of Sociology* 71 (March 1966a): 535–44.

———— "Reply." *American Journal of Sociology* 71 (March 1966b): 547–48.

———— *Symbolic Interactionism: Perspective and Method.* Englewood Cliffs, N.J.: Prentice-Hall, 1969.

———— "A Note on Symbolic Interaction." *American Sociological Review* 38 (December 1973): 797–98.

Boland, Jeanne, and T. R. Young. "The Dramaturgical Society." Paper presented at the annual meeting of the American Sociological Association, August 1972, New Orleans.

Boocock, Sarane S. *An Introduction to the Sociology of Learning.* Boston: Houghton Mifflin, 1972.

Bosserman, Phillip. *Dialectical Sociology: An Analysis of the Sociology of George Gurvitch.* Boston: Sargent, 1968.

Broadhead, Robert S. "Notes on the Sociology of the Absurd: An Under-socialized Conception of Man." *Pacific Sociological Review* 17 (January 1974): 35–45.

Bruyn, Severyn T. *The Human Perspective in Sociology.* Englewood Cliffs, N.J.: Prentice-Hall, 1966.

Burke, Kenneth. *The Philosophy of Literary Form.* New York: Random House, Vintage Books, 1957.

Burns, Sam. "Making the World Available: Ordinary Accounting Practices in Community Development Field Work." Paper presented at the annual meetings of the Pacific Sociological Association, March 1974, San Jose.

Cairns, Dorian. "An Approach to Phenomenology." In *Essays in Memory of Edmund Husserl,* edited by Marvin Farber. Cambridge: Harvard University Press, 1940.

Cancian, Francesca M. "New Methods for Describing What People Think." *Sociological Inquiry* 41 (Winter 1971): 85–93.

Cardwell, J. D. *Social Psychology: A Symbolic Interaction Perspective.* Philadelphia: F. A. Davis, 1971.

Carmen, John B. "The Theology of a Phenomenologist: An Introduction to the Theology of Gerardus van der Leeuw." Harvard Divinity Bulletin, April 1965.

Cassirer, Ernst. *An Essay on Man.* New York: Bantam, 1970.

Chinoy, Ely. *The Automobile Worker and the American Dream.* New York: Doubleday, 1955.

Chomsky, Noam. *Syntactic Structures.* The Hague: Mouton, 1957.

———— *Aspects of the Theory of Syntax.* Cambridge, Mass.: MIT Press, 1965.

———— *Language and Mind.* New York: Harcourt, Brace and World, 1968.

Chua, Beng-Huat. "On the Commitments of Ethnomethodology." *Sociological Inquiry* 44:241–56.

Churchill, Lindsey. "Ethnomethodology and Measurement." *Social Forces* 50 (December 1971): 182–91.

Cicourel, Aaron V. *Methods and Measurement in Sociology.* New York: Free Press, 1964.

———— *The Social Organization of Juvenile Justice.* New York: John Wiley, 1968.

———— "The Acquisition of Social Structure: Toward a Developmental Sociology of Language and Meaning." In *Understanding Everyday Life,* edited by Jack D. Douglas, pp. 136–68. Chicago: Aldine, 1970.

———— *Cognitive Sociology.* New York: Free Press, 1974.

———— "Gestural Sign Language and the Study of Non-Verbal Communication." *Sign Language Studies* 4. The Hague: Mouton, 1974.

———— "Interviewing and Memory." In *Theory and Decision,* edited by C. Cherry, pp. 50–79. Dordrecht: Reidel Publishing Co., 1974.

Cicourel, Aaron V., and John I. Kitsuse. *The Educational Decision Makers.* Indianapolis: Bobbs-Merrill, 1963.

Coleman, James S. "Review Symposium of Harold Garfinkel." *American Sociological Review* (February 1968): 126–30.

Collins, Randall, and Michael Makowsky. *The Discovery of Society.* New York: Random House, 1972.

Conklin, Harold C. "Lexicographical Treatment of Folk Taxonomies." In *Problems of Lexicography,* edited by F. W. Householder and S. Saporta, pp. 119–41; supplement to *International Journal of American Linguistics* 2:28:2. Publication 21 of the Indiana University Research Center in Anthropology, Folklore, and Linguistics, 1962.

———— "Ethnogenealogical method." In *Explorations in Cultural Anthropology,* edited by W. H. Goodenough. Hightstown, N.J.: McGraw-Hill, 1964.

Cooley, Charles Horton. "The Roots of Social Knowledge." *American Journal of Sociology* 32 (July 1926): 59–79.

———— *Social Organization.* New York: Schocken, 1962.

———— *Human Nature and the Social Order.* New York: Schocken, 1964.

Couch, Carl J. "Collective Behavior: An Examination of Some Stereotypes." *Social Problems* 16 (Winter 1968): 310–22.

Coulter, Jeff. "Language and the Conceptualization of Meaning." *Sociology* 7 (May 1973): 173–89.

———— "Deconceptualized Meaning: Current Approaches to *Verstehende* Investigations." In *Verstehen: Subjective Understanding in the Social Sciences,* edited by Marcello Truzzi, pp. 134–64. Reading, Mass.: Addison-Wesley, 1974.

Cumming, Elaine, and William Henry. *Growing Old.* New York: Basic Books, 1961.

Dallmayr, Fred R. "Phenomenology and Marxism: A Salute to Enzo Paci." In *Phenomenological Sociology: Issues and Applications,* edited by George Psathas, pp. 305–56. New York: John Wiley, 1973.

Dawe, Alan. "The Two Sociologies." *British Journal of Sociology,* June 1970, pp. 207–18.

Denzin, Norman K. "Symbolic Interactionism and Ethnomethodology: A Proposed Synthesis." *American Sociological Review* 34 (December 1969): 922–33.

———— "Symbolic Interactionism and Ethnomethodology: A Comment on Zimmerman and Wieder." In *Understanding Everyday Life,* edited by Jack D. Douglas, pp. 295–98. Chicago: Aldine, 1970.

Deutscher, Irwin. *What we say/What we do.* Glenview, Ill.: Scott, Foresman, 1973.

Dewey, Richard. "The Theatrical Analogy Reconsidered." *American Sociologist* 4 (November 1969): 307–11.

Diquattro, Arthur W. "Verstehen as an Empirical Concept." *Sociology and Social Research* 57 (October 1972): 32–42.

Douglas, Jack D. *Understanding Everday Life.* Chicago: Aldine, 1970.

Douglas, Mary, ed. *Rules and Meanings.* Harmondsworth, Eng.: Penguin Books, 1973.

Dreitzel, Hans Peter, ed. *Patterns of Communicative Behavior.* Recent Sociology, no. 2. New York: Macmillan, 1970.

Duncan, Hugh Dalziel. *Symbols in Society.* New York: Oxford University Press, 1968.

Durkheim, Émile. *The Rules of Sociological Method.* New York: Free Press, 1938.

Durkheim, Émile, and Marcel Mauss. *Primitive Classification.* London: Routledge and Kegan Paul, 1963. First published in 1903.

Edie, James M. *Phenomenology in America.* Chicago: Quadrangle Books, 1967.

Eliot, T. S. *Four Quartets.* New York: Harcourt, Brace and World, 1943.

Emerson, Joan P. "Behavior in Private Places: Sustaining Definitions of Reality in a Gynecological Examination." In *Patterns of Communicative Behavior,* edited by Hans Peter Dreitzel, pp. 74–97. Recent Sociology, no. 2. New York: Macmillan, 1970.

Esslin, Martin. *The Theatre of the Absurd.* New York: Anchor Books, 1969.

Farber, Marvin. *The Foundation of Phenomenology.* New York: Paine-Whitman, 1962.

Farber, Marvin, ed. *Essays in Memory of Edmund Husserl.* Cambridge: Harvard University Press, 1940.

Filmer, Paul, Michael Phillipson, David Silverman, and David Walsh. *New Directions in Sociological Theory.* London: Collier-Macmillan, 1972.

Filstead, William J. "Qualitative Methodology: Firsthand Involvement with the Empirical Social World." Paper presented at the American Sociological Meeting, 1973, New York.

Fishman, Pamela M. "Interaction: The Work Women Do." Paper presented at the annual meeting of the American Sociological Association, 1975, San Francisco.

Form, William H. "Auto Workers and Their Machines: A Study of Work, Factory, and Job Satisfaction in Four Countries." *Social Forces* 52 (September 1973.

Frake, Charles O. "How to Ask for a Drink in Subanun." In *The Ethnography of Communication,* edited by John J. Gumperz and Dell Hymes, pp. 127–32. Special publication of *American Anthropologist* 66:6:2 (December 1964).

———— "Notes on Queries in Ethnography." In *Transcultural Studies in Cognition,* edited by A. Kimball Romney and Roy Goodwin D'Andrade, pp. 132–45. Special publication of *American Anthropologist* 66:3:2 (June 1964).

———— "Struck by Speech: The Yakan Concept of Litigation." In *Directions in Sociolinguistics: The Ethnography of Communication,* edited by John J. Gumperz and Dell Hymes, pp. 106–29. New York: Holt, Rinehart, 1972.

Freudiger, Patricia, and Elizabeth M. Almquist. "Male and Female Roles in the Lyrics of Three Genres of Contemporary Music." Paper presented at the annual meeting of the American Sociological Association, August 1975, San Francisco.

Freund, Julien. *The Sociology of Max Weber.* New York: Vintage, 1968.

Fried, Barbara R. *The Middle Age Crisis.* New York: Harper and Row, 1967.

Friedrichs, Robert W. *A Sociology of Sociology.* New York: Free Press, 1970.

Gans, Herbert. "The Positive Functions of Poverty." *American Journal of Sociology* 78 (September 1972): 275–89.

Garfinkel, Harold. "The Rational Properties of Scientific and Common-Sense Activities." *Behavioral Science* 5 (January 1960): 72–83.

———— "Common-Sense Knowledge of Social Structures: The Documentary Method of Interpretation." In *Theories of the Mind,* edited by Jordan M. Scher, pp. 689–712. New York: Free Press, 1962.

———— "A Conception of and Experiments with 'Trust' as a Condition of Stable Concerted Actions." In *Motivation and Social Interaction,* edited by O. J. Harvey. New York: Ronald Press, 1963.

———— "Studies in the Routine Grounds of Everyday Activity." *Social Problems* 11 (Winter 1964): 225–50.

———— *Studies in Ethnomethodology.* Englewood Cliffs, N.J.: Prentice-Hall, 1967.

Garfinkel, Harold, and Harvey Sacks. "On Formal Structures of Practical Actions." In *Theoretical Sociology: Perspectives and Developments,* edited by John C. McKinney and Edward A. Tiryakian, pp. 337–66. New York: Appleton-Century-Crofts, 1970.

Gaskell, Ronald. *Drama and Reality: The European Theatre since Ibsen.* London: Routledge and Kegan Paul, 1972.

Geertz, Clifford. *The Interpretation of Cultures.* New York: Basic Books, 1973.

Gerth, Hans H., and C. Wright Mills. *From Max Weber: Essays in Sociology.* New York: Oxford University Press, 1946.

Giddens, Anthony. *Capitalism and Modern Social Theory: An Analysis of Marx, Durkheim, and Max Weber.* Cambridge, Eng.: Cambridge University Press, 1971.

Gidlow, Bob. "Ethnomethodology—A New Name for Old Practices." *British Journal of Sociology* 23 (1972): 395–405.

Giglioli, Pier Paolo, ed. *Language and Social Context.* Middlesex, Eng.: Penguin Books, 1972.

Glock, Charles Y., and Philip Hammond, eds. *Beyond the Classics? Essays in the Scientific Study of Religion.* New York: Harper and Row, 1973.

Goffman, Erving. *Encounters.* Indianapolis: Bobbs-Merrill, 1961.

———— *Asylums.* New York: Doubleday, 1961.

———— *Stigma.* Englewood Cliffs, N.J.: Prentice-Hall, 1963.

———— *Behavior in Public Places.* New York: Free Press of Glencoe, 1963.

———— *Interaction Ritual.* New York: Doubleday, 1967.

———— *The Presentation of Self in Everyday Life.* New York: Doubleday, 1969.

———— *Relations in Public.* New York: Harper Colophon, 1972.

———— *Frame Analysis.* New York: Harper and Row, 1974.

Goldthorpe, John H. "Review Article: A Revolution in Sociology?" *Sociology* 7 (September 1973): 449–62.

———— "Correspondence: A Rejoinder to Benson." *Sociology* 8 (January 1974): 131–33.

Goodwin, Glenn A. "On Transcending the Absurd: An Inquiry in the Sociology of Meaning." *American Journal of Sociology* 76 (March 1971): 831–46.

Gordon, Chad, and Kenneth Gergen, eds. *The Self in Social Interaction.* New York: John Wiley, 1968.

Gouldner, Alvin W. "The Sociologist as Partisan: Sociology and the Welfare State." *American Sociologist* (May 1968): 103–16.

———— *The Coming Crisis in Western Sociology.* New York: Avon, Equinox, 1971.

Greeley, Andrew W. *Unsecular Man.* New York: Dell, 1972.

Grimshaw, Allen D. "Sociolinguistics and the Sociologist." *American Sociologist* 4 (November 1969): 312–21.

Gumperz, John J. and Dell Hymes, eds. *Directions in Sociolinguistics.* New York: Holt, Rinehart, 1972.

Gurwitsch, Aron. *The Field of Consciousness.* Pittsburgh: Duquesne University Press, 1964.

Hall, Edward T. *The Silent Language.* New York: The Ronald Press, 1963.

———— *The Hidden Dimension.* New York: Doubleday, 1969.

Harvey, O. J. *Motivation and Social Interaction.* New York: Ronald Press, 1963.

Heap, James L. "A Note on Husserl's Phenomenological Sociology." Paper presented at the Pacific Sociological Association meeting, May 1973, Scottsdale, Arizona.

———— "The Cognitive Style of Reading." Paper presented at the annual meeting of the American Sociological Association, August 1974, Montreal.

Heap, James L., and Phillip A. Roth. "On Phenomenological Sociology." *American Sociological Review* 38 (June 1973): 354–67.

Heller, Joseph. *Something Happened.* New York: Alfred Knopf, 1966.

Hendricks, Jon. "Common Sense Typologies and Sociological Theory: The Perspective of Alfred Schutz." Paper presented at the annual meetings of the American Sociological Association, August 1970, Washington, D.C.

Hewitt, John P., and Randall Stokes. "Disclaimers." *American Sociological Review* 40 (February 1975): 1–11.

Hinckle, Gisele. Review of *The Structures of the Life World,* by Alfred Schutz and Thomas Luckmann, in *Contemporary Sociology* 3 (March 1974): 112–14.

Horton, John. "Combatting Empiricism: Toward a Practical Understanding of Marxist Methodology." *Insurgent Sociologist* 3 (Fall 1972): 24–34.

Huber, Joan. "Symbolic Interaction as a Pragmatic Perspective: The Bias of Emergent Theory." *American Sociological Review* 38 (April 1973): 274–84.

————— "Reply to Blumer: But Who Will Scrutinize the Scrutinizers?" *American Sociological Review* 38 (December 1973): 798–800.

Hudson, Liam. *The Cult of the Fact.* New York: Harper Torchbooks, 1972.

Husserl, Edmund. *Ideas: Pure Phenomenology.* London: George Allen and Unwin, 1931.

Hymes, Dell. "Introduction: Toward Ethnographies of Communication." *American Anthropologist* 66 (1964) 12–25.

Hymes, Dell, ed. *Reinventing Anthropology.* New York: Pantheon, 1972.

Ionesco, Eugène. *Four Plays.* New York: Grove Press, 1958.

————— *Notes and Counter Notes.* New York: Grove Press, Evergreen, 1964.

Ireson, W. Randall. "Socio-economic Components of Agricultural Decision-Making: The Adoption of Multiple Cropping in Northern Thailand." Ph.D. dissertation, Cornell University, 1976.

Israel, Marvin. "Comment on James Coleman's Review of Harold Garfinkel's Studies in Ethnomethodology." *American Sociologist* 4 (November 1969): 335–36.

Jacobs, Jerry. "A Phenomenological Study of Suicide Notes." *Social Problems* 15 (Summer 1967): 60–72.

James, William. *Psychology.* Cleveland: World Publishing Co., 1948.

————— "The Self." In *The Self in Social Interaction,* edited by Chad Gordon and Kenneth Gergen. New York: John Wiley, 1968. First published in 1892 by Henry Holt of New York.

Jay, Martin. *The Dialectical Imagination.* Boston: Little, Brown, 1973.

Jehenson, Roger. "Social Construction of Reality and Social Distribution of Knowledge in Formal Organizations." Paper presented at the American Sociological Association meeting, August 1974, Montreal.

Johnson, Jacqueline. "A Phenomenological Alternative to the Analysis of Sex Role Conflict." Paper presented at the annual meetings of the American Sociological Association, August 1975, San Francisco.

Kahl, Joseph A. "Educational and Occupational Aspirations of 'Common Man' Boys." *Harvard Educational Review* 23 (1953): 186–203.

Kalish, Richard A., and Ann I. Johnson. "Value Similarities and Differences in Three Generations of Women." *Journal of Marriage and the Family* 34 (1972): 49–54.

Keesing, Roger M. "Paradigms Lost: The New Ethnography and the New Linguistics." *Southwestern Journal of Anthropology* 28 (Winter 1972): 299–332.

Keller, Robert L. "Marxism and Methodology: Toward a Dialectically Empirical Sociology." Paper presented at the Pacific Sociological Association meetings, March 1974, San Jose.

Kierkegaard, Søren. *Concluding Unscientific Postscript.* Princeton: Princeton University Press, 1941.

——— *Either/or: A Fragment of Life.* Princeton: Princeton University Press, 1944.

Kinch, John W. "A Formalized Theory of the Self-Concept." *American Journal of Sociology* 68 (January 1963): 481–86.

Kockelmans, Joseph J., ed. *Phenomenology: The Philosophy of Edmund Husserl and Its Interpretations.* Garden City, N.Y.: Doubleday, Anchor, 1967.

Komarovsky, Mirra. *Women in the Modern World: Their Education and Their Dilemmas.* Boston: Little, Brown, 1953.

Kuhn, Manford H. "Major Trends in Symbolic Interaction Theory in the Past Twenty-five Years." *Sociological Quarterly* 5 (Winter 1964): 61–84.

Kuhn, Manford H., and Thomas S. McPartland. "An Empirical Investigation of Self-Attitude." *American Sociological Review* 19 (February 1954): 68–76. (Reprinted in *Symbolic Interaction,* ed. by Jerome G. Manis and Bernard N. Meltzer, pp. 112–24.

Kuhn, Thomas S. *The Structure of Scientific Revolutions.* Chicago: University of Chicago Press, 1962. Enlarged second edition 1970.

Kusisto, D. V. "A Summary of Phenomenology as a Potential Sociological Theory." Paper presented at the Pacific Sociological Association meetings, March 1974, San Jose.

Labovitz, Sanford. "The Nonutility of Significance Tests: The Significance of Tests of Significance Reconsidered." *Pacific Sociological Review* 13 (Summer 1970): 141–48.

Lafferty, William M. "Externalization and Dialectics: Taking the Brackets off Berger and Luckmann's Sociology of Knowledge." Paper presented at the American Sociological meetings, August 1975, San Francisco.

Laing, R. D. *The Divided Self.* New York: Pantheon Books, 1960.

Lessing, Doris. *The Summer Before the Dark.* New York: Alfred Knopf, 1973.

Lichtman, Richard. "Symbolic Interactionism and Symbolic Reality: Some Marxist Queries." *Berkeley Journal of Sociology* 15 (1970): 75–94.

Luckmann, Thomas. *The Invisible Religion.* New York: Macmillan, 1967.

Lundberg, George A. "The Postulates of Science and Their Implications for Sociology." In *Philosophy of the Social Sciences: A Reader,* edited by Maurice Natanson. New York: Random House, 1963.

Lyman, Stanford M., and Marvin B. Scott. *A Sociology of the Absurd.* New York: Appleton-Century-Crofts, 1970.

Lynd, Robert S. *Knowledge for What?* Princeton: Princeton University Press, 1939.

Lyons, John. *Noam Chomsky.* New York: Viking, 1970.

McCall, George J., and J. L. Simmons. *Identities and Interactions.* New York: Free Press, 1966.

McHugh, Peter. *Defining the Situation*. Indianapolis: Bobbs-Merrill, 1968.

McHugh, Peter, Stanley Raffel, Daniel C. Foss, and Alan F. Blum. *On the Beginnings of Social Inquiry*. London: Routledge and Kegan Paul, 1974.

Macintyre, Alasdair. "The Self as Work of Art." *New Statesman*, March 28, 1969, pp. 447–48.

McKinney, John C., and Edward A. Tiryakian, eds. *Theoretical Sociology: Perspectives and Developments*. New York: Appleton-Century-Crofts, 1970.

Macmurray, John. *The Structure of Religious Experience*. New Haven: Yale University Press, 1936.

McNall, Scott G., and James C. M. Johnson. "The New Conservatives: Ethnomethodologists, Phenomenologists, and Symbolic Interactionists." *Insurgent Sociologist* 4 (Summer 1975): 49–65.

McTavish, Donald G. "Perceptions of Old People: A Review of Research Methodologies and Findings." *The Gerontologist* 11, Part II (1971): 90–102.

Mandelbaum, Maurice. *The Phenomenology of Moral Experience*. Glencoe, Ill.: Free Press, 1955.

Manis, Jerome G., and Bernard N. Meltzer, eds. *Symbolic Interaction: A Reader in Social Psychology*. 2d ed. Boston: Allyn and Bacon, 1972.

Mannheim, Karl. *Ideology and Utopia*. New York: Harcourt, Brace and World, 1936.

——— *Essays on the Sociology of Knowledge*. London: Routledge and Kegan Paul, 1952.

Martindale, Don. *The Nature and Types of Sociological Theory*. Boston: Houghton Mifflin, 1960.

Marvin, Israel. "Comment on James Coleman's Review of Harold Garfinkel's Studies in Ethnomethodology." *American Sociologist* 4 (1969): 335–36.

Marx, Karl. *Economic and Philosophical Manuscripts of 1844*. Moscow: Foreign Language Publishing House, 1961.

——— *The Grundrisse*. New York: Harper and Row, 1971.

——— "Theses on Feuerbach." In *The Marx-Engels Reader*, edited by Robert C. Tucker, pp. 107–9. New York: W. W. Norton Company, 1972.

Marx, Karl, and Frederick Engels. *The German Ideology*. New York: International Publishers, 1947.

Mead, George Herbert. *The Philosophy of the Present*. La Salle, Ill.: Open Court Publishing Co., 1932.

——— *Mind, Self, and Society*. Chicago: University of Chicago Press, 1934.

——— *Movements of Thought in the Nineteenth Century*. Chicago: University of Chicago Press, 1936.

——— *Philosophy of the Act*. Chicago: University of Chicago Press, 1938.

——— *Mead: Selected Writings*. Indianapolis: Bobbs-Merrill, 1964.

Melbin, Murray. *Alone and with Others*. New York: Harper and Row, 1972.

Mennell, Stephen. *Sociological Theory: Uses and Unities*. New York: Praeger, 1974.

Merleau-Ponty, Maurice. *The Structure of Behavior*. Boston: Beacon Press, 1963.

——— *The Primacy of Perception*. Evanston: Northwestern University Press, 1964.

——— *Sense and Non-Sense*. Evanston: Northwestern University Press, 1964.

Millett, Kate. *Sexual Politics*. New York: Equinox Books, 1971.

Mills, C. Wright. "Situated Actions and Vocabularies of Motive." *American Sociological Review* 5 (December 1940): 904–13.

Monica B. Morris. "Newspapers and the New Feminists: Black-Out as Social Control?" *Journalism Quarterly* 50 (Spring 1973): 37–42.

——— "The Public Definition of a Social Movement: Women's Liberation." *Sociology and Social Research* 57 (July 1973): 526–43.

——— "Creative Sociology: Conservative or Revolutionary." *American Sociologist* 10 (August 1975): 168–78.

——— "Excuses, Justifications, and Evasions: How Newspaper Editors Account for Their Coverage of a Social Movement." *Sociolinguistics Newsletter* 7 (February 1976): 20–25.

Mullins, Nicholas C. *Theories and Theory Groups in Contemporary American Sociology*. New York: Harper and Row, 1973.

Nash, Jeffrey E., and James M. Calonico. "Sociological Perspectives in Bernstein's Sociolinguistics." *Sociological Quarterly* 15 (Winter 1974): 81–92.

Natanson, Maurice. "A Study in Philosophy and the Social Sciences." *Social Research* 25 (Summer 1958): 158–72.

——— *Literature, Philosophy, and the Social Sciences: Essays in Existentialism and Phenomenology*. The Hague: Martinus Nijhoff, 1962.

——— "Phenomenology and Typification: A Study in the Philosophy of Alfred Schutz." *Social Research* 37 (Spring 1970): 1–22.

Natanson, Maurice, ed. *Philosophy of the Social Sciences: A Reader*. New York: Random House, 1963.

——— *Phenomenology and the Social Sciences*. 2 vols. Evanston: Northwestern University Press, 1973.

Neisser, Hans P. "The Phenomenological Approach in Social Science." *Philosophy and Phenomenological Research*, December 1959, pp. 198–212.

Neugarten, Bernice L., ed. *Middle Age and Aging*. Chicago: University of Chicago Press, 1968.

Neugarten, Bernice L., and Joan W. Moore. "The Changing Age-Status System." in *Middle Age and Aging*, edited by Bernice L. Neugarten, pp. 5–21. Chicago: University of Chicago Press, 1968.

Newman, John H. "From Space to Place: Locating a Rural Drug Program." Paper presented at the annual meetings of the Pacific Sociological Association, March 1974, San Jose.

Oleson, Virginia L., and Elvi W. Whittaker. *The Silent Language: A Study in the Social Psychology of Professional Socialization*. San Francisco: Jossey-Bass, 1968.

O'Neill, John. *Perception, Expression and History: The Social Phenomenology of Maurice Merleau-Ponty*. Evanston: Northwestern University Press, 1970.

——— *Sociology as a Skin Trade*. New York: Harper Torchbooks, 1972.

Paci, Enzo. *The Function of the Sciences and the Meaning of Man*. Evanston: Northwestern University Press, 1963.

Paige, Karen E. "Women Learn to Sing the Menstrual Blues." *Psychology Today*, September 1973, pp. 41–46.

Pascal, Blaise. *Pensées.* London and New York: Everyman's Library, 1960.

Percy, Walker. "Symbol, Consciousness, and Intersubjectivity." *Journal of Philosophy* 55 (1958): 631–41.

Perinbanayagam, R. S. "The Definition of the Situation: An Analysis of the Ethnomethodological and Dramaturgical View." *Sociological Quarterly* 15 (Autumn 1974): 521–41.

Perinbanayagam, R. S., and Rosanne Martorella. "The Radical Critique of Social Theory: The Case of Symbolic Interactionism." Paper presented at the Midwest Sociological Convention, April 1975, Chicago.

Peters, William. *A Class Divided.* New York: Doubleday, 1971.

Philibert, Michel. "The Phenomenological Approach to Images of Aging." *Sounding: An Interdisciplinary Journal* 57 (Spring 1974): 33–49.

Pinter, Harold. *The Caretaker and the Dumb Waiter.* New York: Grove Press, 1961.

———— "Writing for the Theatre," In *The New British Drama,* edited by Henry Popkin. New York: Grove Press, 1964.

Pirandello, Luigi. *Naked Masks.* New York: Dutton, 1952.

Pivćević, Edo. "Can there be a phenomenological sociology?" *Sociology* 6 (September 1972): 335–40.

Pollner, Melvin. "Sociological and Common-Sense Models of the Labelling Process." In *Ethnomethodology,* edited by Roy Turner, pp. 27–40. Middlesex, Eng.: Penguin Books, 1974.

Popkin, Henry, ed. *The New British Drama.* New York: Grove Press, 1964.

Poskocil, Art. "Encounters between Blacks and White Liberals: A Situationalist-Interactionist Perspective." Paper presented at the American Sociological Association meeting, August 1975, San Francisco.

Pronko, Leonard Cabell. *Theater East and West.* Berkeley: University of California Press, 1967.

Psathas, George. "Ethnomethods and Phenomenology." *Social Research* 35 (September 1968): 500–520.

———— *Phenomenological Sociology: Issues and Applications.* New York: John Wiley, 1973.

———— "Goffman and the Analysis of Face-to-Face Interaction." Paper presented at the American Sociological Association Meetings, 1973, New York.

———— "Ethnomethodology as a Phenomenological Approach." Paper presented at the meetings of the Eastern Sociological Society, April 1974, Philadelphia.

———— "Goffman's Image of Man." Paper presented at the annual meeting of the American Sociological Association, August 1975, San Francisco.

Reinach, Adolf. "Concerning Phenomenology." *The Personalist* 50 (Spring 1969): 194–221.

Reynolds, Larry T., et al. "The 'Self' in Symbolic Interaction Theory: An Examination of the Social Sources of Conceptual Diversity." In *The Sociology of Sociology,* edited by Larry T. Reynolds and Janice M. Reynolds, pp. 422–38. New York: David McKay, 1970.

Ricoeur, Paul. "New Developments in Phenomenology in France: The Phenomenology of Language." *Social Research* 34 (Spring 1967): 1–30.

Ritzer, George. *Sociology: A Multiple Paradigm Science.* Boston: Allyn and Bacon, 1975.

Robertson, Roland. *The Sociological Interpretation of Religion.* New York: Schocken, 1972.

Roche, Maurice. *Phenomenology, Language and the Social Sciences.* London: Routledge and Kegan Paul, 1973.

Rose, Edward. "The English Record of a Natural Sociology." *American Sociological Review* 25 (April 1960): 193–208.

———— *A Looking Glass Conversation.* Program on Cognitive Processes, report no. 102. Boulder, Colorado: Institute of Behavioral Science, University of Colorado, April 1967.

Rosenthal, Robert, and Lenore Jacobson. "Teachers' Expectancies: Determinants of Pupils' IQ Gains." *Psychological Reports* 19 (1966): 115–18.

Sacks, Harvey, Emanuel A. Schegloff, and Gail Jefferson. "A Simplest Systematics for the Organization of Turn-Taking for Conversation." *Language* 50 (December 1974): 696–735.

Sartre, Jean-Paul. *Existentialism.* New York: Philosophical Library, 1947.

———— *Existentialism and Human Emotions.* New York: Wisdom Library, 1957.

———— *Search for a Method.* New York: Alfred Knopf, 1963.

———— *The Problem of Method.* London: Methuen, 1963.

Scheff, Thomas J. "Negotiating Reality: Notes on Power in the Assessment of Responsibility." *Social Problems* 16 (Summer 1968): 3–17.

Schegloff, Emanuel A. "Sequencing in Conversational Openings." *American Anthropologist* 70 (1968): 1075–95.

Schegloff, Emanuel A., and Harvey Sacks. "Opening Up Closings." *Semiotica* 8 (1973): 289–327.

Scheler, Max. *The Nature of Sympathy.* London: Routledge and Kegan Paul, 1970.

Scher, Jordon M. "Husserl's Transcendental-Phenomenological Reduction." *Philosophy and Phenomenological Research* 20 (December 1959).

———— *Theories of the Mind.* New York: Free Press, 1962.

Schervish, Paul G. "The Labeling Perspective: Its Bias and Potential in the Study of Political Deviance." *American Sociologist* 8 (May 1973): 47–57.

Schmitt, Raymond L., and Stanley E. Grupp, "Self Theory and the Twenty-Statement Test." Paper presented at the American Sociological Association meetings, August 1975, San Francisco.

Schmitt, Richard. "Husserl's Transcendental Phenomenological Reduction," *Philosophy and Phenomenological Research* 20 (December 1959): 238–45.

Schmitt, Richard. "In Search of Phenomenology." *Review of Metaphysics* 15 (March 1962): 450–79.

Schutz, Alfred. "The Stranger: An Essay in Social Psychology." *American Journal of Sociology* 49 (May 1944): 499–507.

———— "Concept and Theory Formation in the Social Sciences." *Journal of Philosophy* 51 (April 1954): 257–73.

———— *Collected Papers,* Vol. I. Edited and introduced by Maurice Natanson. The Hague: Martinus Nijhoff, 1962.

———— "Common-Sense and Scientific Interpretation of Human Action." In *Philosophy of*

The Social Sciences: A Reader, edited by Maurice Natanson, pp. 302–46. New York: Random House, 1963.

——— *Collected Papers,* Vol. II. Edited and introduced by Arvid Brodersen. The Hague: Martinus Nijhoff, 1964.

——— *Collected Papers,* Vol. III. Edited by I. Schutz, introduced by Aron Gurwitsch. The Hague: Martinus Nijhoff, 1966.

——— *The Phenomenology of the Social World.* Translated by George Walsh and Frederick Lehnert. Evanston: Northwestern University Press, 1967.

——— *On Phenomenology and Social Relations.* Edited and introduced by Helmut Wagner. Chicago: University of Chicago Press, 1970.

Schutz, Alfred, and Thomas Luckmann. *The Structures of the Life-World.* Translated by Richard M. Zaner and H. Tristram Engelhardt. Evanston: Northwestern University Press, 1973.

Scully, Diana, and Pauline Bart. "A Funny Thing Happened on the Way to the Orifice: Women in Gynecology Textbooks." *American Journal of Sociology* 78 (January 1973): 1045–50.

Secord, Paul F., and Carl W. Backman. "Personality Theory and the Problem of Stability and Change in Individual Behavior: An Interpersonal Approach." *Psychological Review* 68 (January 1961): 21–33.

Segal, A. "Portnoy's Complaint and the Sociology of Literature." *British Journal of Sociology* 22 (September 1971).

Shearing, Clifford D., and Michael G. Petrunik. "Normative and Phenomenological Approaches to the Study of Deviance." Paper presented at the American Sociological Association meetings, August 1972, New Orleans.

Shepherd, William C. "Religion and the Social Sciences: Conflict or Reconciliation?" *Journal for the Scientific Study of Religion* 11 (September 1972): 230–39.

Shibutani, Tamotsu. *Society and Personality.* Englewood Cliffs, N.J.: Prentice-Hall, 1961.

——— "Reference Groups and Social Control." In *Human Behavior and Social Processes,* edited by Arnold M. Rose, pp. 118–47. Boston: Houghton Mifflin, 1962.

Shumsky, Marshall E. "A Sociolinguistic Approach to Encounter Groups." *Sociological Inquiry* 41 (Spring 1971): 161–74.

Simmel, Georg. "A Contribution to the Sociology of Religion." *American Journal of Sociology* (November 1905): 359–76.

——— "How is Society Possible?" *American Journal of Sociology* 6 (1910): 372–91.

——— "The Adventure." In *Georg Simmel: 1858–1918,* edited by Kurt Wolff, pp. 243–58. Columbus: Ohio State University Press, 1959.

——— *The Sociology of Georg Simmel.* New York: Free Press, 1950.

Sparks, Mike. "The Phenomenon of Aging." Unpublished paper, October 1971.

Sparks, Mike, and Frank Adshead. "Phenomenology and Gerontology." Paper presented at the International Gerontological Society meeting, October 1970, Toronto.

Speier, Matthew. "Some Conversational Problems for Interactional Analysis." In *Studies in Social Interaction,* edited by David Sudnow, pp. 397–427. New York: Free Press, 1972.

Spiegelberg, Herbert. *The Phenomenological Movement: A Historical Introduction.* 2 vols. The Hague: Martinus Nijhoff, 1965.

Spradley, James P. "Down and Out on Skid Road." In *Life Styles: Diversity in American Society,* edited by Saul D. Feldman and Gerald W. Thielbar, pp. 340–50. Boston: Little, Brown, 1972.

Stone, Gregory P. "Appearance and Self." In *Human Behavior and Social Processes,* edited by Arnold M. Rose, pp. 86–118. Boston: Houghton Mifflin, 1962.

Strasser, Stephen. *Phenomenology and the Human Sciences.* Pittsburgh: Duquesne University Press, 1963.

———— *The Idea of Dialogal Phenomenology.* Pittsburgh: Duquesne University Press, 1969.

Strauss, Anselm. *Mirrors and Masks.* Glencoe, Ill.: Free Press, 1959.

Stryker, Sheldon. "Conditions of Accurate Role-Taking: A Test of Mead's Theory." In *Human Behavior and Social Processes,* edited by Arnold M. Rose, pp. 41–62. Boston: Houghton Mifflin, 1962.

Sudnow, David. *Passing On: The Social Organization of Dying.* Englewood Cliffs, N.J.: Prentice-Hall, 1967.

Sykes, Gresham M., and David Matza. "Techniques of Neutralization: A Theory of Delinquency." *American Sociological Review* 22 (December 1957): 664–70.

Szymanski, Al. "Marxism or Liberalism: A Response to Pozzuto." *Insurgent Sociologist* 3 (Summer 1973): 56–62.

Taylor, John F. A. "The Masks of Society: the Grounds for Obligation in the Scientific Enterprise." *Journal of Philosophy* 15 (June 1958).

Thio, Alex. "Class Bias in the Sociology of Deviance." *American Sociologist* 8 (February 1973): 1–12.

———— "The Phenomenological Perspective of Deviance: Another Case of Class Bias." *The American Sociologist* 9 (August 1974): 146–49.

Thomas, Darwin L., David D. Franks, and James M. Calonico. "Role Taking and Power in Social Psychology." *American Sociological Review* 37 (October 1972): 605–14.

Thomas, W. I. *Source Book for Social Origins.* Chicago: University of Chicago Press, 1909.

———— *The Child in America.* New York: Knopf, 1932.

———— *On Social Organization and Social Personality.* Chicago: University of Chicago Press, 1966.

———— *The Unadjusted Girl.* New York: Harper Torchbooks, 1967. First published in 1923 by Little Brown & Co.

Tillich, Paul. *Theology of Culture.* New York: Oxford University Press, 1964.

Tiryakian, Edward A. "Existential Phenomenology and the Sociological Tradition." *American Sociological Review* 30 (October 1965): 674–88.

———— "Reply to Kolaja and Berger." *American Sociological Review* 31 (1966): 260–64.

Truzzi, Marcello, ed. *Sociology and Everyday Life.* Englewood Cliffs, N.J.: Prentice-Hall, 1968.

———— *Verstehen: Subjective Understanding in the Social Sciences.* Reading, Mass.: Addison-Wesley, 1974.

Turner, Ralph H. "Role Taking: Process Versus Conformity." In *Human Behavior and*

Social Processes, edited by Arnold M. Rose. Boston: Houghton Mifflin, 1962.

———— "Role-Taking, Role Standpoint, and Reference Group Behavior." *American Journal of Sociology* 62 (January 1956): 316–28.

Turner, Roy. "Words, Utterances, and Activities." In *Understanding Everyday Life,* edited by Jack D. Douglas. Chicago: Aldine, 1970.

———— *Ethnomethodology.* Middlesex, Eng.: Penguin Books, 1974.

Tyler, Stephen A., ed. *Cognitive Anthropology.* New York: Holt, Rinehart, 1969.

Van der Leeuw, G. *Religion in Essence and Manifestation.* London: George Allen and Unwin, 1938.

Van de Vate, Dwight. "The Problem of Robot Consciousness." *Philosophy and Phenomenological Research* 32 (December 1971): 149–65.

Volkart, Edmund H., ed. *Social Behavior and Personality: Contributions of W. I. Thomas to Theory and Social Research.* New York: Social Science Research Council, 1951.

Vonnegut, Kurt, Jr. *Wampeters, Foma, and Granfalloons.* New York: Delacorte Press, 1974.

Wagner, Helmut R. "Types of Sociological Theory: Toward a System of Classification." *American Sociological Review* 28 (October 1963): 735–42.

———— "Displacement of Scope: A Problem of the Relationship between Small-scale and Large-scale Sociological Theories." *American Journal of Sociology,* 69 (May 1964): 571–84.

———— "The Scope of Phenomenological Sociology: Considerations and Suggestions." In *Phenomenological Sociology,* edited by George Psathas, pp. 61–87. New York: John Wiley, 1973.

———— "Signs, Symbols, and Interaction Theory." *Sociological Focus* 7 (Spring 1974): 101–11.

Ward, Dawn McNeal, and Ira E. Robinson. "The Relationship of Meaning and Behavior: An Empirical Investigation." Paper presented at the annual meeting of the American Sociological Association, August 1974, Montreal.

Weber, Max. *The Theory of Social and Economic Organization.* New York: Free Press, 1947.

———— *The Methodology of the Social Sciences.* New York: Free Press, 1949.

———— *The Protestant Ethic and the Spirit of Capitalism.* New York: Scribner's, 1958.

———— *Basic Concepts in Sociology.* New York: Citadel Press, 1962.

———— *Economy and Society.* New York: Bedminster Press, 1968.

Weitzman, Lenore J., Deborah Eifler, Elizabeth Hodaka, and Catherine Ross. "Sex-Role Socialization in Picture Books for Preschool Children." *American Journal of Sociology* 77 (May 1972): 1125–50.

West, Candace, and Don H. Zimmerman. "Women's Place in Conversation: Reflections on Adult-Child Interaction." Paper presented at the annual meeting of the American Sociological Association, August 1975, San Francisco.

Wieder, D. Lawrence. "On Meaning by Rule. In *Understanding Everyday Life,* edited by Jack D. Douglas. Chicago: Aldine, 1970.

———— "Telling the Code." In *Ethnomethodology,* edited by Roy Turner, pp. 144–72. Middlesex, Eng.: Penguin Books, 1974.

Wieder, D. Lawrence, and Don H. Zimmerman. "On Explaining by Rule: Scientific and Ethnoscientific Sociology." Unpublished paper, 1973.

Wild, John D. *Existence and the World of Freedom*. Englewood Cliffs, N.J.: Prentice-Hall, 1963.

Wilkins, James. "Review of Harold Garfinkel's Studies in Ethnomethodology." *American Journal of Sociology* 73 (March 1968): 642–43.

Wilson, Thomas P. "Conceptions of Interaction and Forms of Sociological Explanation." *American Sociological Review* 35 (August 1970): 697–710.

Winch, Peter. *The Idea of a Social Science, And Its Relation to Philosophy*. London: Routledge and Kegan Paul, 1958.

Wittgenstein, Ludwig. *Philosophical Investigations*. London: Oxford University Press, 1953.

———— *Tractatus Logico-Philosophicus*. London: Routledge and Kegan Paul, 1971. First published 1921.

Wolff, Kurt, ed. *The Sociology of Georg Simmel*. New York: Free Press of Glencoe, 1964.

Wolff, Kurt. "Toward Radicalism in Sociology and Every Day." In *Phenomenological Sociology*, edited by George Psathas, pp. 47–58. New York: John Wiley, 1973.

Wrong, Dennis. "The Oversocialized Conception of Man in Modern Society." *American Sociological Review* 26 (April 1961): 183–93.

Young, T. R. "The Politics of Sociology: Gouldner, Goffman, and Garfinkel." *American Sociologist* 6 (November 1971): 276–81.

Zaner, Richard M. "Theory of Intersubjectivity of Alfred Schutz." *Social Research* 28 (Spring 1961): 71–93.

———— *The Way of Phenomenology*. New York: Pegasus, 1970.

———— "Solitude and Sociality: The Critical Foundations of the Social Sciences." In *Phenomenological Sociology*, edited by George Psathas. New York: John Wiley, 1973.

———— "Context and Reflexivity: The Genealogy of Self." Paper presented at the First Trans-Disciplinary Symposium on the Interface of Philosophy and Medicine, May 1974, The University of Texas Medical Branch, Galveston.

Zeitlin, Irving. *Rethinking Sociology*. New York: Appleton-Century-Crofts, 1973.

Zijderveld, Anton. *The Abstract Society*. New York: Doubleday, 1970.

Zimmerman, Don H., and Melvin Pollner. "The Everyday World as Phenomenon." In *Understanding Everyday Life*, edited by Jack D. Douglas, pp. 80–103. Chicago: Aldine, 1970.

Zimmerman, Don H., and Candace West. "Sex Roles, Interruptions and Silences in Conversation." In *Language and Sex: Difference and Dominance*, edited by Barrie Thorne and Nancy Henley, pp. 105–29. Rowley, Mass.: Newbury House, 1975.

Zimmerman, Don H., and D. Lawrence Wieder. "Ethnomethodology and the Problem of Order: Comment on Denzin." In *Understanding Everyday Life*, edited by Jack D. Douglas, pp. 285–98. Chicago: Aldine, 1970.

Zimmerman, Don H., and Thomas P. Wilson. "Prospects for Experimental Studies of Meaning-Structures." Paper presented at the American Sociological Association meetings, August 1973, New York.

Index